Automation Anxiety

Automation Anxiety

Why and How to Save Work

CYNTHIA ESTLUND

OXFORD
UNIVERSITY PRESS

OXFORD
UNIVERSITY PRESS

Oxford University Press is a department of the University of Oxford. It furthers the University's objective of excellence in research, scholarship, and education by publishing worldwide. Oxford is a registered trade mark of Oxford University Press in the UK and certain other countries.

Published in the United States of America by Oxford University Press
198 Madison Avenue, New York, NY 10016, United States of America.

Library of Congress Cataloging-in-Publication Data
Names: Estlund, Cynthia, author.
Title: Automation anxiety : why and how to save work / Cynthia Estlund.
Description: New York, NY : Oxford University Press, 2021. |
Includes bibliographical references and index.
Identifiers: LCCN 2021011887 (print) | LCCN 2021011888 (ebook) | ISBN 9780197566107 (hardback) | ISBN 9780197566121 (epub) | ISBN 9780197566114 (updf) | ISBN 9780197566138 (online)
Subjects: LCSH: Labor laws and legislation—United States. | Labor supply—Effect of technological innovations on—United States. | Employees—Effect of automation on—United States.
Classification: LCC KF3321.E88 2021 (print) | LCC KF3321 (ebook) | DDC 344.7301—dc23
LC record available at https://lccn.loc.gov/2021011887
LC ebook record available at https://lccn.loc.gov/2021011888

DOI: 10.1093/oso/9780197566107.001.0001

1 3 5 7 9 8 6 4 2

Printed by Sheridan Books, Inc., United States of America

Note to Readers

This publication is designed to provide accurate and authoritative information in regard to the subject matter covered. It is based upon sources believed to be accurate and reliable and is intended to be current as of the time it was written. It is sold with the understanding that the publisher is not engaged in rendering legal, accounting, or other professional services. If legal advice or other expert assistance is required, the services of a competent professional person should be sought. Also, to confirm that the information has not been affected or changed by recent developments, traditional legal research techniques should be used, including checking primary sources where appropriate.

(Based on the Declaration of Principles jointly adopted by a Committee of the American Bar Association and a Committee of Publishers and Associations.)

For Sam

Table of Contents

Preface

By 2015, when I was looking for a new big project, the gig economy and the larger phenomenon of "fissured work" had taken scholars of work law by storm. A particular obsession was Uber and its treatment of drivers as independent contractors. All this attention was well warranted. The growing ability of firms to extract value from human workers without hiring them as employees was in the process of undermining the whole edifice of laws, norms, and institutions built through more than a century of political agitation and organizing by workers and their allies. Perhaps this would be my next project.

As I started to immerse myself in the gig economy, however, I was struck by two thoughts. First, these issues had already attracted an outpouring of scholarly talent and energy among labor and employment law scholars. Second, by contrast, there was almost no work being done on another potentially existential challenge that appeared to be right around the corner from fissuring and the gig economy: automation. On Uber's own telling, the transformation of jobs into gigs is only an intermediate step toward a more complete escape from the hassles and burdens of employing human labor through self-driving vehicles. The end game in many cases—and ever more cases as machines grow more capable—is not the shift from employment to gig work but from humans to machines.

We have all seen the steady stream of stories about how robots, algorithms, autonomous vehicles, and the like are poised to displace human workers in droves. That is a profoundly unsettling prospect, and not only for those of us who have devoted our professional lives to the study, regulation, or improvement of work and working lives. I found it especially eye-opening when Andy Stern, who had spent much of his life organizing workers and agitating for better wages and working conditions, emerged from a years-long deep dive into the future of work as a convert to the automation-as-job-killer narrative and a proponent of universal basic income (UBI).[1]

Some of my particular anxieties about a future of much less work are suggested by the title of my first book, *Working Together: How Workplace Bonds Strengthen a Diverse Democracy* (OUP, 2003). If the seemingly relentless process of automation left growing numbers of people unmoored from work and work relationships, that would not only unsettle and impoverish individual lives and identities but also dissolve part of the social glue that helps to holds a diverse society and polity together. And that was true even if a guaranteed basic income cushioned the economic blow. It seemed well worth delving into the challenges posed by automation to the future of work and the law of work. And so I did.

One challenge that I faced early on in this project was to re-examine my perhaps-too-sanguine view of work and its social value. (My daughter Jess usefully nudged me on this point, among others.) I had to take on board the long-standing aspirations of many working people not only for better wages and working conditions but for lives less consumed by work. The history of the shorter hours movement, and especially its moment of reckoning in the New Deal, was instructive and inspiring on this front.[2] Still, if a future of less work meant little or no work for a growing share of adults, as I feared it would, I remained convinced that would be corrosive in both more and less obvious ways.

A second challenge was to figure out what was really going on, and to get beyond both the Silicon Valley-inflected hype about a jobless future and the economists' ingrained confidence in "creative destruction." Predictions that machines would supplant human labor have been a recurring source of anxiety, and of utopian and dystopian speculation, practically since the dawn of industrial capitalism. Yet neither past hopes for a future of much more leisure nor fears of mass unemployment and immiseration have been realized. For one thing, those who are immersed in the high-tech world tend to fasten on the amazing technological breakthroughs themselves, and to underestimate the daunting organizational, political, psychological, and even technological hurdles to implementation. (Autonomous vehicles, for example, have supposedly been a few years from widespread adoption for at least a decade.) But those past hopes and fears about automation have also been upended by the history of economic growth under capitalism. The market economy has proven to be a prodigious if temperamental engine not only of job destruction but also of creation—creation of new goods and services, new consumer appetites for those goods and services, and new demand for labor. That history leads some observers (and some of my colleagues) to view the current wave of automation anxiety as economically illiterate naiveté. (The term "Luddite" often seemed on the tips of their tongues.)

An extended side trip into the economic literature on the impact of automation on labor markets, the highlights of which are reflected in Chapter 2, persuaded me that this time was indeed different, and that job destruction was more likely this time around to outpace job creation, at least for the great majority of workers without higher education and specialized skills. The weight of expert opinion seems to be moving modestly in that direction, especially with the COVID-19 calamity, which has accelerated trends toward automation and destruction of lower-skill jobs (as discussed in Chapter 1). One or another version of a future of less work is likely enough, I concluded, that we should be thinking about how to respond to it. For how we respond will determine whether automation yields widely shared dividends—including the long-yearned-for boon of more time for life beyond work—or an even more skewed winner-take-all economy.

A third challenge was to figure out what an effective response would look like—in terms that were more granular than standard prescriptions for more and better education and training and public job creation, and more realistic and balanced than the high-profile rival proposals on the left for UBI or a federal job guarantee. On the premise that we should start where we are—within a particular legal and regulatory landscape and within what is likely to remain a predominantly market economy—I set out in this book to grapple seriously with the question of how, in view of a more automated future, we ought to reshape and recalibrate the law and policies governing work. Much of what follows here—especially proposals for unburdening the employment relationship and for work spreading—is grounded in the particulars of US labor and employment law and policy. But I have steered clear of technicalities and tried to keep in sight the problems and possibilities around work that are common across the developed world so as to reach readers beyond the academy and beyond the United States.

I began this project with much more anxiety than optimism about a future of less work. I now think it is possible, and I have tried here, to chart a path toward a more humane and equitable society and toward more balanced lives that are still anchored but not consumed by work. Still, the political heavy lifting that would be required to bring about that better future of less work—including some major redistributive programs—might seem to be beyond the capacity of our currently polarized polity and political institutions. The difficult politics of all that is proposed here, and how the politics might be further complicated as job losses begin to mount, occupy my concluding chapter.

The book draws on ideas and arguments developed in my previous book, *Working Together*; and more recently in two law review articles, "What Should We Do After Work? Automation and Employment Law," in volume 128 of the *Yale Law Journal*; and "Three Big Ideas for a Future of Less Work, and a Three-Dimensional Alternative," in volume 82 of *Law and Contemporary Problems*. The student editors of those publications, and especially Luis Calderon Gomez, YLS 2019, were thorough and thoughtful in their queries, comments, and editorial suggestions, and have made for a better book as well as better articles. Finally, parts of the conclusion draw on my chapter, "Coming Apart: How Union Decline and Workplace Disintegration Imperil Democracy," to be published in *Labor and Challenges to Democracy* (Mark Barenberg & Angela Cornell, eds., 2021), on which Mark Barenberg provided exceptionally thoughtful editorial feedback. Thanks also to my editors at Oxford University Press, Jamie Berezin and Alex Flach, for shepherding the book to publication.

I'm greatly indebted to many colleagues and interlocutors for their insights, criticisms, and suggestions. A few hardy souls worked through the whole manuscript in its final stages, and offered valuable comments throughout—Daron Acemoglu, William Forbath, and Brishen Rogers (only two of whom might have felt bound by ties of friendship to put in that time). In addition, I received invaluable input and feedback on various chapters or precursors of chapters, or on particular passages and puzzles from Jeremias Adams-Prassl, Einat Albin, Charlotte Alexander, Mark Barenberg, Arianne Barzilay, Lily Batchelder, Steven Berkenfeld, Samuel Bowles, Ryan Bubb, Brendan Burchell, Joshua Cohen, Tyler Cowen, David Estlund, John Ferejohn, David Garland, Clayton Gillette, Catherine Fisk, Richard Freeman, Samuel Issacharoff, David Kamin, Mitchell Kane, Thomas Kochan, Wilma Liebman, Lawrence Mischel, Suresh Naidu, Philippe Van Parijs, John Roemer, Debra Satz, Jason Schultz, Daniel Shaviro, Seana Shiffrin, Hila Shamir, Valerio De Stefano, Andy Stern, Arun Sundararajan, Frank Upham, and Ulrich Zieran. In addition to these individual exchanges, I learned a great deal from workshop or conference discussions at Boston College School of Law, Duke Law School, Hebrew University Law School, NYU School of Law, Rutgers University, St. Louis University School of Law, and at Yale Law School, and at the meetings of the Labor Law Research Network and Law and Society Association.

Over the life of this project I was also fortunate to have the research assistance of several outstanding students at NYU School of Law, including

Bridget Ansel, Alexander Arnold, Colin Bradley, Rachel Sommer, Matthew Stolz, and especially Molly Jacobs-Meyer. Molly has my deepest gratitude for her research and close readings of several versions and portions, including near-final drafts of every chapter, and for her warmly supportive but critical engagement with everything from the economics of the minimum wage to the roots of ethnonationalist politics.

New York University, and especially the School of Law, gave me not only excellent research assistants, of course. It has also afforded me the best co-workers, workplace environment, and terms and conditions of work that one could wish for. That includes generous financial support, some of it through the Filomen D'Agostino and Max E. Greenberg Research Fund, and a sabbatical for all of 2020, during the final drafting (not to mention during the strangest year in recent history).

While prowling around the internet for cover images that might evoke the themes of the book while steering clear of cliché, I found a photograph that practically jumped off the screen. Its melding of humanity and machine and of change and permanence, and its depiction of human sociability through metal gears and screws seemed perfect. I'm deeply grateful to the sculptor and photographer, Penny Hardy, a UK-based artist (http://www.pennyhardysculpture.com), for granting me permission to use an image from her *Blown Away* series for the cover.

As for my family, I hope they do not need these paltry words to know how much my life has been enriched and my work made possible by their love and support. Among my greatest gifts have been my adult children Jess (also thanked above) and Lucas Issacharoff and his wife Maurene Comey, all of them extraordinarily smart, grounded, and loving (and remarkably congenial housemates and occasional trivia teammates during the first couple of months of the pandemic). Then there is Sam. Sam Issacharoff and I have been colleagues as well as life partners for most of our forty years together, and he manages to be both a devoted fan and a valued critic. Among the upsides of the past year of near-quarantine has been the remarkable discovery after all these years that we actually enjoyed spending a simply ridiculous amount of time alone together.

1
Is This Time Different?

Let's start with fun and games. Artificial intelligence (AI) research scored a big public relations coup with the 2011 victory of IBM's Watson over reigning *Jeopardy!* champion Ken Jennings. As his defeat revealed itself, Jennings wrote on his answer board, "I, for one, welcome our new computer overlords."[1] Watson's 2011 victory was sandwiched between two other famous computer victories in notoriously complex board games. When IBM's Deep Blue program beat reigning world chess champion Gary Kasparov in 1996, Kasparov initially accused IBM of cheating by channeling the moves of a human grandmaster.[2] When Google's AlphaGo program beat champion Lee Sedol at the ancient and much more intricate Chinese game of Go in 2016, Lee was more gracious: "AlphaGo made me realize that I must study Go more."[3]

AlphaGo's victory amazed cognoscenti of both AI and Go. "Artificial intelligence experts had predicted that a computer program needed at least 10 more years of development before it would be able to beat Go masters like Lee."[4] AlphaGo worked by analyzing a vast database of actual human games of Go and choosing the most successful or highest-percentage moves, all at warp speed. But just one year after AlphaGo's triumph, Google introduced a successor, AlphaGo Zero, which learned the game and chose its moves based solely on the rules and logic of the game itself. "AlphaGo Zero . . . trounced the older program 100 games to zero, [while running] on just four processors, compared with the older AI's 48."[5] The advance from AlphaGo to AlphaGo Zero is quite illuminating on what is new in the new technologies, as we'll see, for it illustrates the shift from attempting to mimic human intelligence to exploiting the very different capabilities of machines themselves.

Another telling example of technological progress is in the field of natural language translation. Google Translate and its sometimes-entertaining foibles once seemed to underscore the lopsided rivalry between computers and human translators. In July 2016, leading economist Jason Furman used natural language translation as a prime example of humans' enduring advantages over computers: "AI today can do decent translations but cannot

Automation Anxiety. Cynthia Estlund, Oxford University Press. © Cynthia Estlund 2021.
DOI: 10.1093/oso/9780197566107.003.0001

come close to what a human can do with his or her knowledge of both languages, social and cultural context, and sense of the author's argument, emotional states, and intentions."[6] A few months later, however, Google launched a new version of Google Translate that used machine learning. Literally overnight, results had "almost immeasurably improved."[7] One translation company found that the percentage of machine-translated documents that required human tinkering to meet quality standards dropped from 80 percent to 10 percent.[8] Overnight, Google Translate began to rival human translators in some settings—except that the former is free and instantaneous.

The availability of free and instantaneous translations on a pocket-held device, even if it is only pretty good, will enable people to manage linguistic challenges at times and in places where human translators were never available. That is a boon to humanity. But that technology will also inevitably supplant human translators in some settings where they are now in demand. Even pretty good will often be good enough when it is free and fast.

Of course, not many jobs call for strategic gaming or natural language translation. But the examples suggest how fast technology is advancing—often surprising even technology experts—with the advent of machine learning and AI. The examples also hint at the potential for replacing human labor. Once these software systems are developed and set loose, they can be replicated and deployed innumerable times at little or no marginal cost, with eye-opening implications for many white-collar and professional jobs.[9]

The job-killing potential of emerging technologies is central to this book, and we'll eventually turn to the statistics, theory, and data that inform economic forecasting about automation's aggregate impact on the labor market. But it's worth first taking a look at some of the technologies that are transforming work in various fields. As we do so, let's be clear: the reality does not always live up to the hype.[10] The imaginations of techies in Silicon Valley and elsewhere often run a bit wild, seeing the potential more than the flaws of their inventions and heedless of the human and institutional frictions, hurdles, and costs that slow or impede their implementation. Occasionally—as with the biotech start-up Theranos—the hype masks outright fraud.[11] Often—as with Amazon's Mechanical Turk—the technology is parasitic on human knowledge and experience, albeit boosted by ever-faster data processing. One way or another, we might be reminded of the original Mechanical Turk—a chess-playing automaton that amazed Napoleon, Ben Franklin, and others, but that turned out to hide a human chess player within.[12]

So we should clearly not swallow whole the prophecies emanating from the tech world about the imminent end of work. But neither should we ignore machines' growing capabilities and their potential to displace human workers. Let's take a look at some examples from the last few years.

A. Tales from Technology's Frontier

Much of the work of lawyers—drafting contracts, performing "due diligence" on a transaction, doing legal research and writing, or negotiating deals—seems comparatively invulnerable to automation for now. Yet technology, and especially machine learning (ML), is making breakthroughs in nearly all aspects of legal work.[13] It has already transformed the process of discovery—the identification, review, and exchange of evidence in civil disputes.[14] Discovery used to engage armies of lawyers in combing through paper files to respond to discovery requests, and then in poring through the dozens, hundreds, even thousands of cardboard boxes of paper produced by the other side. Those days are long gone. Most documents are now in electronic form, and computer software does most the work of identifying and reviewing documents for discovery.[15] Systems of "technology-assisted review" and "predictive coding" use algorithms to screen documents that should presumptively be withheld or surrendered to the other side.[16]

Beyond discovery, AI is also now reportedly able to "draft [legal] documents, undertake due diligence work, isolate the most relevant documents from litigation bundles, predict the outcome of deals and disputes, and offer legal guidance," and often performs "at a higher standard than junior lawyers."[17] For example, JP Morgan developed software to review commercial loan agreements; it takes a few seconds per document to do what had taken 360,000 hours of work by human lawyers and loan officers.[18] A recently launched product, Compose, can generate a "first draft of a legal brief or motion," complete with text and authorities, once the lawyer enters a few pieces of information.[19] While fully automated contract drafting faces several obstacles, advances in ML are chipping away at those obstacles.[20] These technological shortcuts might work only for relatively routine matters, and will probably still require lawyers to review first drafts. But they will drastically reduce the lawyer hours required for these recurring (if not mind-numbing) tasks.

In the burgeoning field of online dispute resolution, a new software platform, Modria, can assemble facts, highlight areas of contention, and propose solutions in disputes.[21] In 2019, a so-called "robot mediator" was able to settle a small-stakes dispute in a public court in under an hour.[22] AI has also made huge strides in predicting "the outcome of judicial decisions, often more accurately, it is claimed, than human lawyers."[23] It could be a short step from there—technologically speaking—to replacing human judges in many disputes (though judges will obviously have something to say about that).[24]

All of these innovations can both replace lawyers and make them more productive, freeing their time for the more creative and challenging aspects of lawyering. (Nobody who did document review in the old days—and I'm speaking from experience—misses that work.) But how many lawyers will be needed? One 2017 study found that over 40 percent of law firm lawyers' billed hours were for tasks in which automation was expected to have a "strong" or "moderate" effect.[25] That could add up to a lot fewer hours and jobs once law firms (and clients) catch up to what technology makes possible—and more is becoming possible every day. In law as elsewhere, rising demand for lawyers' services might offset the impact of labor-saving technology on jobs.[26] But it might not.

AI is also transforming the medical field. Five years after IBM's Watson "went to medical school"—that is, was fed a gigantic trove of research papers and medical cases—it was able to diagnose "a 60-year-old woman's rare form of leukemia—a diagnosis that had eluded her doctors for months."[27] AI has reportedly been able to accurately detect and recommend treatment for illnesses that lead to blindness,[28] to uncover sleep apnea, Alzheimer's, and heart disease based on analysis of patients' voices,[29] and to detect cancers.[30] An AI system reading mammograms decreased false positives by 5.7 percent and false negatives by 9.4 percent when compared with US radiologists.[31] Some radiologists are concerned for their future. "Radiology, at its core, is now a human being, based on learning and his or her own experience, looking at a collection of digital dots" in search of patterns; but "[c]omputers are awfully good at seeing patterns."[32] In short, clinical experience that once took years to accumulate can now be uploaded to databases and searched in seconds.

Again, the most breathless accounts of these innovations may be misleading. For example, image recognition is only one part of what radiologists do,[33] and that is true of most other currently automatable tasks in medicine (as in lawyering). Moreover, most AI-based advances in medicine (and lawyering) are parasitic on information and experience that is itself the product of human intelligence. So for example, three years after its introduction by IBM as a revolution in cancer diagnoses, Watson for Oncology, "[wasn't] living up to the lofty expectations IBM created for it." It was less seamless and less comprehensive in its knowledge base than promised.[34] At least so far, technology is more of an aid to human doctors, and indeed for most professionals, than a replacement.[35] Still, these are early days.

Beyond the professions, the prospects of wholesale job destruction loom larger. Consider the long-heralded advent of autonomous vehicles. About five million people in the United States work as drivers, and two to four million of them could be replaced by autonomous vehicles.[36] When? Early predictions had pegged 2020 as the year autonomous vehicles would become ubiquitous; that proved optimistic, due in part to safety concerns.[37] Yet studies suggest that autonomous vehicles are already safer than human-driven vehicles in many settings. In late 2019, for example, Tesla reported that drivers had nearly twice as many accidents per million miles without the aid of automated safety features than they did with "Autopilot" turned on.[38] Political and regulatory hurdles remain, but most close observers think it is only a matter of a few more years before autonomous vehicles hit the roads—especially the highways on which commercial drivers spend most of their time—and job losses start to pile up.[39]

Then there are the robots, which have long captured the popular imagination. Most robots are not humanoid figures with arms and legs and "eyes" and "ears." They lack many human-like features as well as many human capabilities, and cannot thus far can rarely replace human workers one-to-one. But they can perform a growing range of tasks that humans have long been paid to do. To begin with some good news, robots are replacing humans in some very dangerous jobs like surveying and cleaning up nuclear sites,[40] fighting fires,[41] finding stranded people during natural disasters,[42] inspecting off-shore oil rigs and fixing gas pipelines,[43] and working with highly toxic chemicals and in extreme temperatures.[44]

Robots are also entering some bastions of skilled labor, like construction. Economist Daniel Susskind has noted that a human bricklayer "may be able to lay three hundred to six hundred bricks in an eight-hour shift, but a bricklaying robot called Sam100 can place more than three thousand in the same time." One major construction company aims to make its sites "human-free" by 2050.[45] That might be a pipe dream (though growing use of modular construction might bring it closer to reality). But what if they get halfway there?

Robots have already made huge inroads in manufacturing, especially in the automotive industry.[46] They help account for a peculiar fact about the decline of US manufacturing: while US manufacturing *employment* as a share of the labor force declined by nearly 20 percent between 2000 and 2015, *output* increased by 5 percent in roughly the same period.[47] Robots have had their biggest impact on skilled manufacturing jobs—that is, some of the best jobs once available to those without a college education.[48]

According to some observers, the future of manufacturing may be in "dark factories" with so few human workers that "you could switch the lights off and leave the place to the machines."[49] Lights-out manufacturing—purged of the biological, psychological, social, and political challenges and limitations of human workers—was long a dream of industrial visionaries, but is now becoming a reality. Fanuc, a Japanese robotics company, manufactures its robots in a lights-out factory in Japan, which operates twenty-four hours a day and employs humans only to perform occasional maintenance and troubleshooting.[50] Those robots in turn are spreading nearly human-free manufacturing across the world in pharmaceuticals, food processing, electronics, and beyond.

Logistics is another field of rampant roboticization. In the last few years, warehouses and distribution centers—which have proliferated in the era of e-commerce—have seen two big waves of robotic innovation. The first was embodied in the Kiva robots, which debuted in 2011. Small but powerful, "Kiva robots pick up shelves of products from the warehouse floor and bring them to a human employee who picks items and then packs them for shipping. . . . [T]hey avoid running into each other by using sensors that talk to one another.[51] While humans still carried out the more intricate "picking and packing" of items, the Kiva robots cut costs and sped up operations by enabling "pickers" to hit a target of 300 to 400 items per hour, compared to about 100 items per hour without robotic help.[52] Their human co-workers were ambivalent. "While walking the aisles was 'good cardio,' " reported one Amazon employee, "the new system lets him get through more orders."[53] "We don't socialize as much," he said, "but it's more efficient."[54]

"Picking and packing" itself has long posed a notorious engineering challenge, and has served for some robot skeptics as an illustration of humans' enduring advantages over machines in a large swath of less-skilled jobs. It seemed that "the job's steep requirements for flexibility, object recognition, physical dexterity, and fine motor coordination"—while second nature to most humans—were "too formidable" for robots.[55] "Shapes vary, as do surfaces. One light switch might be upside down, the other right-side up. The next electrical gadget might be in a plastic bag that reflects light in ways a robot has never seen. A human touch has been needed."[56]

Recently, however, the robot skeptics were shown up by a start-up, Covariant.AI. Its robots learned by trial and error, and were soon able to "pick and sort more than 10,000 different items . . . with more than 99 percent accuracy."[57] One warehouse operator described some of the robot's appealing attributes: "It doesn't smoke, is always in good health, isn't chatting with its neighbors, no toilet breaks"; and, echoing Kiva's human co-workers, "It's more efficient." As for cost, the robots' distributor, Knapp, plans to make it hard for companies to say no. "If a company paid $40,000 per year to a worker, Knapp would charge about $30,000. . . . 'We just go lower. . . . For the customer, it's not very hard to decide.' "[58] The rise of e-commerce and the Amazon juggernaut, especially during the COVID crisis, has made warehouses a growing source of jobs. But these recent advances, if they prove their mettle in the field and are widely adopted, might put an end to that.

Let's be clear: warehouse jobs are pretty monotonous and unpleasant. It would be all to the good if workers moved from those rather dismal jobs to better ones. Maybe the coming wave of automation will free humans to deploy more profoundly human traits and skills in better jobs, much as the mechanization of agriculture liberated the bulk of humanity from the backbreaking business of food production and enabled them to take up more varied and productive work. Maybe. It all depends, as we'll see.

A final sphere of robotic advances is especially eye-opening because it defies widespread assumptions about the growing field of care work. Elder care in particular is often cited as a growing and enduringly human field of lower-skill work because of the predominance of unpredictable physical tasks and the importance of human contact and companionship. But we should think again. To begin with, robots can help human workers with some of the heavy lifting—in bathing, for example—that makes care work so physically demanding.[59] But robots can increasingly perform those once-hard-to-automate "unpredictable physical tasks" by themselves.

Will human patients or their families revolt against the rise of the robots in elder care? Perhaps not.[60] While discussing these issues with a fellow middle-aged professional woman, I was initially taken aback when she said, "at the point that I need help with bathing and toileting, I hope there is a robot to do it." Maybe this is an idiosyncratic preference, or maybe not. In these physically intimate encounters, robotic care might feel less invasive of one's privacy and dignity than human assistance.

Still, what about companionship and emotional support? Those sometimes-incidental aspects of much care work are surely beyond the reach of robots, right? Maybe so, but robots' ability to simulate human kindness and empathy is advancing apace. Sophia, a robot with a remarkably human-like appearance, can emulate and express some emotional states, including frowning, laughing, and smiling.[61] In clinical trials in 2018, a robotic caretaker, Sayabot, assisted elderly patients, "performing tasks such as helping patients use the restroom, providing mental stimulation through conversation and games, 24/7 monitoring, and dispensing food, drinks, and medicine."[62] Zora, a robot deployed in a nursing facility in France, provided companionship and elicited something like affection from many patients; one confided to Zora that she had injured herself by falling out of her bed, a fact the patient had withheld from hospital staff.[63]

The rise of the care robots is sure to continue, for many of the world's richest countries are also the oldest and least fecund, and the birth dearth is contributing to labor shortages.[64] Humanoid care robots are already in widespread use in Japan, an aging (and immigrant-averse) society that has long experienced labor shortages.[65] Robots are poised to take over wider swaths of care work as they become more affordable, even relative to notoriously-underpaid care workers. Perhaps human companionship—once it is no longer supplied incidentally with the work of feeding, toileting, bathing, and moving aging human bodies—will become a luxury for those who can afford it.

This brief tour of labor-saving technologies—so far just a collection of stories—has already surfaced some cross-cutting themes that should counter any monochromatic view of automation. Machines can perform some tasks better than humans, and can save lives. (Think of medical image screening and safer autonomous vehicles.) They can replace humans in work that is grueling or even life-threatening (like robots in firefighting and nuclear clean-up), not to mention tedious. (Think of warehouse work and digital review of litigation documents.) Machines can also help to meet labor shortages in aging societies. (Think of care robots in Japan.) Moreover, automation will create new jobs even as it destroys others. (Think of robot repair workers in "lights-out" factories.) Clearly there is much to gain from technological innovations even if job losses also loom—though the overall gains might be greater if the job losses are slower. And on that score, the COVID-19 crisis sent a wake-up call.

B. How COVID-19 Has Accelerated Automation

The unprecedented COVID-19 collapse of 2020, which brought the biggest jump in unemployment ever recorded in the United States, is also causing a surge in automation. Already in late April of 2020, the CEO of Microsoft observed that "[w]e've seen two years' worth of digital transformation in two months" (happily for Microsoft's business).[66] The COVID-induced acceleration of automation has been widely recognized by leading economists who study automation, from David Autor at MIT and Carl Benedict Frey at Oxford to economists at Brookings and the McKinsey Global Institute.[67] COVID did not fundamentally alter the course of automation, but it did accelerate it, and it did so through several mechanisms.

The biggest spur to automation was the economic contraction itself. Economists have long observed that firms' uptake of new technologies does not follow a smooth path but responds to economic shocks.[68] One study finds that 88 percent of all job losses in "routine occupations" since the mid-1980s occurred within one year of a recessionary period.[69] Perhaps managers are more reluctant to automate away the jobs of incumbent workers than of potential future workers. Or they may lack the bandwidth, when production is running at full tilt, to figure out how to operate more efficiently. But perhaps the main reason is that economic downturns tend to cull out less efficient firms, and to open markets to new entrants using more capital-intensive production modes. All in all, the firms that survive, thrive, or emerge as recession gives way to recovery—that is, the winners in these cyclical surges of creative destruction—tend to make greater use of labor-saving innovations.[70] Upticks in automation have been observed in the wake of past (relatively mild) recessions and in the recovery from the Great Recession,[71] and will recur in more dramatic form as the economy digs out of the worst economic collapse since the Great Depression.

COVID-19 is also likely to spur automation and job destruction by other pandemic-specific pathways. First, by rendering interpersonal contact itself risky, COVID-19 heightened the advantages of robots in a wider range of jobs. So while Amazon staffed up its warehouses to meet ballooning demand during the pandemic, it also found that the virus "makes human labor, increasingly, a liability."[72] Safety was only the beginning. The demands of employees and labor activists for "protective gear, warehouse disinfection, more time off, higher pay, and testing" led some firms "to replace more workers with robots permanently. After all, robots don't need face masks, health care, or social distancing, and they don't go on strike for better conditions."[73]

COVID-19 also accelerated the adoption of robots in health care and elder care. Hospitals deployed robots to clean surfaces, take patients' vital signs, and even conduct preliminary screening interviews.[74] That both reduced workers' exposure to the virus and saved them the time required to get safely in and out of patients' isolation tents with their cumbersome protective gear.[75] In the first wave of the pandemic, with hospital staffs overwhelmed and exhausted, that was a clear gain for patients, workers, and public health. But the robots, having proven their utility, are unlikely to go away as normalcy returns.

The pandemic also tilted customers' habits and preferences away from the interpersonal contact that is endemic to many service jobs.[76] As human contact became associated with risk of contagion, people grew accustomed to impersonal and automated modes of buying goods and services. To take one mundane example, many retail customers (like me) who had habitually headed toward the friendly human cashier instead of automated check-out stations might overcome their resistance to the latter and actually learn to use them. That may pave the way for retail firms to make the leap to fully automated check-out.

That is, if those retailers stay in business at all. Many brick-and-mortar retail giants were felled by the pandemic.[77] Economists David Autor and Elisabeth Reynolds, leading experts on automation and jobs, observed that, in retail, "the COVID crisis will compress into a few short months what would otherwise have unfolded over multiple years."[78] The immediate loss of foot traffic during the shutdown might have dealt the death blow, but major brick-and-mortar chains had already been rocked by the tectonic shift to online shopping; then the pandemic suddenly drove more customers online for a wider range of purchases.[79] Those new habits are likely to outlast the pandemic. The resulting loss of retail sales jobs might be temporarily offset by more warehouse and delivery jobs—at least until the ongoing automation of warehouses and the predicted automation of delivery through autonomous vehicles and drones destroys those jobs.

Finally, as we all know, COVID-19 led to a rapid spike in what MIT economists call "telepresence," itself a form of automation.[80] As remote communications technologies like Zoom got better and more familiar, it became clear they would reshape business practices long after the pandemic faded, with ripple effects through the labor market:

> [R]eductions in office occupancy, daily commuting trips, and business excursions will mean steep declines in demand for building cleaning, security, and maintenance service; hotel workers and restaurant staff; taxi and ride-hailing drivers; and myriad other workers who feed, transport, clothe, entertain, and shelter people when they are not in their own homes.[81]

It will be years before we can assess the economic impact of COVID-19. But faster automation and fewer jobs are likely to be among its lasting effects.

C. What Is Automation Doing to Jobs? A Preview of the Debate

So are super-capable robots and algorithms destined to devour American jobs and idle much of the working population? Predictions of a jobless future have recurred in waves throughout the history of capitalism, only to crest and retreat as new jobs—usually better paid and less grueling jobs—have replaced those lost to machines. Maybe the past is prologue. Yet the astounding pace and distinctive nature of the latest wave of innovations in AI, machine learning, and robotics lead many contemporary observers to believe that this time will be different.

As we have begun to see, machines are replicating and surpassing an ever-wider range of human capabilities, putting more kinds of existing jobs at risk and casting doubt on whether demand for new goods and services will translate as it has in the past into new demand for human labor. Two widely cited studies using different methodologies reach the same bottom line: Nearly half the work that humans perform in the current economy is at risk.[82] And although some new jobs are readily foreseeable—especially skilled jobs working with technology—no large new sectors or industries yet visible on the horizon appear likely to absorb the multitudes of human workers who might be displaced.

Automation recasts several seemingly unrelated developments in the world of work. We've seen that COVID-19, which yielded the worst job losses since the Great Depression, is also causing a surge in automation that will make many of those job losses permanent. Before COVID's arrival, labor scholars across the world were riveted by the rise of platform-based "gigs" in place of real jobs, epitomized by Uber's treatment of its drivers as independent contractors. But if Uber has its way, its drivers will eventually go the way of lamplighters, replaced by self-driving vehicles.[83] And before Uber's rise, a major focus among labor watchers was the steady flow of manufacturing jobs to overseas suppliers, especially in China. But the biggest of those—the Taiwanese company Foxconn, which employs over a million Chinese workers in the production of iPhones and iPads—has begun replacing its factory workers with robots.[84] That process has gone more slowly than expected, mainly because of quality concerns at Apple.[85] Yet the shift to robots in Chinese factories continues, accelerated by COVID.[86] In short, many trends that have unsettled the world of work and drawn the anxious attention of scholars, advocates, and policy wonks—deindustrialization, offshoring, and the disintegration of jobs into gigs, as well as the decline of unions and the steady rise of economic inequality, as we'll see—are intertwined with the ongoing replacement of human workers by machines.

Developments like these lead some observers to predict a jobless future as machines rival or surpass humans at a growing range of tasks.[87] Putting aside fantastical predictions about AI dominating or even devouring its human creators,[88] the prospects for job destruction are eye-opening, as we've begun to see. Advances in both hard and soft forms of technology—robots and algorithms, for example—are replicating a wider range of human capabilities and weaving together those distinct capabilities more seamlessly than ever before. The very terms "artificial intelligence" and "machine learning" hint at what is new: technology is acquiring and refining cognitive and sensory capabilities that had long been thought to be uniquely human, and is outpacing humans at increasingly complex tasks.

On the other side of the debate, many economists dismiss the latest wave of automation anxiety as misinformed scare-mongering by modern-day Luddites.[89] They point out that predictions that machines will supplant human labor have recurred in both utopian and dystopian flavors throughout the history of industrialization.[90] Futurists of the past have predicted that mass automation will usher in an era of human liberation from toil, or that it will immiserate all but the fortunate few who own or create the machines. Time and again, however, the economy has defied such predictions. For centuries, automation has been destroying some jobs while creating other jobs—usually better paid and less grueling—and driving economic growth and prosperity. In short, the history of automation's impact on the labor market has been one of "creative destruction,"[91] a mantra to which many economists still adhere.[92]

To be sure, even on this account, job losses may be devastating to workers and their families and communities even if they are numerically offset by new job opportunities elsewhere in the economy. Apart from the geographic mismatches between jobs lost and jobs gained, those displaced by automation might not have the skills needed in the new jobs, nor any realistic shot at acquiring those skills. So creative destruction is not an altogether-reassuring prediction for those whose jobs are at risk. But if the result is greater productivity and shared prosperity, as in the past, then the challenge will be to manage the temporary dislocations and spread the gains.

Yet some economists who study the impact of automation on labor markets are coming around to the view that this time is indeed different—that automation is already producing not shared prosperity but a more polarized labor market with declining wages and job quality for many workers.[93] So concluded a star-studded MIT task force led by David Autor in 2019:

> Unlike the era of equitable growth that preceded it, the digital era has catalyzed labor market polarization—that is the simultaneous growth of high-education, high-wage and low-education, low-wage jobs at the expense of middle-skill jobs. This lopsided growth has concentrated labor market rewards among the most skilled and highly-educated workers while devaluing much of the non-specialized work that remains. This imbalance contributes to the vast divergence of earnings between college- and noncollege-educated workers in recent decades.[94]

Although the MIT task force did not predict a future of fewer jobs overall, it found that automation is already destroying more decent middle-skill jobs than it is creating, and is likely to continue to do so. Automation, in short, is hollowing out the labor market. Harvard economist Richard Freeman agrees: As robots become better and cheaper substitutes for human labor, "the net impact . . . will be to shift work from humans to the robots, [both] reducing employment and pressuring wages downward in jobs where machines can do the work of humans at lower costs."[95] Technology is contributing to both inequality within the labor market and the growing shift of income from labor toward capital.[96] Indeed, work by Daron Acemoglu and Pascual Restrepo suggests that "*automation may have been the most important factor boosting inequality in the US labor market*."[97]

These diagnoses of the impact of automation on jobs are deeply concerning, even if job shortages (and falling wages) for ordinary workers coexist with high demand (and rising wages) for some skilled workers. The result will be a growing economic chasm between those at the top who own or produce the new technology, or whose high-end skills are complemented by that technology, and most workers who are stuck competing for the shrinking range of low- or middle-skill jobs that humans can still do better or more cheaply than machines but that most humans can also do. On one account, the end of middle-class jobs could spell the end of capitalism as we know it.[98] But it will certainly spell growing misery for workers at and below the middle of the labor market.

Even apart from the adequacy of incomes, working conditions, and living standards at the bottom, economic inequality itself—the erosion of the middle class and the growth of self-perpetuating fortunes at the top, is a serious problem for a society that aspires to collective self-rule. That theme has reverberated through American political thought since before the Declaration of Independence, as Joseph Fishkin and William Forbath chronicle in their book, *The Anti-Oligarchy Constitution.*[99] The growing chasm between the lives and worlds of the rich and the rest is a serious, even existential, concern for American democracy whether or not it translates into either fewer jobs overall or declining living standards at the bottom.

Growing economic polarization is also likely to exacerbate racial stratification in the labor market.[100] If workers are increasingly sorted into high-end and low-end jobs and occupations, with fewer decent middle-skilled jobs in between and fewer pathways for advancement up the ladder, that will impair economic mobility and exacerbate inequality and segregation along lines of race and ethnicity. Since the 1960s, workers of color have made meaningful progress in middle-skill jobs—now endangered—while the best jobs remain predominantly white and the worst jobs are mostly occupied by workers of color and immigrants. Those patterns are likely to become more entrenched if we do not find ways to counter them—and that will require combating not just discrimination but overall economic inequality.

So while debate continues over whether we face a future of less work overall, there is growing evidence that *automation is already destroying more decent mid-skill jobs than it is creating.*[101] Too many of those who are displaced from those jobs are crowding down into the less-skilled but still human jobs that remain instead of climbing up to the better-paid, higher-skilled jobs that require more advanced training. The prospect of net job losses overall would further worsen the outlook for most workers, but the ongoing hollowing out of the labor market should be quite enough to draw the concern of citizens, policy makers, and scholars.

In the meantime, a more value-laden debate is percolating: If the new wave of automation does enable greater economic output with less need for human labor, why not embrace that future? Most humans throughout history have aspired to a life with more leisure and less toil. The goal of shorter working hours animated the labor movement for the better part of a century leading up to the New Deal. Imagine, for example, a world in which everyone could meet their economic needs while working no more than ten or twenty hours per week. If that is one's ideal vision of the future, then one might even aim to accelerate the replacement of human labor with technology while agitating for the radical social and political changes that would be required to bring about a more egalitarian distribution of technology's gains.[102]

Declining demand for human labor could translate into fewer hours of work, greater leisure, and decent pay for all. But without a concerted effort to bring that about, job losses are more likely to descend with a thud on a beleaguered subset of workers, leaving them with little or no paid work and too little income to live a decent life. If that is what a future of less work looks like, then it would be perverse to characterize it as one of greater free time. Free time without an adequate source of household income is just the malaise of long-term unemployment.

The economic fallout of unemployment—periodic and long-term—only begins with the loss of wages. During the twentieth century, employment became the platform for what Harry Arthurs has called "industrial citizenship."[103] The American social model in particular delivers many of the material requisites of a decent life—including retirement security and insurance for health care, disability, and unemployment—mainly through employment.[104] Outside the moderately-regulated employment nexus, and above a rather stingy safety net for the poor (at least in the United States),[105] individuals are largely left to the tender mercies of the market, armed with whatever individual bargaining power they can muster given the intersection of their skill set with changing market conditions. Decent, steady, middle-skill jobs—white collar and blue collar—were the foundation of American prosperity, albeit only for some. Those are among the jobs most at risk from automation.

The stakes are not only economic. Useful paid work is central to most people's identity and to our social and political life. I'll return to these points in Chapter 4, but let me put down a marker for now: The experience of shared work fosters social interaction and integration, solidarity and friendship, and cooperation and compromise, and it does so among relatively diverse groups of co-workers—not as diverse as they should be but more diverse than just about any other social setting in most adults' lives.[106] If a growing segment of the population finds itself detached from the world of work, our social fabric will become even more frayed and our politics even more fraught. And that would be true even if people's basic material needs were met by something like universal basic income.

So we have plenty to worry about, especially but not only if job losses outpace job gains. Whether we're facing the labor market equivalent of a tropical storm or a Category 5 hurricane, we had better start thinking about what to do about it even as we continue to keep our eyes on the forecast.

Speed matters. The faster jobs are destroyed, the harder it will be for public and private job creation and worker retraining to keep pace, and the harder it will be to put in place the policies that could steer clear of a hyper-polarized dystopia. In short, faster job destruction will yield more wrenching social consequences and less hospitable conditions for a serious political debate and policy making over how to spread the gains and mitigate the losses from automation. The COVID-19 pandemic suggests an analogy. Recall public health officials' arguments for "flattening the curve": If infections mounted too fast, they would overwhelm the capacity of medical institutions to treat the sick. But if the rise in infections were slower and spread out over a longer period, the system could better cope, even with existing capacity but also by expanding the capacity for treatment. Putting aside the dubious analogy of job losses to human infections and deaths, there is a parallel logic here: even if job losses from automation are inevitable, a slower and flatter pace of job destruction will allow more time for new job creation, more time for workers to prepare for those new jobs, and more time to devise and put in place policy innovations for a more automated world.

The idea of slowing down automation is anathema to the enthusiasts of innovation and automation as engines of growth and prosperity (not to mention to those who see rapid automation and job destruction as a welcome way to accelerate the end of capitalism[107]). The aim can't be to slow down automation as much as possible. So how much and what kind of slowing makes sense, and how to achieve it? Those are among the hard questions I'll tackle here.

Still, slowing down automation, however judiciously, is not a strategy for building a humane future of less work. Or rather it's only one part of a more comprehensive strategy for realizing and spreading the gains and mitigating the losses from the ongoing automation of work. We can't achieve those goals with any one big idea—with either universal basic income (UBI), or a federal job guarantee (JG), or a shorter work week, each of which is touted by some proponents as the best response to the prospect of automation-based job losses. Even if we bracket the daunting practical and political hurdles they face, each of those big ideas falls short on one dimension of a good livelihood and a good economy—widely-distributed decent work, more free time, and adequate incomes. None of those big ideas by itself promises a satisfactory future of less work. Big ideas are urgently needed given the challenges we face. But big ideas do not necessarily come in a single neat package; and those that do—especially UBI and the federal job guarantee—have crucial blind spots. What is needed is a big suite of ideas for conserving, creating, and spreading work while supporting incomes for ordinary workers.

D. What This Book Is (and Is Not) About

The impact of technological innovation on work and workers goes far beyond the hotly contested prospect of job losses. AI and machine learning are also changing the quality of work and processes of hiring, supervising, and firing of workers. Jeremias Adams-Prassl explores how "algorithmic management" and tracking of workers' movements, keystrokes, attentiveness, and emotional states threatens to render human work itself increasingly robotic, and to undercut existing strategies for constraining managerial overreach.[108] Ifeoma Ajunwa is examining how workplace technologies and the quantification of human performance affect hiring, promotions, and discipline, and especially the operation and efficacy of anti-discrimination laws.[109] Brishen Rogers highlights managers' use of technology to enhance their power over workers, and especially to squelch collective action, with or without accompanying improvements in productivity.[110] Valerio DeStefano explores how workplace technologies exacerbate problems of "subordination and submission" at work.[111] Others target the use of technology to shift risk from firms to workers.[112]

For some of these observers, fears about job losses risk distracting us from the clear and present dangers of technological degradation of the quality and fairness of work and workplaces.[113] But those urgent problems should not in turn divert us from the prospects for job destruction—which have gotten lots of attention from economists and technology experts, but little from legal scholars. That is the topic of this book, which aims to bring some clarity to societal goals and public policy strategies for a future of less work.

There's widespread skepticism across the political spectrum about whether we face such a future—whether automation in fact threatens net job losses. Chapter 2 digs more deeply into the forecast for job destruction and job creation, and adds some theory and data to this chapter's string of anecdotes about how algorithms and robots are replacing human workers. It reports both the emerging view that automation is further polarizing an already polarized labor market, and the even more concerning prediction—still a minority view—that machines are destined to produce overall net job losses as they continually whittle away at humans' comparative advantages. My working premise for the rest of the book straddles those two forecasts: *We are facing a future of less work—at least less work for those with ordinary human skills and without advanced education, and possibly less work overall.* That straddle might seem untenable; but when it comes to policy prescriptions, not much will turn on the space between the two forecasts. One need not buy into the contested prediction of net overall job losses to recognize that *most workers* do face a future of both less work and worse work unless we do something about it. And most of what we should do about it doesn't turn on whether large *net* job losses are in the offing.

Chapter 3 fills in some institutional features of the landscape of work—the evolving law of labor and employment and recent trends in the organization of work—that shape and illuminate managerial decisions about automation. Labor scholars and advocates have been rightly preoccupied with the rise of "fissuring," or outsourcing of labor needs, as illustrated by both Apple's offshoring of production to China and Uber's treatment of its drivers as independent contractors. Chapter 3 argues that automation confounds old and new legal strategies for improving the lives of ordinary workers. In short, many of the mandatory legal rights, protections, and benefits that workers have won over the past century tilt firms' calculus toward both fissuring and automation; and the prevailing legal responses to fissuring tend to strengthen the business case for automation.

To construct a better future of less work, we have to know what we're aiming for. Should we set our sights on full-time full employment for all? Should we instead aim to free people from the compulsion to work and replace work-based income with guaranteed basic income? Chapter 4 argues that we should be looking to ensure a wide distribution of three goods: adequate income, more free time, and decent work (though less of it). It's the last of these—the value of work—that is most contested, but that most animates this book. Widespread engagement in work—in particular, "decent work"—has profound psychic, social, and political benefits even apart from the goods and services it produces and the income it yields. We should aim to maintain decent work at the center of most people's lives and livelihoods even in a world where there's less of it to go around.

Proceeding from goals to means: Chapter 5 takes up the Three Big Ideas that some tout as all-purpose solutions for a future of less work: UBI, a federal job guarantee, or a shorter work week. Each faces practical and political hurdles, but more importantly each fails on one of the three dimensions of a good livelihood and a good economy. What we need is a more eclectic but nonetheless bold strategy that simultaneously saves and spreads work while supporting incomes for those who are otherwise unlikely to capture the dividends of a more automated economy.

Chapters 6 and 7 lay out the components of a three-dimensional strategy for a future of less work—one that aims for a more balanced distribution of work and free time, as well as adequate incomes, across the society. Chapter 6 focuses on creating and conserving decent jobs—that is, creating public jobs by serving public needs, and conserving decent private sector jobs by "unburdening employment," or shifting the cost of some worker entitlements off the platform of employment and onto a broader foundation. Chapter 7 focuses on work spreading—that is, shifting work from those with too much of it toward those with too little of it, and reaching a more equitable and healthy work-life balance across the society. Some work spreading can be accomplished by supporting workers' own choices to work less than full-time; other work-spreading techniques may be more controversial. Fortunately, work spreading is not an all-or-nothing proposition; we can pursue it in steps, beginning with those that make sense in the present and in light of widely accepted forecasts for the future.

That underscores a point made earlier: Most of what is proposed in this book makes sense here and now—it would counter growing economic polarization and improve the lives of most workers and the society as a whole—whether or not we face a future of less total demand for human labor. The three-dimensional strategy proposed here pursues a wider and fairer distribution of work, free time, and decent material living standards by creating, conserving, and spreading work. That offers a better future for individuals and the society—better than complacent reliance on market forces of creative destruction to replace lost jobs, and better than more single-minded strategies like UBI or a job guarantee.

Chapters 8 and 9 address concerns about money and politics, concerns that will be refracted through the prism of automation and popular anxiety about its impact on jobs. Chapter 8 takes up two questions about funding these proposals, each quite briefly: first, how to structure the funding of new and existing benefits—through payroll taxes, general revenues, or some combination—so as to advance policy goals in a politically pragmatic way; and second, how to raise the public revenues that will be needed to fund many of the proposals and to achieve some equitable redistribution along the way. The concluding chapter turns finally to politics, and how to navigate the turbulent political seas through which any major redistributive programs will have to cross.

This book aims to point the way to a better future of less work—one that mitigates the losses that automation will otherwise inflict on ordinary workers and that captures and spreads the prodigious gains from technological innovation in the form of lives that are less dominated but still anchored by shared work.

2
Forecasting the Impact of Automation on Jobs

Since the invention of the plow and the wheel, machines have been replacing human labor. Machines transformed the production of food, textiles, and clothing, which had occupied the bulk of humanity for millennia.[1] With the Industrial Revolution, machines and the collective modes of production they enabled supplanted most artisanal production, vastly increased efficiency, drove down the cost of basic consumer goods, and freed up human labor for new industries that catered to the evolving appetites of a more prosperous population.[2] In particular, major innovations from the mid-1800s to the mid-1900s both displaced workers—sometimes whole occupations, like weavers, lamplighters, and horse carriage drivers—and vastly improved most people's lives and standards of living.[3] Since the mid-twentieth century, technology has continued to destroy some jobs, to create others, to reduce misery and drudgery on and off the job, and to generate economic growth and prosperity.[4]

So what's not to like about automation going forward? One answer lies in the role of automation in growing inequality. Thomas Piketty famously documented and diagnosed a pattern of growing economic inequality under capitalism, with a few decades' reversal during the middle of the twentieth century, after the Great Depression and the socializing, humanizing, reforms adopted in its wake.[5] Notoriously, the growth of inequality has resumed since the early 1970s, as the economic gains from innovation and growth have been increasingly skewed toward the top of the income scale. For just one indicator, the share of US income that has gone to the top 1 percent of US families has grown from under 10 percent in 1972 to 22 percent in 2018.[6] Ours has been described as the New Gilded Age, and that is not meant to be celebratory.

Economic inequality partly reflects the growing share of income accruing to capital versus labor; rich people derive more of their income from capital than the rest. But it also reflects the growing polarization of labor earnings

Automation Anxiety. Cynthia Estlund, Oxford University Press. © Cynthia Estlund 2021.
DOI: 10.1093/oso/9780197566107.003.0002

both *within* firms—as seen in the exploding ratio of CEO pay to median wages[7]—and *between* firms in an increasingly concentrated "winner-take-all" economy.[8] As we've begun to see, there is mounting evidence that automation is exacerbating inequality.

More controversial is the claim that, as emerging technologies replicate or surpass human performance on a wider range of tasks, job destruction is likely to outpace job creation. The two claims are intertwined, for automation is contributing to economic polarization partly by destroying decent mid-level jobs, or hollowing out the labor market. Moreover, the two claims—net losses of mid-skill jobs and overall net job losses—point in much the same depressing direction for most workers, who are likely to face less demand for the skills they can muster, greater competition for jobs, and lower wages.

A. Dueling Economic Indicators

For those who doubt that new technologies are more likely than past ones to yield net job losses, Exhibit A is sluggish productivity growth in recent years. Stated simply: "If automation were rapidly accelerating, labor productivity and capital investment would also be surging as fewer workers and more technology did the work. But labor productivity and capital investment have actually decelerated in the 2000s."[9] The coexistence of dazzling technological advances and sluggish productivity growth is puzzling to many observers. As Larry Summers put it, "Any fully-satisfactory synthetic view has to reconcile those two observations. I have not heard them satisfactorily reconciled. This is something we have to figure out."[10]

Economists are hard at work on this puzzle. A 2019 MIT task force report suggests two possible answers. One is the proliferation of what Daron Acemoglu and Pascual Restrepo call "so-so technologies," like automated customer service and self-checkout kiosks, which "disrupt employment and displace workers without generating much of a boost in productivity."[11] A second explanation, suggested by Erik Brynjolfsson and others, is that the up-front costs of acquiring and implementing new technologies might be temporarily masking productivity gains.[12]

A third hypothesis is offered by Tyler Cowen: Maybe more workers are being diverted from productive jobs into the protean but zero-sum quest for market share. He points to the proliferation of jobs in branding, marketing, social media management, and the like: "[M]achines are not effective at persuading, at developing advertising campaigns, at branding products or corporations, or at greeting you at the door in a charming manner. . . . Those activities will remain the province of human beings for a long time to come."[13] But those jobs don't actually produce anything; they are mostly part of a "zero- or negative-sum game" in which "[e]ach business tries to pull customers away from the other brands."[14] That could explain the puzzle of rising automation without either rising productivity or (so far) net job losses.

Consider the advent of ATMs, featured in David Autor's canonical article, "Why Are There Still So Many Jobs?": How is it that, after the introduction of ATMs in the 1970s, bank teller employment held steady in the next few decades? "[W]hat are all of these tellers doing?"[15] It seems that, as tellers were liberated from counting and accounting for deposits and withdrawals, many were redeployed "as salespersons, forging relationships with customers and introducing them to additional bank services like credit cards, loans, and investment products."[16] In other words, bank tellers shifted into marketing—persuading customers to borrow money, to open credit card accounts, or to finance or refinance mortgages . . . and perhaps to take on debt that was ill-advised and eventually disastrous for the economy. Some hyperactive marketing schemes even veered into fraud, as with the Wells Fargo workers who, pressed to meet unrealistic sales quotas, signed up customers for new accounts without their consent.[17] The transformation of productive workers into marketers is a dubious basis for sustaining a healthy economy over the long run. But it suggests one answer to the question of "why are there still so many jobs?" and why productivity growth is still sluggish despite advances in automation.

Another top-line economic indicator that seemed to point against automation-based job losses is—or rather was—the unemployment rate: Before the COVID-19 collapse, it had fallen to historic lows, and employers in parts of the country were reporting labor shortages, even in less-skilled jobs.[18] In general, unemployment had been following a familiar cyclical pattern, except for severe shocks to the system like the financial crisis and the recent pandemic crisis.

But the impact of automation on jobs may show up not just in higher unemployment rates—which include only active job seekers—but in labor force participation rates. The latter have steadily declined for younger and older men over the past century or more,[19] and for prime working-age men since the 1950s.[20] Nationwide, 12 percent of men ages 25 to 54, and 17 percent of those with only a high school degree or less, were out of the labor force in 2015; that compares to 2 percent and 3 percent, respectively, in 1954.[21] Women's workforce participation increased over that period, though it has also fallen since 2000.[22] Even at the height of the pre-COVID boom, workforce participation for prime working-age men was well below the levels of a half-century ago.[23]

The best measure of the US jobs gap, and the number to watch, is the so-called "U-6" unemployment rate. That includes those who are actively seeking work as well as "discouraged" workers who have given up on seeking work, those who are "marginally attached" to the labor force, and those who are working part-time though they would prefer full-time work.[24] To illustrate, in April 2020 at the peak of COVID-19 job losses, the unemployment rate—that is, those without work but actively seeking it—spiked to 14.7 percent; but the more inclusive U-6 unemployment rate was 22.8 percent.[25]

Those numbers would be even higher but for the astronomical US rate of incarceration. Incarcerated and other institutionalized individuals, as well as those in the military, don't count in the denominator for any official unemployment statistics.[26] Yet a high percentage of the more than 2.2 million individuals occupying US prisons and jails at any one time come from demographic groups—especially young Black men—with very high jobless rates.[27] Incarceration takes those individuals off the books for unemployment purposes for the duration of their sentences (and then devastates their employment prospects thereafter).[28] The point here is obviously not just statistical, but it is also that. Mass incarceration—which took off in the 1970s just as wages began to stagnate for ordinary workers[29]—is masking what would otherwise be an even higher rate of unemployment, especially in predominantly Black communities.[30]

Alongside declines in workforce participation, there was a longer-term decline in average working hours per employee—from nearly sixty hours per week in the 1890s (for non-agricultural workers) to just under thirty-five hours per week in 2010.[31] In February 2020, just before COVID-19 began to ravage labor markets, private non-agricultural employees worked, on average, 34.4 hours per week.[32]

The point is not necessarily to lament the decline either in workforce participation or in working hours per employee. Some young people are not in the active labor force because they are in school, and many older folks have left the active labor force because they have been able to retire. The virtual demise of child labor, the long-term decline in the standard work week and the advent of the weekend, and the rise of retirement are among the greatest joint accomplishments of industrial capitalism and organized labor in the twentieth century. They underscore the fact that technological innovation has a long history of enabling the production of more goods and services with fewer total hours of human labor. Those who now predict significant net job losses due to automation, far from ignoring history, expect a continuation of those trends: more production with less labor (though unfortunately without the higher wages that went along with those trends until the 1970s).

These trends also remind us that the prospect of declining demand for human labor evokes not just fears but also fond hopes. After all, less work might sound more like a blessing than a curse to many hard-working people, now and throughout history. That depends of course on how declining work hours are distributed—in the form of shorter hours for many or of joblessness for an unlucky subset—and on what happens to incomes, especially for those below the top of the increasingly polarized income distribution. For now, let's turn to recent efforts to estimate both job losses and job gains going forward.

B. Estimating Automatability and the Pace of Job Destruction

Work tasks can't be automated unless they are "automatable." Automation is an organizational decision; automatability is a technological fact, though a tricky one to observe. Recent studies of the automatability of existing work have reached varying estimates.[33] But the state of the art is well reflected in a 2017 report by a research team at the McKinsey Global Institute (MGI), which analyzed at a fairly granular level how much human work in today's economy can be automated.[34] The team's US results capture both the dramatic potential for job losses and the uncertainty about their pace and extent.

The MGI team first identified eighteen distinct human capabilities in five categories—sensory perception, cognitive skills, natural-language processing, social and emotional skills, and physical skills—and assessed how current technology (as of 2016) stacked up against human performance on these dimensions.[35] Not surprisingly, humans outperform technology at sensing others' emotional states and responding in emotionally appropriate ways (though technology is making headway, as with the care robots).[36] By contrast, technology already outperforms humans in many physical and cognitive skills, and leaves even the most skilled human beings in the dust on both speed and accuracy in, for example, data processing.[37]

Chronicling the growing capabilities of machines is only the first step in estimating how much actual human work can be automated. The MGI team broke down human work activities into seven large categories and analyzed what percentage of those activities is capable of being automated "by adapting currently demonstrated technology."[38] The least automatable activities are management and development of people (9 percent automatable); application of expertise to decision-making, planning, and creative tasks (18 percent); interacting with stakeholders like customers, suppliers, or the public (20 percent); and unpredictable physical activities (26 percent). Much more automatable are collecting data (64 percent); processing data (69 percent); and predictable physical activities (81 percent).[39]

The mix of workers' activities varies widely by sector and by occupation, and so does automatability.[40] The MGI team estimated that work in the accommodation and food services sector is 73 percent automatable; that is, 73 percent of the time for which humans are now paid in that sector is spent in activities that could be automated with existing technology. By comparison, work in health care and social assistance is just 36 percent automatable. Those of us in "educational services" might be happy to learn that it is the least automatable large sector at 27 percent.[41] At the finer level of occupations, the work of both sewing machine operators and graders of agricultural products is nearly 100 percent automatable, while that of psychiatrists is less than 10 percent automatable.[42]

The MGI team found, unsurprisingly, that many professional jobs are relatively insulated from automation (though other studies predict much greater exposure down the line[43]). Some low-wage jobs are also hard to automate because they involve unpredictable physical tasks (janitors, landscape workers, and domestic workers, for example) or social and emotional skills (child care or elder care workers, for example). Of course. the tech sector is hard at work dismantling some of those technological hurdles, as seen in the advent of care robots and "picking and packing" robots. In any case, low-wage workers in those fields are unlikely to reap wage gains: although less exposed to competition from robots, they will be *more* exposed to human competition as other workers are displaced from automatable mid-level jobs.

Putting together their assessments of what humans currently do at work and what machines currently *can* do, the MGI researchers estimate that *46 percent of the time for which people are now paid in the US economy is spent in activities that could be automated based on "currently demonstrated technology."*[44] That estimate doesn't take into account future innovations, or even technology that exists today but hasn't yet been adapted to perform work in today's economy. And it doesn't take into account innovations like the "picking and packing" robots that came online just in the past couple of years, after blasting past seemingly-obstinate technological barriers. All in all, it's a pretty eye-opening figure.

Still, automatability does not equate to job destruction. Technical automatability is only the threshold factor in firms' decisions about whether to automate. For one thing, it is not easy to disaggregate automatable tasks from those that humans still do better. As Autor writes, "many of the tasks currently bundled into . . . jobs cannot readily be unbundled . . . without a substantial drop in quality."[45] Think, for example, about the automation of customer service. Those endless automated phone trees save on labor costs, but they also annoy and alienate customers.[46]

It takes time and managerial skill to reconfigure jobs and organizations to take advantage of what technology makes possible. Highly skilled workers are needed to implement and work with the new technology; and skills shortages in those fields create a bottleneck that will slow down the process of automation.[47] McKinsey & Co. (the consulting outfit, not its research arm) highlights another bottleneck in the retail sector: managerial inertia. Although existing technologies could "already operate a typical retail grocery store with up to 55 to 65 percent fewer hours" of human labor, "few retailers are moving quickly to implementation." (McKinsey offers its consulting services to those who want to be among the "disruptors" instead of the laggards.[48])

Given all these challenges and uncertainties, the MGI study is highly circumspect about the time frame for large-scale automation. Based on historical data on the diffusion of past innovations, its estimates range from *two to six decades*. Uptake will be faster for software (which is easier and cheaper to implement) than for robots, faster for higher-wage but still-automatable jobs, and faster in high-wage countries like the United States than in China or India.[49]

A big factor in managers' decisions about automation is labor costs. If an existing technology—a robot or a software solution—is capable of performing certain tasks currently performed by humans, then firms must weigh the potential gains against the costs of acquiring, operating, and maintaining the technology, and of reorganizing operations accordingly.[50] Chief among the gains are labor cost savings: How many hours of human labor could be saved, and what are the direct and indirect costs associated with that labor? Other gains in safety, reliability, or quality might be even greater. But labor costs are crucial factors in the pace of automation.

One upshot is that the most automatable jobs may not be the first to disappear. For example, jobs in "accommodations and food services" are among the most automatable in the US economy (73 percent); but because wages are so low in that sector, there is simply less to be gained by firms in replacing humans.[51] Unfortunately, human workers in that sector are still indirectly competing with robots, which are growing cheaper almost by the day.

The MGI folks conclude that automation is currently proceeding too slowly. Firms are missing out on efficiency gains, and countries are missing out on productivity gains that could drive economic growth.[52] The MIT task force report reaches a similar conclusion, though with greater emphasis on the disruptive losses for displaced workers and the lopsided distribution of gains from automation. Much turns on whether and how quickly displaced workers land on their feet in new jobs. And that brings us to the other side of the equation.

C. Will New Job Creation Keep Pace? Some Grounds for Concern

Estimates of new job creation are much less empirically grounded than estimates of job destruction. It's hard enough to assess the impact of existing technology on existing jobs; predicting the creation of new jobs, and even new kinds of jobs, is a more speculative enterprise that involves many debatable assumptions. Indeed, when the MGI team predicted in early 2017 that automation would underwrite economic growth in the United States and across the globe, that was based on an explicit assumption that "human labor displaced by automation would rejoin the workforce and be as productive as it was in 2014, that is, new demand for labor will be created."[53] That looked like a colossal leap of faith. But MGI had in the works, and soon issued, a second report that sought to identify and quantify sources of new or increased demand for labor that might absorb workers displaced by automation.[54]

Automation can create new jobs through several channels. First, there will be new jobs for those who create, implement, maintain, and work with the new technology.[55] Second, automation will make some workers more productive and increase demand for their labor.[56] Third, productivity gains and cost savings from automation can increase consumers' disposable incomes, which can generate new demand for human labor both in existing jobs and in new kinds of jobs that don't exist in the current economy. The MGI economists predict that, by 2030, "9 percent of the US labor force could be employed in occupations that do not exist today."[57]

The MGI estimates of job creation, like their estimates of the pace of actual automation, are based on evidence of how past labor-saving innovations affected labor markets. Economic forecasts customarily rely on historical data, which has the virtue of being actual data versus sheer speculation. As *The Economist* put it in assessing the failed economic forecasting in the lead-up to the financial crisis, "Does the past predict the future? Maybe not, but it's all we've got."[58] Unfortunately, when the question is whether this time is different, historical data and assumptions derived from that data have their limitations, and we should be alert to them.[59]

The MGI report's bottom-line prediction for the United States is that *job creation could just about keep pace with job destruction, and maintain existing employment levels, up to 2030.*[60] At first glance that "break-even" prediction might look like a reassuring affirmation of the virtuous dynamics of creative destruction—at least over the short period until 2030. But a closer look reveals several qualifications, contingencies, and contestable assumptions, all of which should unsettle any complacency about the impact of automation on jobs.

First, the MGI researchers explicitly base their break-even prediction on what they call a "step-up scenario," which envisions a fulsome set of new public and private investments in training and education, human services, infrastructure, and income support.[61] Depending on how one fills in the blanks, it might resemble the platform of the US Democratic Party; in any case, it's very far from the status quo, and even further from "small government" aspirations on the right. But what if political polarization and paralysis prevent us from "stepping up" and making those investments? The MGI report supplies an answer—though it is hidden in the small print: In a "trendline scenario," in which existing trends and policies continue without any "stepping up," job losses outpace job creation by some 10 million jobs by 2030.[62] In short, the MGI report buries the lede—what should be an urgent call to action on the policy front—beneath its headline break-even prediction.

Second, the break-even prediction is based on the assumption that the pace of job destruction is at the midpoint of its large estimated ranges for uptake of existing technologies, based on historical patterns of technological diffusion.[63] But what if innovations diffuse faster in the more competitive and wired economy of the twenty-first century than they did historically?[64] In that case, then job losses are likely to outpace job creation even under the "step-up" scenario, with its various stimulating and mitigating measures.

Third, the MGI expects the lion's share of new jobs—well over half—to stem from the higher consumer incomes and higher demand for goods and services that more productive machines will help to generate.[65] But what if consumers don't earn those higher incomes (through decent jobs) and spend them as in the past? Since the 1970s, wage gains have sharply diverged from productivity gains; and income growth in a more automated world is likely to be even more skewed toward the rich, and especially toward owners of capital, rather than being widely distributed through decently paid jobs.[66] That's bad enough in itself, but it would also depress job growth because rich people save more and spend less of their income on goods and services.[67] That suggests a worrisome circularity within the MGI's predictions of new job creation from consumer surplus: Ordinary people have to have decent jobs in order to earn and spend the money that helps to create those new jobs.

Fourth, "job creation" as the MGI defines it does not represent jobs occupied by actual workers but rather employer *demand* for workers. But what if workers displaced by automation fail to acquire—and our chronically deficient educational and training institutions fail to cultivate—the different and often higher skills demanded by employers going forward? In that case, "job creation" will translate into unfilled job vacancies due to skill shortages of the sort that employers are already reporting.

Other doubts about the MGI's break-even projection are more hypothetical: What if newer technologies prove to be bigger or faster job killers than "currently demonstrated technologies"? Or if machines can produce a growing share of the new stuff that people want in the future, so that growing demand for goods and services doesn't translate into demand for *labor* as it did in the past?[68] Or if consumer appetites are not inexhaustible—if the so-called "full closet effect" dampens new consumer demand?[69] It makes good sense to ground estimates in historical facts and existing technologies, unlike the feverish speculation that fuels some predictions of "the end of work." Yet it might also feed complacency about the future pace and extent of automation.

There is, in short, a whole raft of reasons to question the MGI's break-even prediction. Once we take those qualifications on board, far from being reassuring, the MGI estimates might foretell a grim future in which workers displaced from mid-level jobs find themselves competing for jobs lower down the ladder—jobs that are hard to automate but that require no specialized human skills, or jobs that are not worth automating because wages are so low.

D. Assessing Economic Assessments of Automation in Light of "Task Encroachment"

More basic concerns with the MGI estimates stem from the economic models on which they rest, and what those models might fail to grasp about the nature of the ongoing wave of technological innovation. So argues Daniel Susskind, a U.K. economist. Let's first back up and review how economic thinking on automation has evolved.[70]

Predictions of technological unemployment have recurred since the onset of the Industrial Revolution. But the recurring reality was one of economic growth through creative destruction. Yes, machines destroyed lots of jobs, often with devastating effects on displaced workers for whom new jobs were often too late or out of reach. Over time, however, job destruction freed up labor and capital that went into new and usually better jobs and higher incomes. That is because technology both *substitutes* for labor—in particular, less-skilled labor—and *complements* labor, or makes it more productive, thus generating new demand for labor. Casual observers have often tended "to overstate the extent of machine substitution for human labor," which was readily observable; they "repeatedly underestimated the demand for the work of human beings that would remain."[71]

The view that technology's complementary effect would always counter its substitutive effect congealed into conventional wisdom among economists during the twentieth century. Indeed, says Susskind:

> in the dominant model used in the field, it was impossible for new technologies to make either skilled or unskilled workers worse off; technological progress always raised everyone's wages, though . . . some more than others. This story was so widely told that leading economists referred to it as the "canonical model."[72]

But the canonical model could not explain why, starting around 1980, demand for mid-level, moderately skilled workers was stagnating, depressing both wages and employment.

By the early 2000s, leading labor economists were challenging the canonical model. In particular, David Autor, Frank Levy, and Richard Murnane recognized that automation's substitution effect was greatest not for *unskilled jobs* but for *routine tasks*—that is, tasks that a worker could fully explain step by step.[73] Many less-skilled jobs (like care work and maintenance) involved social or physical tasks that required tacit knowledge and were hard to automate, while many mid-skilled white-collar jobs consisted largely of routine and eminently automatable tasks.[74] Autor, Levy, and Murnane formalized their insights into the so-called "ALM hypothesis," which become the new canonical model. That is the model that underpins the MGI studies and most contemporary research on the economics of automation.[75]

In the past decade or so, economists using the ALM hypothesis have continued to poke holes in the old consensus and to highlight the double-edged nature of technological innovation for workers. As Daron Acemoglu and Pascual Restrepo explained in a 2018 paper, contrary to the prior consensus, some technological innovations might "simultaneously reduce wages and employment."[76] In other words, this time might be different.

Acemoglu and Restrepo distinguish three effects of technology: a *displacement effect*, replacing workers and destroying jobs; a *productivity effect*, increasing overall productivity and "demand for labor in non-automated tasks"; and a *reinstatement effect*, generating "new tasks in which labor has a comparative advantage" and even wholly new occupations.[77] The net impact on wages and jobs depends on the mix of those three effects, and there is no guarantee that the latter two effects will outweigh the displacement effect. Indeed, they find "stronger displacement effects and considerably weaker reinstatement effects during the last 30 years than the decades before."[78] Those patterns "hint at an acceleration of automation and a deceleration in the creation of new tasks," and help to account for "a slowdown in the growth of labor demand and an almost complete stagnation over the last two [decades]."[79]

The 2019 MIT task force report previewed in Chapter 1 reflects an emerging body of evidence that automation not only can but has hurt many workers. In particular, the "digitalization of work . . . made highly-educated workers more productive and made less-educated workers easier to replace with machinery."[80] In the end, they conclude that "this time is different," and that "Americans are right to be worried" about growing inequality and declining job quality and wages.[81] Still, the MIT report did not project an overall deficit of jobs relative to the expected supply of labor.[82] Indeed, "demographic trends point towards rising labor scarcity in the decades ahead."[83] Let's take a quick look at those trends.

Demographic trends affect both demand for and supply of labor in cross-cutting ways. *Lower birth rates* mean fewer new entrants to the labor force (potentially offset by younger immigrants). Countries with shrinking working-age populations might face labor shortages; in any case, they will need fewer new jobs to offset jobs lost. But *longer life expectancies*—rising toward one hundred years in the next several decades—throw a curveball into these estimates.[84] The MIT researchers note that growth in the elderly population will increase demand for workers in health care and elder care. But they don't factor in the prospect of *longer working lives*—that is, older workers seeking or holding onto jobs past "normal" retirement age. Why should we expect that? Mainly because it will take more years of work—and of retirement savings and contributions—to support more years of retirement.[85] Going forward, most people will have to work longer, if they can, to provide for a decent retirement.[86] Good news, bad news.

Back to the job gap: In some aging societies of Europe and Asia, a cohort of healthy older workers might help offset the birth dearth and shrinking flow of new entrants into the labor market.[87] But the United States is not an aging society in that sense; both birth rates and immigration rates are higher than in much of the developed world.[88] Longer working lives may thus contribute to a job deficit in a more automated future.

With that caveat, the new betting line among economists working with the ALM hypothesis, as of 2019, was greater economic polarization but not fewer jobs overall relative to labor supply. That forecast was plenty concerning, but it was soon unsettled (like everything in our lives) by COVID. Two of the three authors of the 2019 MIT report, Autor and Elisabeth Reynolds, wrote in 2020 that "the COVID crisis has upended our confidence" in predictions of continued growth and labor scarcity.[89] As noted in Chapter 1, they concluded that COVID was likely to accelerate job destruction through automation, perhaps yielding lasting labor surpluses, especially in low-wage service jobs.[90] Whether those developments will topple the newly canonical ALM hypothesis remains to be seen; for now it is still the reigning model.

Now let's take on board Susskind's doubts about that model: He argues that it fails to reckon with a recent paradigm shift in AI research and development. The ALM hypothesis defines "non-routine work" as work that humans can do but can't fully explain. We know more than we can say, according to "Polanyi's paradox"; and jobs that require tacit knowledge have been deemed beyond the reach of automation.[91] That, says Susskind, "has encouraged us to believe that there is a wide range of tasks that can never be automated, a refuge of activity that will always provide enough work for human beings to do."[92] That belief seemed reinforced by AI researchers' slow progress toward replicating actual human intelligence. So far so good for the ALM team.

More recently, however, AI research has shifted away from seeking to mimic human intelligence, and has galloped ahead by unleashing machines' ability to forge alternate paths to task completion—paths that deploy machines' own capabilities that are mostly inaccessible to humans. Recall AlphaGo Zero's blazing triumph based on nothing more than the rules and the objective of the game—that is, without human instructions or a database of human experience.[93] Susskind calls this the "pragmatist revolution" in AI. It recognizes that, "just as Darwin found a century before, remarkable capabilities can emerge gradually from blind, unthinking, bottom-up processes that do not resemble human intelligence at all."[94]

The pragmatist revolution has accelerated the process of "task encroachment," whittling away at humans' advantages and repeatedly outstripping AI experts' beliefs about what machines could do.[95] That process goes in only one direction, and is bound to continue, says Susskind:

> Machines will not do everything in the future, but they will do more. And as they slowly, but relentlessly, take on more and more tasks, human beings will be forced to retreat to an ever-shrinking set of activities. It is unlikely that every person will be able to do what remains to be done; and there is no reason to imagine there will be enough demand for it to employ all those who are indeed able to do it.[96]

That is a sobering assessment. As task encroachment continues, says Susskind, job losses will mount not with a "big bang" but through steady erosion of humans' comparative advantages.[97]

E. A Working Premise (and the Illusory Answer of More Training)

Between the lines of these sometimes-arid academic accounts, one can glimpse a feverishly competitive future—a high-stakes tournament in which the winners will include firms with the agility and perhaps ruthlessness to exploit labor-saving technology, and individuals who learn to "race with the machines."[98] The losers are likely to outnumber the winners.[99] Firms will lose out if they continue to employ people to do things that machines can do more efficiently, and if they lack the human talent and organizational agility to constantly adopt and adapt to new technology. (Big firms have advantages in this contest, and are likely to get bigger.[100]) And people will lose out—without dramatic changes in the regulation and governance of work—if they fail to acquire the high-end, hard-to-automate skills that will be in greatest demand, or if they lack the resources and opportunities needed to acquire those skills, or if they crumple under the pressure of the tournament itself.

Somewhat paradoxically, many workers at both the top and the bottom of this even-more polarized economy might end up working long hours for very different reasons. Those with scarce skills, along with their employers, might rationally converge on long hours of work, as those extra hours will garner high marginal returns for both. By contrast, some low-wage workers will scramble to work multiple jobs or gigs just to make ends meet.[101] We know this is realistic, for it is already happening in today's US economy, as explored by sociologist Jamie McCallum in a recent book, *Worked Over.*[102] But it can get worse.

The human contestants in this tournament economy will need to be intelligent, adaptable, and entrepreneurial about their working lives, and willing and able to continually retrain and redeploy their talents to meet the ever-changing demands of technological innovation and dynamic market conditions.[103] That in turn will require a high level of psychological resilience and tolerance for risk and change, as well as a strong basic education that equips them to learn how to learn. Not everyone is blessed by nature and nurture with the makings of those traits, and not everyone in our egregiously unequal society has an opportunity to cultivate them. Even those who succeed in this tournament, or who could succeed, might pine for a more balanced life that is not dominated by the competition to get ahead and stay ahead.

Again, we're already seeing features of this tournament economy and some of its costs. Daniel Markovits has recently underscored the psychic costs to the current tournament's top young contenders, who suffer high levels of drug use, depression, anxiety, and suicide.[104] As for the tournament's losers, Angus Deaton and Anne Case's recent account—*Deaths of Despair and the Future of Capitalism*—chronicles rising death rates from suicide, drug abuse, and alcoholism among those left behind by economic change.[105]

Undoubtedly, better institutions of training and education are essential, and would help to prepare many workers displaced by automation for higher-skill jobs. That could modestly mitigate both the polarization of the labor market—by increasing the supply of in-demand skills and reducing the downward wage pressure on lower-skill jobs—and the exodus of displaced workers from the labor force. Reports and policy papers on automation invariably emphasize the importance of both "learning to learn" and "lifelong learning"—better basic education and better structures for training and retraining workers for the new jobs that will be created directly and indirectly by automation.[106] I doubt one could find a single observer of automation trends—whether wary or enthusiastic—who does not think we need to overhaul and upgrade our institutions of education and training.

Suppose we managed to do that. (I will offer a few proposals in this vein in Chapter 7.) Would more and better education and training be enough to head off either economic polarization or a growing exodus from the active labor market? Sadly, that seems unlikely. Automation is destroying many of the decent mid-level jobs—jobs that require diligent completion of mostly routine tasks—that have long sustained the broad middle of the working population, and that provided stepping stones to higher-skill jobs. Assuming no differences in the capacity to acquire in-demand social and technical skills at birth, the social conditions associated with poverty systematically decimate much of that capacity—much of that potential "human capital"—long before individuals enter the labor market, and even before they enter formal schooling.[107] A massive social transformation would be required to enable every individual to develop the skills that will be demanded in a more automated future.

Recall Susskind's prognosis: With continuing technological task encroachment, it is "unlikely that every person will be able to do what remains to be done; and there is no reason to imagine there will be enough demand for it to employ all those who are indeed able to do it."[108] All in all, placing a big bet on re-engineering humans for the more frenetic tournament economy that lies around the bend seems both doomed and misguided.

F. Five Futures of Work

This book is about what we should be aiming for in a future of less work and how best to get there. But it is worth conjuring at the outset some alternative futures, including what awaits us if we *don't* get our act together and formulate a constructive response to the challenge of automation-based job losses. If we merge the varying forecasts of automation's impact on labor markets with some speculation about how society might or should respond, we can glimpse several stylized versions of the future:[109]

First, more of the same, but with more and better stuff: Some enthusiasts of markets and market-driven innovation—especially those who still hew to the old conventional wisdom—believe that jobs lost to automation will be replaced by new and better jobs that satisfy evolving and bottomless consumer appetites, and that, although we can't yet imagine what we'll want decades hence, surely people will be needed to produce much of it.[110] But we've seen that markets alone cannot perform the magic of matching new job creation with job destruction. For those who believe they can, the views of the MGI economists should be especially sobering, for they found that net job losses are likely to mount in the United States *absent an ambitious suite of mitigating and stimulating measures* (even if their other assumptions hold true).[111] (And that is without considering concerns about sustainability that we have ignored thus far.) The old vision of continuing growth and prosperity through markets and market-driven innovation is too complacent and outdated.

Second, a hyper-polarized dystopia: Aiming for the first future by trusting in markets and innovation might instead yield a deeply dystopian future of economic struggle and misery for many alongside ever more concentrated wealth for the few. On the MGI's forecast, if we stay on the current trendline and fail to "step up" to the challenge of faster automation, then job losses are likely to mount. This is also the MIT Task Force's forecast of growing economic polarization—though it emphasizes institutional changes that could bend this trajectory. Without those changes, workers who lack in-demand skills will compete, and drive down wages, for the jobs that that machines can't do as well or as cheaply as humans, but that most humans can do, and growing numbers may get squeezed out of the active labor force altogether. The winners—those who make or own the technology or whose scarce skills are augmented by technology—might win access to private enclaves fortified against the resentment and desperation of the losers.[112] This is a future we should strive mightily to avoid.

Third, a stepped-up, super-charged capitalism: Suppose now that firms and governments rise to the challenge of automation more or less along the lines of the MGI's "step-up scenario" with large investments in training and education, income support, infrastructure, and social services. On that scenario, job creation might keep pace with job destruction, and we can enjoy continuing growth and prosperity. But the MGI's favored future seems to require ever-agile and endlessly resilient humans constantly retraining and remarketing themselves to slot into higher rungs of a constantly innovating economy. There is very little room in this future for human frailty or balanced lives. And even if this vision seems congenial, it may be out of reach if predictions of job creation prove too sanguine, or if the pace of automation is on the high side of current estimates (or if we finally come to grips with the unsustainability of perpetual economic growth[113]). Sobering indeed.

Fourth, a utopian post-scarcity future of little or no work: A fourth vision of the future is frankly utopian and post-capitalist: Automation will banish scarcity, and a benevolent state will orchestrate the production of ample public goods and redistribute the large economic gains from technological progress, probably in the form of universal basic income, so that everyone can live a decent life free from the compulsion and drudgery of paid work. For some readers, this might be the very meaning of human liberation. Others might recoil at the hugely expanded role of the state and the massive redistribution that this future would require. Still others might worry that the end of work will lead to aimless anomie rather than human liberation. But many readers, however favorably or unfavorably they might rate this future, are likely to view it as hopelessly unrealistic.

Fifth, a fairer and more humane market economy: A fifth possible future would steer between the last two paths toward a fairer distribution of the gains from a well-regulated market economy. Shorter work weeks and periodic paid leaves from work (for family, rest and recreation, education, and civic work) would be coupled with ample public goods and universal basic benefits. This future would build on basic features of social policy in some European countries, which are grounded in a belief that it is necessary to "constrain the free market in the name of the public interest" in order to lay the foundation for a just society.[114]

This last vision might appeal to many readers, as it does to me. Others will disagree about what is desirable or achievable. But that is a debate we urgently need to have. We need to choose and shape our future lest we fall into the dystopian, hyper-polarized future by default. For that is where complacent trust in creative destruction might land us.

* * * * *

We've seen two lines of thought about where we are headed, absent an effective policy response. First, as automation displaces workers from many mid-level jobs, it is very likely to exacerbate inequality and deepen the economic troubles of ordinary working people and their families even without any overall loss of jobs. That prediction defies the old conventional wisdom about creative destruction, but it is gaining adherents among leading economists who study automation. Second, as technology encroaches on humans' comparative advantages, job losses are likely to mount. That is still a minority view, but it is plausible, and may become more so with every new and surprising breakthrough in what machines can do (some of which might occur in the short time between my completion of this book and its publication).

The premise for the rest of this book straddles those two predictions. That might seem untenable, but in fact the two forecasts will point to many of the same prescriptions. I'll often use the shorthand phrase "a future of less work." By that I mean at least less work for ordinary workers without scarce skills, and very possibly less work overall.

The main agenda for this book is figuring out how to respond to the prospect of future job losses—how to avoid the worst possible futures and to steer toward the better ones. That will require us to identify goals—what we want to achieve or to avoid—for a future of less work. But I want to postpone further discussion of both goals and strategies. Whatever future we aim to construct, we have to start from where we are. We need a more complex picture of the existing landscape of work and the role of the law in shaping it. Automation is obviously not the only trend that is affecting the number and quality of jobs, and responding to one trend without keeping others in mind risks making things worse.

3

What's Law Got to Do with It?

How the Law of Work Affects Automation (and Fissuring)

Our economy is becoming increasingly polarized, with steep gains at the top of the income distribution and stagnant wages and eroding labor standards for most workers.[1] Leading economists now believe that automation is a major driver in those trends. Most worker advocates and labor scholars have been looking elsewhere for causes and solutions to workers' economic woes. And there surely are other causes. One is the decline of unions, which enabled many working people to claim a bigger share of a growing pie during the middle of the twentieth century. Another is the erosion of the minimum wage. And then there is "fissuring," David Weil's evocative term for firms' growing proclivity to outsource, offshore, or otherwise contract out their labor needs.[2] Fissuring in turn has contributed to both the erosion of labor standards and the decline of unions.

When it comes to solutions, worker advocates have accordingly focused on fortifying the right to form a union, raising minimum wages and expanding mandatory employee rights and benefits, and extending firms' responsibilities for workers in their supply chains. Yet these sensible strategies fail to reckon with the prospect of automation-based job losses. While both automation and fissuring are driven in part by the costs, risks, and hassles associated with direct employment of human labor automation offers firms a more complete and increasingly cost-effective escape from those costs, risks, and hassles, and an end run around prevailing legal strategies for improving the quality of work. In this chapter I'll develop that argument while introducing some of the institutional factors—the law of work and the changing organization of work—that are shaping the trajectory and impact of automation and that will be critical in crafting responses.

Automation Anxiety. Cynthia Estlund, Oxford University Press. © Cynthia Estlund 2021.
DOI: 10.1093/oso/9780197566107.003.0003

A. A Brief Tour of the Fortress of Employment

Since the mid-nineteenth century, US workers have fought to improve their work lives through collective self-help and political mobilization. Their efforts met resistance and repression, led by the Supreme Court under the constitutional banner of "liberty of contract."[3] But public confidence in *laissez-faire* capitalism buckled and judicial recalcitrance gave way in the Great Depression. Beginning with the New Deal in the United States, and by the mid-twentieth century across the industrial democracies, employees gained an array of rights, labor standards, and benefits, all backed by employer duties and liabilities. The US law of work is illustrative though distinctive.

Federal labor law, embodied in the National Labor Relations Act of 1935 (NLRA), granted most private sector employees the right to form unions, to engage in strikes and other concerted activities, and to bargain collectively. The NLRA codified certain basic labor rights—especially workers' freedom of association—that are now deemed foundational for a free and democratic society.[4] It also sought to achieve a sustainable form of "industrial peace" by giving workers a democratic voice in their working life and enabling them to bargain for more than what public law required, or could require, across the board. For several decades, the NLRA model worked pretty well for many workers in core industries. But the law (especially as later amended) also imposed harsh restrictions on some union tactics, and left employers with ample means of resisting unionization. Changes in the economy—globalization, deindustrialization, deregulation, fissuring, and, yes, automation of highly unionized industries—took their toll as well.[5] With unions now representing about 6 percent of private sector employees,[6] the NLRA is widely seen as a failed statute. We will return to collective labor law later, but the main focus here will be on the mandatory entitlements created by employment law.[7]

Since the New Deal, legislatures have created an array of employee entitlements—legal rights, minimum labor standards, and mandatory benefits. (Although the term "entitlement" carries political baggage in the United States, I will use it here as shorthand for all of those legal mandates.) Among key *employee rights* are protections against discrimination because of race, religion, sex, age, disability and other traits; and rights to engage in certain protected activities—such as union organizing or disclosing or complaining of unlawful activity—free from employer retaliation. (Most

US workers still lack legal protection against unjustified dismissal, which are otherwise ubiquitous across the developed world.[8] The vast majority can be fired "at will"—at any time and for any reason not forbidden by law, even without a legitimate justification—and the resulting fear of arbitrary dismissal tends to undermine all other legal rights on the job.[9]) Key *labor standards* laws include restrictions on child labor, minimum wage rates and overtime premiums, and workplace health and safety laws. Mandatory *employee benefits* include Social Security retirement and disability benefits; worker compensation for occupational injury and illness; unemployment compensation; and, under the "employer mandate" of the Affordable Care Act (ACA), employer-subsidized health insurance.

Nearly all employment statutes leave out some employees and some employers. But most US employees enjoy most of those entitlements, at least on paper; and many in left-leaning states and cities enjoy additional ones under state or local law. The federal minimum wage is a paltry $7.25 per hour, but many states and cities have enacted higher minimum wages.[10] Federal law doesn't guarantee paid sick leave or parental leave, but some states do. Federal law does little to combat abusive scheduling practices that wreak havoc in the lives of many low-wage service workers; but some states and localities have enacted fair scheduling laws.[11] US employment law is a varied and changing patchwork of entitlements; but it almost only expands as a formal matter. Employment rights tend to be sticky, and to resist repeal.[12]

The mandatory terms imposed by the public law of employment add up to a sturdy but spare social minimum that is supposed to protect nearly all workers, regardless of their individual or collective bargaining power. In principle, that social minimum includes the "core labor standards" that bind all member states of the International Labor Organization (ILO):[13] workers' freedom of association and right of collective bargaining (embodied very imperfectly in the NLRA), along with freedom from "all forms of forced or compulsory labour," child labor, and "discrimination in respect of employment and occupation."[14] Everything else—minimum wages and benefits, job security, and even health and safety—is governed by national judgments,[15] and, in the United States, by a federal floor and a patchwork of state and local embellishments.

I will use the term "decent work" here to describe work that meets both core international labor standards and the mandates set by positive law at any given time and place. That usage of decent work might seem to set the bar too low, to defer unduly to the results of skewed political processes, and to undercut the normative thrust of "decent work" as an agenda and a rallying cry for improving the quality of work. I don't mean to do that; indeed, I'll argue for some improvements. Yet existing law in any given jurisdiction approximates society's current conception of decent work. In a reasonably democratic society, we can credit the political and legal processes that yield the existing law of work, even while continuing to argue and agitate over what the law should be.

Employment laws set a non-waivable lower boundary on wages and working conditions, but they leave lots of room for private ordering above that floor through both unilateral employer action and individually or collectively bargained agreements.[16] Most employees earn much more than the minimum wage, and more-than-mandatory benefits. Indeed, after the New Deal, the mostly white and male workers in the core of the US economy—blue and white collar alike—came to enjoy an economic package that underwrote the expansion of the American middle class. The so-called "standard employment relationship" included rising wages over a worker's career; internal promotion ladders; formal or informal job security; paid vacations; employer-funded health insurance; retirement security; and insurance against injury, illness, disability, or unemployment. Employers rather than the government became responsible for providing basic benefits like health insurance and pensions (beyond Social Security).[17] The standard employment relationship spread from the union sector to much of the labor market, though never to its lower tiers. It was what women and racial and ethnic minorities sought access to, and what some eventually got, especially after the enactment of civil rights laws in the 1960s. Unfortunately, by the time exclusionary hurdles began to fall, the standard employment relationship itself was starting to crumble.

Many private sector workers—especially the college-educated full-time employees of leading companies—still enjoys much more generous wages, benefits, and conditions of employment than the law requires. But today's version of the standard employment relationship, if we can still call it that, is far from standard; its reach has shrunk and its terms are more varied, with much less by way of job security and longevity, for reasons we'll soon see.

Together, the laws that define minimum standards of decent work and the private and contractual commitments that exceed that minimum create a kind of fortress of protections against many of the risks and insecurities of life at work and beyond. The *fortress of employment*, like any medieval fortress, has more and less privileged precincts; yet its outer walls afford protection that is lacking outside, where individuals are largely left to fend for themselves. Those equipped with skills and capital and a tolerance for risk might choose to make a go of it on their own outside the fortress. Others who are left outside are forced to rely on scraps of independent work and a patchy social safety net to stave off destitution. For the great majority of workers, the key to economic security for themselves and their families lies in securing a place inside the fortress of employment in the form of a steady decent job and all that goes with it. Ever since the wage-labor relationship eclipsed independent production, workers and their organizations have struggled to expand and shore up the fortress of employment by agitating for more and broader entitlements.

Here's the rub, though: The fortress is costly to maintain, and much of the cost falls on employers, who have nearly unfettered power to decide who gets in and considerable power over who stays. The costs of employing humans—including those that stem from the mandatory provisions of employment law—inevitably enter into firms' calculus about whether to automate automatable work and to shed workers or not hire them. Yet automation is only one kind of managerial decision that affects the quality and number of jobs, and that is affected in turn by labor costs. So let's situate automation within the broader landscape of changes in the organization of work.

B. Fissuring and the Growth of Outsourcing, Offshoring, and the Gig Economy

The heartland of the standard employment relationship was in the profitable branded corporations that reigned at the top of the economy during the twentieth century. AT&T, IBM, General Motors, and other large vertically integrated firms once hired their own employees to supply nearly all of their labor needs, from manufacturing and maintenance on up. Back in the day, one could find top executives in those large firms who had started on the production line or in the storied mailroom.[18] A combination of collective bargaining commitments and market-driven efforts to attract and keep good workers (and to divert union sentiment) induced firms to establish relatively high wages and benefits, promotion ladders, and formal or informal job security even at the bottom of those lead firms' internal labor markets. Those were relatively well-appointed quarters within the multi-tiered, sprawling fortress of employment.

Over the past several decades, however, leading firms have been busily shedding workers and contracting out labor functions—especially manufacturing, maintenance, cleaning, security, and food services.[19] Some outside contractors supply specialized services or components. Some, like temporary employment agencies, supply nothing but labor. Others, like franchisees, take over all daily operations subject to standards set by the lead firm (and in turn contract out some of those operations). Outsourcing is not new. Early twentieth-century garment manufacturers sought to avoid child labor laws and union organizing through their "putting out" system.[20] But outsourcing has metastasized in the past few decades, earning the new name of "fissuring" in the process.

Fissuring usually leaves workers worse off—without the generous benefits and pathways to advancement that their predecessors enjoyed inside lead firms,[21] and usually without union representation, which is sparse and vehemently opposed in supplier sectors. Intense cost-based competition and thin profit margins among suppliers sharpen the incentive to cut corners, leading to lower wages and widespread labor violations. And many supplier firms have little capital or reputation on the line; they are less able and less motivated than branded lead firms to treat their employees decently or even comply with the law. Fissuring allows lead firms to reduce costs while insulating themselves from the stench of the lawless practices that may underlie those lower costs.

Fissuring has exacerbated economic inequality in part by widening disparities between firms. *Intra*firm inequality is alive and well, as seen in the growing ratio between CEO pay and ordinary workers' compensation in the same firm—on average, 320-to-1 among the 350 largest US companies in 2019.[22] But a growing component of overall economic inequality is *inter*firm disparities—that is, the gap between high-profit branded firms and their relatively cosseted employees, on the one hand, and the lower-profit firms that employ most low-wage workers on the other.[23] Interfirm inequality and the concentration of low-wage workers in less-profitable supplier sectors are driven largely by fissuring.

Two kinds of fissuring have drawn especially anxious attention from scholars, advocates, and the wider public: the offshoring of jobs to overseas suppliers (think China), and the splintering of jobs into "gigs" that are or purport to be outside the employment nexus (think Uber). Outsourcing raised China's share of global manufacturing output from under 3 percent in 1990 to nearly 25 percent in 2015.[24] India, with its large reservoir of English-language skills, became the epicenter of outsourced information-based services.[25] The cost savings from offshoring stem partly from much lower wages and weaker regulatory institutions and trade unions in these poorer countries, and partly from the same forces that depress labor standards among domestic suppliers: cost-based competition in a concentrated low-profit environment. Offshoring allows lead firms to escape the reach of collective and regulatory efforts in more advanced economies to protect workers or improve their wages or working conditions.

Uber stands for another kind of fissuring and another exit option—one that shifts work outside the employment nexus by disintegrating jobs into "gigs." Uber thus treats its drivers as independent contractors, while setting prices and performance standards and assiduously monitoring them. Some platforms, like Task Rabbit, allow workers to set their own prices, and to bid against each other in real time. And where work can be done remotely—like the microtasks posted on Amazon Mechanical Turk[26]—the bidders may include poor workers in developing countries, thus allowing firms to escape both employment laws and higher-wage labor markets.

Platform-based work is just one high-profile aspect of the larger practice of outsourcing work to individuals. Drivers, writers, accountants, cleaners, artists, carpenters, care workers, web designers, software programmers, fitness instructors, and therapists are among those attempting to piece together a living from a string of short-term gigs in today's economy. Although it is unclear how much independent contracting, or "self-employment," has grown,[27] one large recent study found that 20 to 30 percent of working-age adults in the United States and Europe engaged in some "independent work."[28] By hiring independent contractors, lead firms don't just pass the burdens of employer status down to less visible, profitable, and capable firms; they eliminate the corresponding employee protections.

Some freelancers prosper outside the fortress of employment, and some plainly value the greater autonomy and flexibility of independent work.[29] But for many US workers and their families, the devolution of decent and stable jobs into contingent work and gigs is an economic disaster. Workers lose rights, economic security, and benefits that are linked to employment by law, contract, or widespread practice, especially in large companies. The shift of work from lead firms to leaner and meaner supplier firms, and from steady full-time employment to contingent work and gigs, is shaking the foundations of the fortress of employment not only in the United States but across the developed world.[30]

C. How Automation Is Like and Unlike Fissuring

Automation and fissuring share some common causal roots; yet automation is different.

1. Common Causes: Technology, Competition, Labor Costs

Technological innovation underlies not just automation but nearly every aspect of fissuring, including outsourcing to lower-wage countries and platform work.[31] Technology has lowered the transaction costs associated with explicit contracting for goods and services, or of "buying" versus "making" necessary inputs.[32] It enables lead firms to disintegrate products and processes into component parts, to set precise standards and specifications, and to monitor performance and outputs of remote outside suppliers. Technology in the form of container ships and barcoding allows Walmart to reliably track goods from a factory in Shenzhen, China, to a store in Lexington, Kentucky.[33] Technology allows Apple to maintain scrupulous quality standards for its iPhones and iPads while tapping into the much cheaper Chinese labor market. And technology enables Uber to monitor drivers, connect them with customers, and capture a large share of the fares they generate, without directly supervising them.[34] Technology has greatly expanded firms' "outside options" or exit strategies from existing employment relationships.[35]

Technology is just the means, however, and not the motivation for these developments. Both fissuring and automation are driven in part by supercharged global capital markets, in which billions of dollars move across national borders in microseconds, and globalized product markets.[36] Firms that falter in the pursuit of cheaper means of producing goods and services risk losing both investors and market share to lower-cost producers. The pursuit of profits and customers and the basic dynamics of price, supply, and demand are hardwired into a market economy, but deliberate policy decisions have done much to foster the growth of transnational firms; networks; and supply chains; and to facilitate the movement of goods, services, and capital across national boundaries.[37] Technology has accelerated all of those movements, but firms use technology to eliminate or outsource jobs when it generates returns to capital through lower costs, higher productivity, or both. Those who supply the robots and algorithms that replace human labor are responding to demand from firms seeking more profitable ways to produce other goods and services.

Automation is thus part of a larger menu of options by which owners and managers of capital seek to maximize their returns. Fissuring in all its forms—domestic and transnational outsourcing, franchising, the rise of platform-based work—reflects the growing ability of lead firms to deploy labor without directly employing people. But if robots or algorithms can supply those inputs more reliably or cheaply, then firms will turn to them instead of human labor.

That points to a third factor driving both fissuring and automation: the costs and risks of employing human beings. Investment banker Steven Berkenfeld made the point in vivid terms at a 2015 Department of Labor (DOL) conference on the future of work:

> As I talk to companies, yes, it's about labor savings, but that's just the starting point. It's also about indirect cost savings. . . . It's about health care liabilities, lawsuits[,] and insurance and disabilities benefits. And . . . people need people. There is a whole management infrastructure that needs to go on top of every person that you employ; it's a multiplier effect.[38]

Moreover, managers report that "*people are a pain to manage*":

> They have to be identified and recruited, hired [and] trained. They want performance reviews and promotions. They take vacations, they get sick, their kids get sick, their parents get sick, they get pregnant; they get injured on the job. Sometimes they don't get along with each other. They sue for harassment. They need all kinds of insurance and benefits. They want raises and career development, and then sometimes they quit. Then you have to start it all over again. . . . [People] have needs, issues, and ambitions. And perhaps most significantly from a CEO's standpoint they do dumb things. They give bribes and kickbacks, they discriminate and harass, they expose companies to cyber-attacks, they commit . . . acts of negligence, misconduct, and violence, and sometimes they even deliberately sabotage. They create liabilities, they damage brands, and they sometimes get CEOs fired.[39]

Berkenfeld's bottom line drew an audible gasp from the mostly labor-friendly audience: "*[S]ome CEOs . . . will do anything possible, they'll explore all other alternatives so as not to hire another full-time employee.*"[40] Putting the point succinctly elsewhere, Berkenfeld reported that CEOs these days ask, "Can I automate it? If not, can I outsource it? If not, can I give it to an independent contractor?" In other words, "[h]iring an employee is the last resort."[41]

"Labor costs" is a bland term for the varied reasons that lead managers to avoid hiring human workers, but it will have to do for now. The role of labor costs in fissuring is plain.[42] Their role in spurring automation can come as no surprise. A basic postulate of labor economics holds that increases in the cost of labor—whether due to market forces, legal mandates, or collective bargaining—tend to lead firms to substitute capital, including technology, for labor.[43] That substitution is bound to accelerate with the growing capabilities and falling cost of labor-saving technology.

Some labor costs, and some part of the impetus for both automation and fissuring, stem from the legal obligations of employers vis-à-vis employees. Some laws add direct costs, like payroll taxes for workers' compensation and unemployment insurance, Social Security, and Medicare, which together can add 18 to 26 percent to the base salary cost.[44] Minimum wages obviously affect direct labor costs at the bottom of the labor market. Overtime laws and the ACA's "pay or play" employer mandate increase direct costs much further up the wage scale.[45] At least some of those mandates function like taxes on the hiring of humans, *distorting* firms' demand for labor versus labor-saving robots.[46]

Other laws increase the cost of employing people less predictably; they create *risk*. Firms clearly regard federally-protected union organizing as a risk, and they pay union avoidance consultants a lot of money to manage that risk.[47] The bevy of laws against discrimination, harassment, and retaliation also generate risks, including the intangible risks of litigation to reputation and morale as well as the tangible costs of attorneys, judgments, and settlements. Employees both trigger lawsuits and file them, as when employees sue employers over supervisory harassment. Employees—as whistleblowers or as wrongdoers—can also trigger liabilities under laws governing taxation, corporate securities, or environmental and consumer protection. Large corporate compliance departments and battalions of outside lawyers are devoted to managing those risks and liabilities at the cost of billions of dollars per year.[48]

We should pause to note that, while it might seem self-evident that the law-related costs and risks of employing people fall on employers, labor economists generally assume that *employees* ultimately bear those costs through lower wages.[49] If that's so, those costs should not affect employers' hiring decisions. But that assumption comes with several caveats.[50] First, because minimum wage laws constrain wage cuts, other legal mandates and payroll taxes do add to the cost of employing low-wage workers.[51] Second, because employers usually can't (or rarely do) reduce wages of existing employees, it can take a long time for new mandates to get priced into wage packages.[52] In any case, employers seem to *believe* they bear the costs of legal mandates above and beyond wages.[53] We should probably assume they act accordingly.

The point is *not* that we should give up on employment mandates. Some mandates protect basic values of fairness and dignity.[54] Some overcome collective action problems among workers or force firms to internalize externalities,[55] and might improve national economic performance.[56] Others might enhance workers' productivity.[57] Unfortunately, most of the benefits of employment mandates accrue to workers or the society at large, not to employers. Firms might still reap gains from avoiding or evading those laws and their costs if they can.

Once upon a time, community norms (or union strength and the threat of industrial conflict) might have restrained cost-cutting measures that destroyed or degraded jobs. But both union strength and community norms came under pressure as corporations became "delocalized" and their managers answerable to anonymous capital markets.[58] The watchword of corporate law became "shareholder primacy,"[59] nicely (or not so nicely) captured in Milton Friedman's injunction fifty years ago that "the social responsibility of business is to increase its profits."[60] Business leaders themselves have lately questioned the norm of shareholder primacy.[61] But financial markets still pressure firms to reduce costs if that increases profits. And increasingly firms can reduce labor costs without violating the law by shedding workers through either fissuring or automation.

2. Why Automation Is Different

So automation is in one sense just another tool in the toolbox for firms seeking to reduce the many costs and risks associated with in-house labor. But it is also different. Rather than separating human workers from those who use and profit from their labor, automation replaces some human labor altogether. It can offer the ultimate exit from the costs, risks, and hassles of employing people, including those that stem from the law of work.

Fissuring can partially but not completely insulate lead firms from the blowback that may hit lead firms when their suppliers' workers suffer abuse. Apple was hit by brand-bruising scandals when a dozen employees of its supplier Foxconn committed suicide in 2010, and when others were injured by toxic chemicals in the manufacture of iPhones and iPads.[62] Foxconn's plan to replace most of those workers with robots will avert this risk. Machines have no human rights to be violated and no bodies to be bruised or battered. Nor can they catch and spread infectious diseases.[63] "Lights-out" factories, automated check-out kiosks, or robotic warehouses are much less likely than their human-staffed counterparts to become vectors of viral transmission.

Robots and algorithms also do not demand higher wages, form unions, or go on strike, as humans sometimes do. The high wages and benefits that unionized US workers had won over many rounds of collective bargaining helped drive the exodus of manufacturing operations to China. After average real wages in China rose by a factor of ten from 1990 to 2015, some suppliers headed to poorer countries with cheaper labor, and others began to automate their Chinese factories.[64] Some manufacturing has even returned to the United States, but to factories equipped with robots or 3D printers and staffed with a relative handful of skilled workers.[65]

Rising wages in the United States, China, and elsewhere reflect some profound social and economic forces. Karl Polanyi famously argued that the commodification of labor under capitalism tended to provoke a countermovement—both collective agitation and political mobilization—in pursuit of social protection against harsh market forces.[66] That happened across the industrial world over the course of the twentieth century, and yielded collective bargaining rights as well as the higher wages, job security, and benefits associated with the standard employment relationship. Even China's unelected leaders found it necessary, in the face of rising labor unrest, to improve labor standards and to briefly ponder allowing real collective bargaining.[67] Over the history of industrial capitalism, wages have tended to rise, and rising wages affect managers' decisions about automation once work becomes automatable.

Even if workers demand only a living wage—as in the "Fight for Fifteen" in many US cities—they may bolster the business case for automation. In the words of Andrew Puzder, the fast-food CEO who was then-President Trump's first nominee for Secretary of Labor: "If you're making labor more expensive, and automation less expensive—this is not rocket science."[68] The first burger-flipping robots might cost more than low-wage fast-food workers. But at some point, as the robots get cheaper and more efficient, the up-front investment will be worthwhile, if not obligatory, for firms in a competitive market.

To generalize the point: Over time, machines get cheaper and more capable relative to human labor.[69] Recall Susskind's account of inexorable task encroachment, especially in the wake of the pragmatic revolution in AI. The falling cost and growing capabilities of technology stem from the mysterious dynamics of innovation and the more transparent dynamics of supply and demand: In response to firms' demand for ways to lower costs and raise productivity, tech firms on the supply side race to improve the capabilities and lower the cost of the technologies that enable both fissuring and automation.[70]

Some readers might detect the fallacy of "technological determinism" here.[71] Undoubtedly, policy decisions and human agency are crucial in speeding, slowing, or directing the flow of technological change. But the fallacy of technological determinism has its counterpart in technological denial—that is, in underestimating the powerful forces of competition and innovation that drive both automatability and automation of work. As long as we have a market economy in which private firms pursue profits—a proviso that not all readers will accept—we should come to grips with the forces that are converging to drive down the costs and drive up the capabilities of machines relative to humans.

In short, technological innovation outpaces human evolution. Yes, educational and cultural institutions and technology itself can enhance human capabilities. But the functional capabilities of machines are rising much faster and with fewer natural limits than those of humans. The organizational innovations that fall under the rubric of fissuring still run up against the upper bounds of human performance and the lower bounds of the cost of sustaining human beings and reproducing their labor. Automation potentially transcends both, and offers firms a more complete exit from the costs of employing human labor. To be sure, automation also obviates some of the problems addressed by the law of work; it can reduce workers' exposure to occupational hazards, discrimination, retaliation, excessive hours, or substandard wages. As robots replace humans in dangerous jobs, for example, there may be fewer hazards for OSHA to abate or regulate.

The law of work is basically concerned with ensuring decent terms and conditions of work in whatever jobs exist, not with ensuring that jobs exist. A "right to work" finds support in international labor law theory and advocacy.[72] It has been a recurring demand from left liberals since the New Deal,[73] and it might be making a comeback in the form of proposals for a federal job guarantee (as we'll see in Chapter 5). But there is no legal right to a job in the US law of work.[74] Rather, the sum total of labor and employment law—that is, the prevailing standard of decent work—represents *a societal judgment about what jobs should exist at all.* And that leads to some dilemmas.

D. How Automation Confounds Prevailing Approaches to the Regulation of Work

Raising the legal floor on terms and conditions of employment strengthens firms' incentive to automate technically automatable jobs, especially at the bottom of the labor market, where minimum wage laws prevent firms from shifting the cost of mandates onto employees through lower wages. I'll trace this argument through two established strategies for improving wages and working conditions: raising minimum labor standards and expanding the reach of employer responsibility under employment laws.

1. Raising Labor Standards in a More Automated Economy

Starting with the minimum wage: When Andrew Puzder suggested, in his 2016 "rocket science" comment, that doubling the minimum wage to $15 an hour would accelerate automation of some jobs, he was excoriated by workers' advocates for preferring robots to workers. It was not a good look for a would-be Secretary of Labor.[75] But if robots can perform as well as or better than humans at a lower cost, firms that deploy them will gain profits, market share, and investors over those that do not. That is indeed "not rocket science"; it is Capitalism 101. And it was conventional economic wisdom for many decades. Daniel Shaviro observed over twenty years ago: "Most economists of all ideological persuasions have long agreed that [the minimum wage] is self-defeating: it destroys jobs in the low-wage sector of the economy and thus hurts many of the people it is intended to help."[76]

Decades of empirical research, beginning with the widely discussed Card and Krueger studies in the 1990s,[77] have painted a more complex picture. Scores of studies have now found that modest increases in the minimum wage led to little or no loss of employment, while yielding higher incomes for poor workers and a stimulus effect on local economies.[78] The idea of a $15 federal minimum wage, first floated in 2012, tested the limits of those findings. Most economists apparently still oppose the $15 minimum wage.[79] And as of 2015, even some left-leaning labor economists who favored minimum wage hikes were skeptical of doubling it in much of the country because of the expected toll on jobs.[80] By 2019, however, over one hundred economists had endorsed a $15 federal minimum wage, to be phased in by 2024:

> [T]he weight of evidence [shows] that previous, modest increases in the minimum wage had little or no negative effects on the employment of low-wage workers. It is time to support a bolder increase to address the fact that wages for workers at the low end of the labor market have continued to stagnate. Even if the growth of aggregate work hours for low-wage workers were to slow somewhat, workers who work less could still break even, or come out ahead, in terms of annual earnings.[81]

These economists recognized that a $15 minimum wage required at least a small leap of faith, for it "would bring the US wage floor above its historical high point," both in absolute real terms and relative to the median wage, and "just slightly beyond the range of minimum wages that have been studied."[82] But they concluded the risk was worth taking. President Biden has since vowed to pursue a national $15 minimum wage.[83]

In the meantime, local minimum wage increases continue to provide grist for the empiricists' mill. Some studies suggest that *capital substitution* in response to those increases, and any resulting job losses might not show up in studies that focus on short-term effects.[84] One study, for example, found that, while existing restaurants did not reduce employment levels after a minimum wage increase, the sector saw both more exits and more new entries in the wake of an increase, and that new entrants to the sector used more capital and fewer workers.[85] It seems that the mix of labor and capital in an existing business is difficult to alter, but that new firms take up more cost-effective automation options.[86] That is, the long-term effect of a large minimum wage increase on employment is likely greater than the short-term effect.) Minimum wage increases also have a bigger impact on jobs and sectors that are more automatable,[87] and in "tradable" sectors where firms compete across jurisdictional lines, like manufacturing and services that can be delivered remotely.[88]

There is plenty of room for significant minimum wage increases in today's economy. But nobody doubts that large minimum wage increases, at some level of magnitude, will tilt the scales toward displacement of low-wage workers, and will hurt those workers more than help them.[89] The growing capabilities and falling costs of labor-replacing machines are likely to lower that threshold and increase that displacement.

What holds for minimum wage increases holds as well for other labor standards or worker entitlements that raise employer costs, whether separately or cumulatively. Higher labor standards won't inexorably or immediately lead to job losses, but at some point, at least over time, those higher standards are likely to spur automation and speed up job destruction. And that's a problem if we can't count on new job creation to pick up the slack as in the past. There are ways to soften that dilemma, as we'll discuss later, but the dilemma is real.

2. Expanding the Fortress of Employment and the Reach of Employer Responsibilities

A version of this dilemma recurs in the legal responses to fissuring and misclassification of workers. Fissuring undermines labor standards by shifting employer responsibility to less-capable and less-compliant supplier firms or by putting workers beyond the reach of domestic employment laws (as with offshoring and use of independent contractors). Faced with this very big problem, labor scholars and advocates have converged around efforts to expand lead firms' responsibility for the wages and working conditions of the workers whose labor they use.[90] Like early labor reformers who targeted the apparel industry's "putting-out" system, they seek to shore up the fortress of employment against the corrosive effects of fissuring. Hence the explosion of scholarship and advocacy aimed at combating misclassification of employees as independent contractors and expanding the reach of employment and joint employment.[91]

Scholars have proposed reforming or reconstructing the concept of employment,[92] dismantling the distinction between employees and independent contractors,[93] or creating an intermediate category of "independent worker" or "dependent contractor."[94] Some state legislatures have rallied to the cause of expanding the scope of employment. When California codified the so-called "ABC test," that made it harder for firms to avoid employee status for the workers they hire.[95] In particular, it would have forced Uber to treat its drivers as employees.[96] Uber and other gig-economy firms pushed back, claiming this was a make-or-break issue.[97] Responses from worker advocates ranged from "we don't believe you" to "we don't care."[98] But Uber spearheaded a successful campaign to overturn the law by referendum—Proposition 22—as to most platform workers.[99] In the meantime, worker advocates are seeking to extend the ABC test to other states.[100]

Even more is at stake in parallel efforts to expand lead firms' responsibility as *joint* employers of their contractors' employees. Most low-wage workers are plainly employed by somebody; but worker advocates have long sought to extend employer responsibility to more capable and profitable lead firms, and to curtail the use of domestic outsourcing to evade minimum labor standards. The issue has become a political football: Obama's Department of Labor expanded the definition of "joint employment"; Trump's DOL contracted it; Biden's is poised to expand it again.[101]

All these reform efforts aim to expand firms' responsibility for the people who supply their labor needs. Business advocates vehemently oppose these efforts, which they say will squelch innovation, flexibility, and growth.[102] Those battles are bound to continue. But the exit option of automation cuts a path around that battleground, and creates a potential dilemma: The more successful worker advocates are in holding lead firms responsible for the workers who supply their labor inputs, the greater the appeal of automation. If the law treats McDonald's, Inc., as the employer of its franchisees' employees, or Uber as the employer of its drivers, those firms are more likely to turn to burger-flipping robots or self-driving vehicles when those become feasible.

An analogous dilemma faces the response to branded firms' offshoring of operations. Advocates and scholars have long sought to hold major corporations responsible—socially if not legally—for labor conditions within their supply chains.[103] In effect, they are following as best they can the domestic strategy of expanding the legal scope of employer responsibility. This long campaign has elicited high-profile professions of corporate social responsibility, and some actual reforms in supply chain management, though mixed results on the ground.[104] Nike, an early target of activists, earned kudos as a model of transparency in 2005 when it became the first major brand to publicly disclose its suppliers.[105] Yet recent reports find safety issues and forced labor among Nike suppliers.[106] After Apple was embarrassed by a spate of suicides and injuries among the Chinese workers who assemble iPhones and iPads, it launched high-profile efforts to improve conditions at Foxconn.[107] Yet Apple now faces new reports of child labor at Foxconn and elsewhere.[108] Still, we are long past the days when big consumer brands could wave off reports of forced labor or child labor in their supply chains by claiming they were "just the buyer."[109]

Automation complicates this transnational strategy in a double-edged way. The more successfully global labor regulators and advocates hold branded firms accountable for labor conditions in their supply chains, the more those firms and their suppliers have to gain from switching to robots. Foxconn's plan to replace most of its Chinese workers with robots—if it eventually comes to fruition—will neatly sidestep future scandals that might hit its major client, Apple. It will also eliminate hundreds of thousands of dangerous and dehumanizing jobs.[110] If those workers end up with better jobs, the episode will show off the virtuous side of innovation and creative destruction. If not, those workers might end up among the losers from the convergence of technological progress and well-meaning efforts to hold lead firms responsible for upstream working conditions.

Workers' rights and the legal, political, and social consequences of labor violations are not the biggest drivers in firms' automation decisions, but they inevitably figure in those decisions. The point is not that we should let profitable lead firms off the hook for the labor violations affecting the workers, foreign and domestic, who supply them with labor. We shouldn't. But this sensible response to fissuring simply does not meet the challenge of automation-based job losses, and may even exacerbate it.

E. The Special Case of Labor Law and Collective Bargaining

Collective labor law in its current form—especially US labor law—presents a pointed version of the same dilemma: Labor law creates a framework through which workers can advance their own interests and participate in employer decisions, including decisions about workplace technologies. Yet labor law and the organizing and bargaining activities it protects are high on the ledger of costs and risks that firms can avoid by replacing workers with machines. In short, collective bargaining could be part of the solution for workers anxious about automation; but for employers it is among the problems that automation can solve by replacing workers.

Labor law aims to equip workers to seek more—more money, benefits, rights, voice, and security—than across-the-board employment mandates provide; and it does so by protecting workers' rights to form a union and to back up their demands by inflicting or threatening economic pain through strikes, boycotts, and public opprobrium. All of this—the economic losses that collective action might inflict, the concessions it might exact, and the union organizing that prefigures both—threatens managerial power and profits. Unionization and all that follows from it are among the risks associated with employing humans, and among the reasons firms might seek to reduce their reliance on human labor through automation.

The particular shape of collective bargaining in the United States has proven to be especially flawed—especially likely to fail as a solution for workers, in part because it is especially likely to provoke resistance from employers. Because unionization and bargaining under the NLRA take place at the enterprise level, the conflict and concessions associated with collective bargaining can put a firm at a competitive disadvantage within their product market. Employers can gain an edge over competitors by resisting unionization; and they can do that—given the NLRA's notoriously lax restraints on anti-union tactics—by intensely propagandizing and pressuring their own employees at the workplace. In short, US labor law gives employers ample means, motive, and opportunity to resist unionization.

The depth and breadth of employer resistance to unionization might seem puzzling given evidence linking unionization with higher productivity in some settings.[111] But the puzzle is not hard to solve. First, as Brishen Rogers emphasizes, employers jealously guard their power as well as their profits, and unionization tends to empower workers and constrain employers.[112] Second, unionized workers use their collective power to secure higher wages and benefits; productivity gains, if any, do not show up in higher profits.[113] Third, the studies suggest that productivity gains hinge on the existence of a positive labor relations climate versus one of the adversarial combat and mutual suspicion.[114] A constructive *modus vivendi* between employers and unions can arise if employers see coexistence as beneficial, or at least inescapable. But that is rare these days in the United States. It takes two to tango, and most US managers opt reflexively for resistance.

Even if workers succeed in forming a union and getting the employer to the bargaining table, their ability to exact concessions is notoriously limited, especially when it comes to labor-saving technologies.[115] What Rogers calls the "political economy of workplace technological change" starts with a strong default of discretionary managerial control. Even in a union setting, an employer's legal duty to bargain over a decision to introduce job-killing technology—or over distribution of any resulting gains—adds little to the sparse economic power workers can muster in that context. Ironically, the legal duty to bargain seems to augment workers' power and constrain employers' power just enough to elicit aggressive resistance to unionization, but rarely enough to enable workers to effectively participate in decisions about the automation of work even if they do manage to unionize.

All told, existing US labor law is profoundly flawed as a mechanism for enabling workers to participate in workplace decisions, including decisions about automation or the distribution of gains from automation. Even so, labor law and the processes of unionization and collective bargaining that it regulates are seen by firms as among the most fearsome risks associated with employing humans versus machines.

Labor law could take a very different shape. In much of Europe, national and EU-level "works council" legislation provides a legal structure for workers' representation more or less by default, without workers having to go the barricades to fight for it. German law in particular requires management to confer with workers' representatives over a wide range of issues, including the deployment of labor-saving technology.[116] Complementing the works council system at the firm level is *sectoral* bargaining over economic terms, including the distribution of gains from technological innovation. Sectoral bargaining attempts to "take wages out of competition" by extending collectively bargained wage levels across an industrial or occupational sector. That makes economic gains for workers more sustainable, for employers are less motivated and less able to escape them. Although sectoral bargaining is under pressure in today's more globalized product markets, collective bargaining has held up better in those systems than in the enterprise-based systems typical in Anglo-American countries.[117] That is one reason why economic inequality is less extreme in the former than in the latter.[118]

Works councils and sectoral bargaining are among the features of European labor law that have long drawn the admiration of US labor advocates and scholars.[119] Those structures, along with high-level processes of "social dialogue" in which trade unions play a leading role, give unions a wider compass, a longer time horizon, and a stronger voice in policy making. All are useful in devising worker-friendly responses to automation, including training structures that allow workers to develop the skills that are still needed.[120]

Still, automation poses a potentially existential threat to collective labor law systems, whatever their particular shape. Those systems aim to secure for workers a kind of industrial citizenship and all that implies by way of equal dignity and a democratic voice in their working lives. But it grafts that ennobling vision onto a wage labor relationship in which employers decide whether to hire workers in the first place, and by and large whether to retain them; and it attempts to realize that vision by enabling workers to collectivize their individual bargaining power. Legal protections against unjustified dismissal—which exist in nearly every industrialized nation except the United States—can play a supporting role, as they tilt toward retraining workers versus dumping them. But workers' bargaining power rests at bottom on employers' need for their labor, and it is ultimately workers' threat to withdraw that labor—individually and permanently by quitting or collectively and temporarily by striking—that motivates employers to make concessions. The easier it is for employers to replace workers, whether with other workers or with machines, the less bargaining power those workers have. Unfortunately, aggregating the sparse individual bargaining power of easily replaceable workers does not add up to much collective bargaining power.

In short, the growing automatability of work strikes at the heart of the grand twentieth-century project of industrial citizenship through collective bargaining. Automatability itself—the technological potential for automation—tends to disempower the workers who could be displaced, and to further tilt the already-skewed balance of power between labor and capital by allowing employers to escape the risk of workers collectivizing their demands.

* * * * *

The current wave of labor-saving technological innovations, given existing US laws and institutions, will tend to produce lower wages, rising insecurity, and underemployment or unemployment for many workers, alongside even longer working hours and higher wages for some in-demand workers. Unfortunately, the dominant pro-worker strategies of the twentieth century—expanding employee entitlements and employer liabilities through both legislation and collective bargaining—won't meet that challenge. When it comes to automation-based job losses, the existing law of work is less of a solution than it is part of the problem.

We should now be looking not to dismantle the law of work—which has done much to improve work and workers' lives—but to reconfigure it for a more automated future. We'll return in Chapter 6 to that project. But first we need to know what we should be trying to achieve in that future of less work, for it is clearly not to preserve all jobs at all costs.

4

Three Goals for a Future of Less Work

What do we worry about when we worry about a future of less work? And what might we welcome in such a world? We can't decide how to respond to the prospect of a future of less work without first thinking through what we should be aiming to achieve or to avoid in that future. In this chapter I ask: Given what is at stake—what people stand to lose or gain—in a more automated economy of less work, what should the society aim to ensure that they have? What people stand to lose is work and work-based income; and what they could gain is time for life beyond work. I'll argue here that a technologically advanced economy should aim to ensure wide access to decent paid work and income sufficient to afford a decent standard of living, as well as more time for life outside of work. In shorthand that I'll use here, *work*, *income*, and *free time* are three dimensions of a good livelihood whose distribution is at stake in a more automated future.

The purpose of this chapter is not to prescribe the overall shape and animating principles of a good and just society or to trace the implications of any particular comprehensive conception of justice, freedom, equality, or democracy. It is to identify broad patches of common ground among thoughtful citizens who are committed at some level to all of those basic values regarding what we should be aiming for in a future of less work. Enough common ground, that is, to give direction to the discussion of means—strategies and policies—that will follow.

On income and free time, I will be brief. I do not think there will be much controversy about people's need for enough income to afford a decent standard of living, or about the value of time for life outside of paid work. My main focus in this chapter will be on the more debatable claim that work itself—specifically, decent remunerative work—is among the three dimensions of a good life and a good livelihood that we should be aiming to preserve and distribute even if the economy is generating less of it. But first, briefly, on income and free time.

Automation Anxiety. Cynthia Estlund, Oxford University Press. © Cynthia Estlund 2021.
DOI: 10.1093/oso/9780197566107.003.0004

A. On "Income" and "Free Time"

Income: People need food, clothing, shelter, furniture, and appliances, as well as access to health care, education, transportation, electricity, information, and means of communication. Everyone needs at least a basic level of these goods and services to live a decent life, and in a prosperous, technologically advanced society it is fair to say they need things (like internet service) that, in another time or place, would be considered comforts or luxuries. Most of these goods and services are allocated through markets in economies across the world, and certainly in the United States.[1] And I assume that will continue to be true for the foreseeable future.

To be sure, much of what is allocated through markets could be—and to varying degrees is, even in the United States—subsidized or supplied in kind by the government, at least at some basic level. Some necessities like health care could (and should) be delivered by the government as a basic social entitlement. Others, like education and transportation, are at least partly "public goods" with spillover societal benefits that have long justified a large state role in their provision and funding. Still, most people in market economies, including the US economy, buy most of the goods and services that they and their dependents need or want throughout their lives with income earned through paid work.

One obvious worry about a future of less work is that many people will see their incomes fall and will be unable to earn enough through paid work to support themselves and their dependents. Labor markets will then fail in their crucial function—the flip side of their function of bringing labor into production processes—of allocating income to those who own little or nothing but themselves and their labor power. To be sure, labor markets haven't been performing that function all that well in recent decades. Still, it has been possible to rely on labor markets as the primary mechanism for generating income for most adults and their families, and to look to government to provide a "social safety net" for the relatively few who are unable, temporarily or permanently, to find decent paid work and who lack other means of support. But if increasingly capable machines deplete the demand for the type of labor most humans can muster, then we'll have to rethink the respective roles of governments and markets in ensuring a basic level of material security for the citizenry. The kind of social safety net that more or less sufficed in the past won't be enough. For now, however, the focus is on goals.

Here is the first such goal for a future of less work: *We should aim to ensure at least adequate incomes, or the means to afford a decent standard of living, to all, and to maintain or improve incomes and standards of living for the broad middle of the income spectrum.* A society might fairly leave to markets the allocation of comforts or luxuries, but it should aim one way or another to ensure that everyone has the means to acquire the necessities—the minimum material requisites of a decent life—even if decent jobs are in short supply. I'll focus here on the goal of adequate incomes at the bottom, or a floor on standards of living, and will clarify a few points.

First, the goal of adequate income for all doesn't require the government to provide that income directly through something like Universal Basic Income (UBI). Far from it. A well-ordered market economy in which most people derive most or all of their income through paid work could largely ensure both adequate incomes and wide access to decent work, a goal that will be developed at length.

Second, the goal is not *equal* incomes. (John Rawls famously offered one reason: The least well-off members of the society could—and should—benefit from the greater overall output and economic vitality of a society that differentially rewards talent and effort.[2]) Extreme *inequality* is still a concern: Beyond maintaining or bringing up incomes at the bottom to a level of sufficiency, we should also aim to counter the hollowing out of the labor market and the decline in middle-class incomes. Beyond that, countering extreme and growing economic *inequality* should inform the shape of public policy responses to automation. But that's far from aiming for income equality.

As for what counts as an adequate income, it must at least cover the costs of food, clothing, shelter, health care, and education—to whatever extent those must be purchased. (An income at the official US poverty line falls short of that in much of the country.)[3] And it should reflect a society's level of development. In a modern developed society, for example, it should afford not only bare shelter from the elements but decent housing by prevailing societal standards, with plumbing, reliable electricity and water, heating and cooling, and other safety features and amenities beyond what might count as adequate in a very poor country.[4]

Obviously, what counts as adequate income will depend on the *cost* of living, or the *prices* of essential goods and services that have to be purchased—for example, the high cost of housing in many urban areas where jobs are concentrated. Perhaps less obviously, it might come to reflect *lower* prices for some basic goods and services, which are expected to be among the upsides of automation.[5] Lower consumer prices might do some of the work of countering the impact of declines in work-based income on standards of living.

Finally, what counts as adequate income will depend on what individuals have to pay for and what they don't. A society could go far toward ensuring adequate incomes for all, even in a world of much less paid work, through universal social entitlements and public goods—for example, free or subsidized health care, higher education, or public transportation. (But we're getting ahead of ourselves.)

This brief account leaves many questions unanswered, but it is enough to give direction to public policy responses to a prospective future of less work: Among the chief social problems posed by a future of less work is the loss of income for those left with too little paid work or none of it. We should set our sights on maintaining a decent floor on incomes, and to avoiding or mitigating the income losses and declining living standards that will otherwise follow from fewer jobs and lower wages among workers with ordinary skills.

Free time: I'll use the term "free time" to include all the time in individuals' lives that is not devoted to paid work.[6] Recalling the slogan of the historical eight-hour-day movement—"Eight hours for work, eight hours for rest, and eight hours for what you will"—"free time" includes both rest and "what you will." It includes time devoted to sleeping, eating, cooking, unpaid family care and domestic chores, reading and studying, cultural and religious activities, hobbies, entertainment, volunteer work, socializing, and sex. It includes time spent in reproducing one's own labor power, and in childrearing and family care, sometimes called "social reproduction." In short, "free time" is a large residual category that includes all time not spent in paid work.

Of course, calling it "free time" does not make it so. In particular, many readers may balk at putting unpaid domestic labor within one's own home in the same category with genuine leisure. That might seem to pointedly ignore, or take sides on, gender-laden issues such as the value and voluntariness of unpaid domestic labor and whether it should be paid.[7] In drawing the line between time spent in paid work and time spent on everything else, I don't mean to discount those concerns, but rather to focus attention on what is at stake in a future of less paid work. A lot of activities—necessary, pleasant, valuable, creative, relaxing, or demanding—have to fit into one's time outside of paid work. All things being equal (like income), most people would prefer to have *more* time for those other activities. Biological imperatives and relational responsibilities will claim their share of time outside of paid work. But the perils or possibilities of a future of less paid work have little to do with the particulars of how people spend that time.

More time outside paid work means more time for "what you will." A future of less paid work opens up the possibility of expanding the time available for the rest of life, or what I am calling here free time. That is a second goal we should embrace in a future of less work: *We should aim to ensure wide access to more free time, or time for life beyond paid work.*

Of course, if free time is defined as all time that is not spent in paid work, then more free time is mathematically ensured in a world of less paid work. But the aim here is not more *total* non-work time across the society but more time for all or most individuals. In other words, in a world of less total work, time outside of paid work should be widely distributed, not bunched together in the form of long-term unemployment for those who are unable to gain their footing in a polarized and shrinking labor market. The point will be underscored when I turn to the third goal of widespread engagement in paid work. The aim is not to maximize non-work time for some subset of the population but to enable people generally to achieve a better balance between work and the rest of life—that is, a better societal work-life balance.

"Time affluence," as some call it, has prodigious physical, psychological, and social benefits. Most people are happier and healthier when they have more time for the rest of life than full-time work normally permits.[8] Indeed, beyond some threshold of adequate income, additional non-work time may boost well-being more than additional income.[9] Up to a point, that is. Nothing *but* time outside of work—at least in the form of involuntary joblessness—takes its own toll on physical and psychological well-being. And when time outside of work translates to unpredictable part-time and just-in-time work schedules, the resulting stress and economic insecurity swamps the benefits of those erratic extra scraps of non-work time. We'll address that problem by way of the value and meaning of decent work. The point for now is that we should set our sights on affording more time outside of work—widely distributed, not concentrated in the form of unemployment or underemployment.

Automation can pay dividends in both overall social wealth and free time, and some portion of both should be distributed broadly for the benefit of all. Perhaps the greatest opportunity that is afforded by a more automated economy is the possibility of more balanced lives, with more time for rest and "for what you will." If that is what a future of less work means, then we should welcome it. But we've already seen that, without some conscious engineering of working time, a more automated economy is likely to find some workers with scarce skills working even longer hours (for high marginal returns), while most workers scramble for whatever hours of work are to be had and many get squeezed out of the labor market altogether.

Before turning to paid work—the third dimension of what we should be aiming for in a future of less work—let's note what income and free time, as defined here, have in common and what sets them apart from work. Income and free time are valued in part because individuals choose how to spend them. Money and time are both *resources*; they have an almost endless variety of uses, and they enhance individuals' freedom to live as they wish. People with more income can enjoy their free time in ways that poorer people cannot; and individuals vary—both among themselves and across their life spans—in their preferred balance of income and free time. Still, everybody needs and wants a decent minimum level of both income and time off work; even workaholics need to sleep. And most people would like to have more of both than they have. For those who believe public policy should aim to improve people's lives, there should be wide agreement that adequate material living standards and more time for life outside of work are two worthy goals against which to assess public policy proposals for a future of less work.

B. The Case for Paid Work as an Individual and Social Good

Work is another matter. Clearly work is not a resource that can be spent as one wishes, nor is it a matter of sheer necessity, as are both income and time away from work. A good life without paid work is plainly possible (though only for those with another source of material support). And paid work comes in the infinitely varied shapes of distinct jobs, most of which entail far more subordination than freedom. In traditional economic analysis, individuals seek to optimize leisure and income, while work is a disutility—a means of gaining income by sacrificing leisure, but not a good in itself.[10] Many people with boring, arduous, or demeaning jobs would surely agree. Even so, work has its fans on both the right and the left (as seen in critiques of UBI, to which we'll turn in the next chapter).[11] In my view, the value of work is profound, many-faceted, and beset by contradictions and paradoxes, all of which are worth a closer look as we face a future of less work.

To begin with, let's be clear that not all work is worth having or preserving. Workers and their allies have long struggled to combat the "bads" of work—forced labor, dangerous or abusive working conditions, or excessive hours, for example—through public law making. Those struggles have yielded a conception of *decent* work as defined in Chapter 3; that is, work that meets both core international labor standards—akin to human rights—and other mandatory rights and labor standards, however a given society or jurisdiction defines them. Taken together, those laws represent an evolving societal judgment about what jobs are worth having at all.

The third of the goals I'll argue for here is thus decent work—work above the local, socially determined floor. That is, *a prosperous and highly automated society of less work should aim to ensure a wide distribution of decent paid work for those who are able.* Decent work is not necessarily intrinsically meaningful or enjoyable work. We might aspire to everyone having work that is fulfilling or uplifting, but that is not the only work worth preserving. I will argue that paid work should remain a central organizing feature of most people's lives for the foreseeable future, and its wide distribution should be one dimension against which we judge public policy proposals for a future in which there is less need for human labor and less work to go around. The question is why.

1. Old and New Arguments for the Value of Paid Work

The idea of work as a moral imperative runs deep in Western religious thought, though its religious foundations bear little weight for many citizens today.[12] As capitalism eventually displaced most independent production, and work became virtually synonymous with selling one's labor in exchange for a wage, the supposed moral imperative to work took on a more ideological hue—a way to legitimize the commodification of labor.[13] And individuals' motivation to work—once stripped of its spiritual content—seemed to boil down to a depressing mix of sheer economic necessity and market-fueled appetites for more stuff, status, and conspicuous consumption.[14]

If that is all there is to the value of work, and if we are facing a future of less of it, then we might do well to wean ourselves off the venerable work ethic and accelerate that future's arrival. In that case, a society that produces enough wealth to enable its citizens to devote their lives not to working for a living but to "what they will"—caring for loved ones; communing with family and friends; producing and enjoying music, art, and literature—should set its sights on making that possible. Something like this utopian vision underlies support for UBI among some on the left.[15] That vision challenges the pro-work camp to scrutinize some deeply rooted but normatively dubious grounds for the attachment to work. If engagement in remunerative work is a virtue—even if it ceases to be an economic necessity—then its virtues should be rationally defensible on other grounds.

Generations of thinkers have explored the normative case for work in the modern world, after disenchantment and apart from sheer necessity.[16] Work has been depicted as a source of fulfillment and self-realization and a means of cultivating human capabilities.[17] To be sure, many of these accounts have little good to say about work as it actually is for most workers, and might ring hollow for the work skeptics. Even decent work that meets minimum societal standards of fair treatment, safety, and the like mostly falls short of the idealized visions of work and its value that emerge from much of this literature.[18]

Others depict work not as a good that should be widely distributed but as an obligation that should be widely shared. The idea that all members of a society are obliged to contribute to the greater good through work has a long history. Marx offered a version of that norm for a post-capitalist future: "From each according to his [sic] ability . . ."[19] In part the idea is that all members of a society are obliged to support *themselves* as best they can. As Jon Elster puts it, "it is unfair for able-bodied people to live off the labor of others."[20] But in a foreseeable future in which the society doesn't need the work that many individuals are capable of doing—in which machines could do that work better or more cheaply—the idea of work as a social obligation might lose its moorings. We might need better reasons as a society to ensure a wide distribution of work, and to inculcate the idea that work is something one *should* do (even if it isn't strictly necessary for one's own livelihood).

Social science offers empirical insights on the value of work. The value of work is seen elliptically in the harms of unemployment, both individual and social—physical illness, stress, unhappiness and depression, and higher rates of suicide and crime.[21] On the flip side, work contributes to individuals' feelings of self-worth, social standing, and overall well-being.[22] Researchers have found that work has "latent psychosocial benefits including time structure, collective purpose and social contacts, identity and activity."[23] The psychic returns to work are greatest for those who have fulfilling and high-status jobs, many of which are also quite well-paid. And work that is degrading, dangerous, monotonous, exhausting, or highly precarious can be worse than no work at all.[24] But relatively low-paid and low-status work still has psychic returns.[25] Even people who say they hate their jobs find that their "sense of dignity and self-worth is caught up in working for a living."[26]

This empirical research is still largely focused on the returns to individuals, but it suggests grounds for believing that the distribution of work in a society—even apart from the income it generates—is a matter of distributive justice.[27] Yet evidence of the psychosocial rewards of work can take us only so far in making the case for work in a society that needs less of it. Those rewards surely reflect in part the pervasive societal drumbeat in favor of work rather than just its intrinsic rewards. Americans in particular have long been socialized to measure their own and others' worth and status largely on the basis of their jobs. If it became possible to eliminate the sheer economic necessity to work, it might also become possible to socialize people out of associating paid work with those psychic rewards, and into finding those rewards elsewhere. Maybe a society facing a future of less work should undertake that reprogramming project. Or maybe there are sound *societal* reasons to cultivate an association between paid work and self-worth, self-realization, and social status. So I will argue below. But first let's take on board Michael Sandel's powerful synthetic account of why work matters.

In his 2020 book *The Tyranny of Merit*, Sandel has woven together several normative threads—work as a mutual obligation, as a source of social recognition, and as an individual good that should be fairly distributed—into the concept of "contributive justice": Everyone deserves a fair "opportunity to win the social recognition and esteem that goes with producing what others need and value."[28] We all have a right, in short, to contribute to the common good through work, and to be recognized for doing so.

Sandel's main point is not about the quantity and distribution of work but about the lack of social recognition accorded to the work most people do. He argues that "[t]he heart of the populist resentments that roil American politics are grievances about work"; but they are not just about "job losses and stagnant wages. . . . The people left behind by globalization haven't just struggled while others prospered; they sense that the work they do is no longer a source of social recognition."[29] Sandel argues that decades of market-centrism and meritocracy have stripped the work of ordinary, non-college-educated workers of dignity and social respect by reducing the value of labor to what others are willing to pay for it.

In Sandel's alternative "civic conception" of the common good, "the most important role we play in the economy is not as consumers but as producers."

It is as producers that "we develop and deploy our abilities to provide goods and services that fulfill the needs of our fellow citizens and win social esteem." If we were able to recover the notion of work as both a reciprocal social obligation and a source of mutual recognition, he argues, we might begin to see "ourselves as members of a community to which we are indebted. This sense of indebtedness would enable us to say 'We are all in this together'—not as a ritual incantation in times of crisis but as a principle that informs our everyday lives."[30]

Sandel's account of why work matters, and how most people's work came to be so devalued, is much more than a reason to worry about a future of *less* work. But it is also that. Seen through the lens of "contributive justice," a society in which growing numbers of people are left without paid work because they can't compete with machines (or with the multitudes of other people who have the same basic human skills they have) is a civic nightmare. While embracing Sandel's argument, I want to offer a complementary argument about how work—decent work, widely distributed—contributes to a sense that "we are all in this together."

2. Paid Work as a Source of Social Capital, Social Integration, and Intergroup Solidarity

What does it take for the members of a sprawling, modern, diverse society—especially one that aspires to collective self-governance—to have a sense that "we are all in this together"? For Sandel it rests on feelings of reciprocal respect and obligation among those who contribute to the greater good through their work. But those feelings can be enriched, and made warmer and more concrete, by the experience of working with others and by the social ties, thick and thin, that form at and through shared work. A sustainably democratic society rests on a substrate of associations and social ties—not just intimate ties among close family and friends, but the looser connections and connectedness that come from cooperating toward shared ends outside those intimate circles. A profusion of ties formed through purposeful cooperative activity, and the millions of overlapping social networks that form among co-workers, generate diffuse feelings of trust and reciprocal obligation that help to hold a society and a polity together.[31]

Paid work has long been the primary locus of purposeful cooperation in our society, but that doesn't mean it must be so. Obviously, voluntary associations with charitable, religious, political, cultural, or even recreational aims can also foster sociability, solidarity, reciprocity, and connectedness.[32] And they are usually less tainted by the economic compulsion and hierarchy that lead many theorists of civil society to discount the value of workplace ties in supporting social cohesion and collective self-governance.[33] Robert Putnam famously argued that it was chiefly in formal and informal voluntary associations where citizens develop "social capital," or the bonds and norms of reciprocity that enable people to cooperate in pursuit of shared objectives, including shared governance.[34] As citizens devote less time to voluntary associations, he argued, social capital and social trust in American society are eroding.[35] He is probably right about that. Yet it is a mistake to overlook the profound and distinctive social value in the ties formed through shared engagement in paid work.[36]

To begin with, most working adults spend much of their waking lives interacting with co-workers in the course of doing the job, before and after work, and during breaks. They talk about shared working conditions—a speed-up of production, a rumor of layoffs, an overbearing new supervisor—and about family, popular culture, sports, and other stuff of daily life. They also talk about politics with some frequency—far more with co-workers than with any group outside family and friends.[37] Over weeks, months, or even years of working together, co-workers often develop weak and strong ties of affection, empathy, loyalty, solidarity, and friendship.[38] (Those ties were sorely missed during the pandemic by some workers relegated to remote work.[39])

Obviously workplace relations can also be fraught, and tainted by conflict, resentment, abuse, or humiliation. But given all that is at stake in a job, people often find ways to avoid conflict, or to work through or around it, and to get along—at least well enough to get the job done—despite friction. Even in the age of fissured, fragmented, virtual, and precarious work, common work brings more people together for more time and over longer periods than any other form of association outside family and friendships—that is, outside the circles in which one either grew up or chooses to associate. Those relationships with once-strangers can form a kind of psychological bridge from family and close friends to the larger society.

Some evidence of the strong bonds that can form among co-workers can be seen in the past and present of the labor movement.[40] Shared work has long provided a rich medium for building solidarity and a platform for organizing and mutual aid among ordinary people. That is partly because common work often generates shared grievances—hardly an unambiguous argument for holding onto the centrality of work. And it might be partly because of the physical interdependency that was common in blue-collar work but that has become exceptional. Still, recent strikes among teachers, fast-food workers, and even Uber drivers reminds us that common work still evokes feelings and expressions of solidarity that are rare outside the sphere of work—and that it does so even among those who do not share a physical workplace or interact face-to-face on the job.

The relative resilience and density of workplace ties is especially important because workplaces are relatively diverse in their make-up—more diverse than families and non-work friendships, and more diverse than most voluntary associations. I'll emphasize two aspects of workplace diversity that are especially important in today's America (and beyond)—diversity of political views and of racial and ethnic identity—and add a few words about gender.

Political diversity: One widely noted sign—both cause and consequence—of ever-greater political polarization in our society is the growing tendency of individuals to associate with like-minded others within politically-homogeneous "bubbles" or "echo chambers."[41] Yet the workplace remains relatively diverse in that respect. A 2019 study by Columbia University political scientist Alexander Hertel-Fernandez found that most workers thought they had "a good sense of how their coworkers think about politics," and that most encountered a high degree of diversity in partisan affiliations: 28 percent reported that their workplace was evenly divided between Democrats and Republicans, and many reported that their own partisan affiliation is in the minority at work.[42] All in all, "over 60% of workers are employed in jobs where they work alongside many individuals who do not share their partisan views."[43]

Political diversity at work is especially important given the variety and density of interactions among co-workers. People talk politics with co-workers (more than with neighbors or fellow members of civic or religious groups though less than with family and friends); they practice "civic skills" of persuasion, communication, and compromise at work;[44] and they often working closely with co-workers as part of a team.[45] In short, the workplace appears to be a rare outpost of regular, varied, and mostly civil interactions across political lines. That is at least partly because workers don't tend to sort themselves politically in choosing a job.[46] Hertel-Fernandez observes that, "[i]n an era of intense political polarization and division, the workplace remains an important site for workers to interact with others who do not necessarily share their own political stands"; it is a "site for '*involuntary association*' with a politically diverse set of individuals."[47] "Involuntary association" turns out to be a crucial and distinctive dimension of workplace relationships, and we'll return to it.

Given the depth of political polarization in our society, one might doubt that these workplace ties across partisan lines are doing much good. Point taken. But I'll take refuge for now in a question: How much worse might things be without the daily informal ties among politically diverse co-workers? And where else would we hope to see those ties arise?

Racial and ethnic diversity at work: One's co-workers also tend to be more demographically diverse than the people one meets within families, neighborhoods, religious congregations, or other voluntary associations.[48] That is partly because employment discrimination law has had some success in countering forms of exclusion, segregation, and self-segregation that are far less regulated, or even constitutionally immune from regulation, in other social settings.[49] The *relative* success of anti-discrimination law at work (compared to, say, neighborhoods) is in turn related to the distinctive nature of workplace relationships and organizations and the role of compulsion in both—the *involuntariness* of workplace associations—which I will take up.

The coexistence of dense and durable ties and relative diversity among co-workers makes the workplace the most prolific site of sustained interaction, and the most frequent source of friendships, among adults of different racial and ethnic identities.[50] Friendships are important not because they offer some magical solution to racial bias or subordination but mainly because they are strong evidence of the larger reservoir of weakly positive ties that can flourish among co-workers. Daily cooperation, informal sociability, and shared experiences among comparatively diverse co-workers can render the unfamiliar more familiar and can break down stereotypes and biases.[51]

Obviously discrimination, and both out-group biases and in-group affinities, persist at work; and their burdens fall most heavily on groups that are underrepresented in the upper ranks of organizations.[52] More than a half-century after the Civil Rights Act of 1964, white (and male) workers still dominate the best jobs, while workers of color are still concentrated in the worst jobs.[53] That enduring legacy of racial stratification needs addressing for reasons that go far beyond the impact on interracial interaction at work. Yet the latter is crucial, in part because it might affect our collective will and capacity to attack racial injustice more broadly. Given the relative homogeneity that prevails in other social settings, the workplace is often the one place where adults of different racial and ethnic groups must find ways of getting along over sustained periods of time.

Let me be clear: The claim is *not* that demographic diversity—at work or elsewhere—facilitates the formation of solidaristic and friendly ties. Sadly, that is not the case. The claim is that societies that are in fact demographically diverse must find ways and places to foster individuals' ability to transcend the differences and frictions that often come with diversity, or to get along in spite of them. Shared work is the most promising medium for doing that.

Gender: It might seem unlikely that anything like this can be said for relations between men and women at work. After all, there is plenty of close and cooperative contact *outside* of work between men and women, who often live together as spouses, siblings, parents, and children.[54] Yet much of that contact takes place within families and domestic or sexual relationships in which traditional gender roles are salient, and in which the law can do very little about that. If we could imagine a law barring the assignment of domestic tasks on the basis of sex, it would presumably be unconstitutional. By contrast, the law prohibits employment discrimination because of sex, and dictates the assignment of workplace roles and responsibilities on the basis of skills, qualifications, and interests, not gender stereotypes. The law also penalizes forms of harassment—unwelcome sexual overtures, offensive sexual slurs, and more—that are unregulated and often unregulable outside work. The normative project of anti-discrimination law, incomplete and complex as it is, makes the workplace a crucial site for cultivating more egalitarian gender relations in the society.[55] And that can have positive spillover effects outside work. Women's progress at work—their higher incomes, status, and authority, often over male workers—might well be the single most powerful force in promoting greater equality within the home.[56]

In sum, more is at stake here than combating intergroup biases, crucial as that is in a diverse society. Personal connections across racial or partisan lines allow for the exchange of experiences and opinions, the discovery of commonalities and differences, and the cultivation of diffuse qualities of empathy and broad-mindedness that shape political preferences, enable compromise, and enrich public discourse. The daily experience of working together, multiplied across legions of adult citizens, strengthens the social foundations for democratic governance in a complex and heterogeneous society.

While work is neither as necessary nor as universally valued by individuals as income and leisure, there is social value in work and working relationships that cannot be replaced by income or leisure, and that is far less likely to arise in other associational settings. That proposition raises concerns about a more automated future. But first I want to drill down into the role of compulsion at work, for it both complicates and deepens the case for the distinctive value of workplace ties.

3. The Paradoxical Role of Compulsion and Necessity in Workplace Ties

Needless to say, work is hardly an oasis of freedom. Most workers face explicitly hierarchical, even autocratic managerial power at work—power that is backed up by the economic necessity that drives workers to seek and hold onto a job.[57] The economic compulsion to sell one's labor to make a living and the managerial compulsion to cooperate in production are at the heart of enduring critiques of capitalism. How does that jibe with the notion that work itself is worth preserving and distributing—assuming we need less of it in the future—and especially with the claim that workplace ties help sustain democratic self-governance?[58]

Paradoxically, it is the economic hold that the workplace has on individuals and the power that managers exercise there, as well as the law's firm regulatory foothold, that makes possible the distinctive convergence of diversity and intense cooperation among co-workers. Those elements of compulsion give workers powerful motivations to find ways to deal with conflict and friction, and to carry on cooperating with co-workers with whom they did not and would not choose to associate, rather than just walking away. That is what sustains what Hertel-Fernandez calls "involuntary association." Anyone who doubts that hierarchy can be useful in promoting intergroup cooperation should consider the transformation of the US military in the wake of its desegregation.[59] People can sometimes be ordered to get along. The example is extreme, but it helps to illustrate the paradoxical role of compulsion in promoting integration.

The point is not that strictly hierarchical managerial control is needed to foster intergroup connections and connectedness. Any organization that is somehow accountable for what it produces, whether through market or political mechanisms, will have to find ways to motivate workers to get things done together, cooperate in work tasks, and overcome differences. That is enough compulsion to generate the kinds of workplace bonds I am touting here.

More democratic workplace organizations—unionized or worker-owned firms, for example—might rely less on hierarchy and more on cooperation to get things done. Democratic institutions at work also create additional spaces and occasions for workers to discuss common concerns, resolve conflicts, and cultivate solidarity. Unions in particular can foster solidarity and civic engagement among co-workers and union members, including solidarity across group lines.[60] In any organizing campaign or strike within a racially mixed workforce, a union must strive to forge trust and solidarity across racial and ethnic divisions even if management seeks to exploit those divisions.[61] Both unions' institutional interests and workers' shared material interests often depend on holding together against divide-and-conquer tactics and damaging divisions and defections.

With or without unions or other democratizing institutions, however, managers have strong motives and organizational means for inducing workers to overcome differences. In the case of diversity along lines of race, ethnicity, and sex, the law plays a crucial role by proscribing segregation and exclusion. If the law does its job, and managers find it necessary to deal with diversity within their workforces, then they will have to find ways to mitigate intergroup tensions and division. (That is so even apart from their fear of Title VII liability for discriminatory harassment.[62]) Those managerial imperatives have generated a profusion of corporate initiatives on diversity and inclusion, not all of which have proven effective.[63] The point is that, for managers of diverse workforces, the bottom line impels them to try to figure out what actually works in promoting intergroup civility and cooperation.

We might like to believe that individuals, if freed from the bare compulsion to work, would enjoy a richer mix of voluntary associations and connections across persistent lines of social division. But many would not. Freed from the need to work for a living, some people would slip out of any constructive social networks and into isolation or destructive behaviors.[64] Others surely would spend more time in diverse and egalitarian voluntary associations. But we see all around us the evidence that many people would choose instead—because they often do choose when they can—to live and associate with others from similar backgrounds, similar political proclivities, and similar racial and ethnic identities.

History suggests that bonds of trust and reciprocity form more easily among those from similar backgrounds and identities. Indeed, the kind of social solidarity that undergirds generous and inclusive social welfare programs appears to be easier to cultivate in racially and ethnically homogeneous societies.[65] Nowadays, nearly all economically developed societies are more or less, and increasingly, diverse due to cross-border migration.[66] That diversity has been exploited by right-wing ideologues and opportunists across the world in the past decade. The weaponization of diversity, and the political polarization to which it has contributed, pose major challenges to the solidaristic social models that put a human face on capitalism in the twentieth century. They also pose challenges to constructing a humane future of less work, the agenda for the remainder of this book.

Now more than ever, it is essential for diverse societies to find ways and places to cultivate bonds of empathy and reciprocity—some sense of being in this together—across group lines and across political divisions. That might require the kinds of legal, economic, and organizational compulsion that shape the experience of working together. Work-based associations can cut across and counter some social divisions, and can foster forms of connectedness that are especially valuable and especially scarce elsewhere.

4. The Troubled Future of Working Together

Unfortunately, the capacity of shared work to generate interpersonal bonds across social divisions is eroding. First, although workplaces became less segregated along lines of race, ethnicity, and gender after the 1960s, progress has lately stalled. And growing economic polarization—due in part to automation—is contributing to racial stratification by destroying middle-skill jobs and pathways for advancement, and entrenching the predominance of white workers in high-level jobs and of workers of color in low-wage jobs.

In other ways, too, work has become less conducive to strong co-worker bonds than were the factories and large integrated organizations that dominated twentieth-century labor markets. All of the major trends in the organization of work since the 1970s—the shift from manufacturing to services, shorter job tenures, more precarious and contingent work, the "fissuring" of supply chains, and the rise of the gig economy and of independent contracting versus employment—seem likely to undercut the potency of work as a source of connectedness and social solidarity. And that is apart from the technologically supercharged efforts of employers—documented by Brishen Rogers and others—to root out and defeat the kinds of co-worker associations that can grow into collective rebellion or union organizing.

Union decline itself raises profound concerns. Unions within diverse workplaces can be especially powerful engines of intergroup solidarity, for unions multiply occasions for constructive and egalitarian engagement among co-workers and underscore both the interests workers share and their shared interest in making common cause. Unions also contributed in their heyday to a less polarized economy and a fairer distribution of income. All this makes the decline of union representation a serious concern not just for workers and for economic fairness but for the future of democracy—a point to which we'll return in the last chapter.[67]

Intertwined with these developments is the decline of work as a source of identity, status, and social recognition since the 1970s, which Sandel, among others, has lamented.[68] The fading association between work, dignity, and social esteem, and the fading sense of reciprocal obligation and mutual respect through work, are deeply troubling at many levels, including their impact on social cohesiveness. It means that the experience of working together is a weaker source of social solidarity.

In the meantime, the rise of remote and dispersed work is thinning work relationships. Since the advent of the factory system, employers have chosen to assemble workers together under one roof in order to control and supervise them, to secure their cooperation in shared production, and to combine their labor with physical capital located at the work site. Solidarity was an incidental byproduct. Nowadays, technology is enabling employers to remotely control workers who are isolated from each other. Gig workers—Uber drivers and Amazon Mechanical Turkers, for example—are highly visible representatives of this trend. But the rise of remote work goes far beyond the gig economy. And for employers, frustrating workers' ability to coalesce around common goals and grievances is at least a welcome consequence of remote work, if not the actual aim.[69]

The COVID-19 crisis accelerated many of these trends, driving many white-collar workers out of common work spaces and into working from home. They were the lucky ones—unlike the "essential workers" and their families who suffered the brunt of infections and deaths. Some workers found a better work-life balance, if only by skipping the daily commute.[70] And technologies for remote meetings and collaboration like Zoom, Slack, and G-Suite proved surprisingly effective. Still, not everybody loved working from home (especially when it overlapped with home-schooling).[71] Old gender norms made a comeback, as mothers diverted more of their time to children's needs and demands than fathers did, even when both were working at home. (One study found that "mothers with young children have reduced their work hours four to five times more than fathers."[72]) Others complained of the further colonization of domestic life by work, even beyond the always-on-call trend facilitated by electronic devices.[73] Some workers simply missed the casual interaction with their co-workers.[74]

Some of these changes will plainly outlast the pandemic. Telework technologies are bound to improve, and to whittle away at the advantages that firms derive from face-to-face interactions and from large and costly common work spaces. But even if both workers and firms, for different reasons, gravitate toward more remote work after the pandemic is behind us, society could end up the loser. Neither firms nor workers capture the social and political spillover benefits of workplace togetherness.

Then again, most work in the post-pandemic era will still entail a good bit of face-to-face interaction with co-workers, even if not all day every day. And recent organizing successes among Uber drivers, Amazon Mechanical Turkers, and domestic workers have shown that, valuable as it is, even face-to-face interaction is not always indispensable to forming bonds based on common work.[75] Shared work is still the best medium we have for generating solidarity and connectedness across social divisions, and it is one that we should strive to preserve, create, and widely distribute even as demand for human labor declines.

5. What Kind of Work and How Much of It?

I've outlined a multifaceted case for keeping paid work at the center of most people's lives and livelihoods. What does that case suggest about what kind of work and how much of it we should be aiming to preserve and distribute in a future of less work?

What kind of work is worth preserving? It is tempting to introduce a whole wish list of worthy reforms here, from democratizing work to ensuring meaningful and socially interactive work. But most of that wish list has little to do with hopes and fears in a future of *less* work. So I'll mostly fall back on the positivist yet changeable standard of decent work as already defined: Work that falls below the floor set by existing law is, by societal consensus, not worth holding onto; but work that meets that standard is worth preserving even if it falls short of higher aspirations for freedom, equality, and democracy at work. Of course those higher aspirations might become law, and might redefine what work is worth preserving. The decent work standard as I've defined it responds to changing social norms and ongoing political agitation, and those are more likely to push that standard up than down (at least as a formal matter). Indeed, I will suggest a few of those upward adjustments in Chapters 6 and 7. Debates about raising the floor on workers' entitlements should take account of potential job losses. But that political process—rather than an abstract discussion of goals for a future of less work—is the right place to make collective judgments about what kind of work is worth preserving.

Take, for example, workplace democracy, a long-standing aspiration of labor reformers. The goal of workplace democracy is already reflected—albeit very imperfectly—in the decent work proviso by way of the NLRA, which protects rights of self-organization, peaceful collective action, and collective bargaining. The NLRA doesn't protect those rights very well, and its mechanism for promoting collective bargaining has largely failed. If the multifaceted campaign for labor law reform succeeds in creating better legal structures for democratizing workplace governance—as I hope it does—then those structures would in turn become part of what decent work entails. In the meantime, we want to have jobs and workplaces within which struggles for democratization by one mechanism or another can continue.

The same goes for most other fronts in the ongoing battle to improve the quality of work, whether through collective self-help or politics and legislation. Problems abound in the domain of paid work, especially in its lower tiers. Some of those problems reflect underenforcement of existing laws; others call for new laws; and I've weighed in on both scores in the past. My point here, however, is that we want to have jobs and workplaces within which those struggles for better work can continue.

How much work? Work is a social good, but that doesn't mean that more of it is necessarily better, or that we should set our sights on maintaining the current norm of full-time work for all. On the contrary, I've argued we should also be aiming for more free time, or time outside of paid work, in a more automated future. So how much work is necessary or sufficient or optimal to yield the various non-pecuniary benefits of work?

The UK-based authors of a recent study call this the "dosage" question. Too much of almost any good thing—protein, medications, or sunshine—can be bad for you. The same is true of work, as evinced by the history of agitation and legislation against excessive working hours. But few have asked, as the UK researchers did, how much work is necessary or sufficient to secure the non-pecuniary benefits of work—specifically, the individual psychosocial benefits of work. Their preliminary empirical study reaffirmed the substantial benefits of paid work for individual well-being, but found that those benefits tapered off and hit a plateau beyond about *eight hours of work per week*![76]

The UK study is hardly the last word on the "dosage" question. For one thing, it does not attempt to reckon with the practicalities of chopping jobs up into much smaller pieces.[77] More importantly, it does not purport to measure the social benefits of work, including the social and intergroup integration that I emphasize here—if that is even possible. Those social gains might continue to rise with hours of work even if individual non-pecuniary benefits do not, and might require more hours of work than would be required for individual well-being.

Still, the UK study opens an intriguing line of inquiry that might recalibrate the debate over whether to welcome or to fear an automated future of less work. If work is good but much less of it is plenty—and that might be about as far as empirical studies can take us on the question of "how much work?"—then the pro-work camp should worry less about a decline in the aggregate demand for labor, and focus on how to *spread work* to more people through shorter hours. And that is indeed where this book is heading.

* * * * *

This chapter has sought to clarify what is at stake in a future of less work—what might be lost (work and income), what might be gained (time outside of work), and what we should be looking to achieve—so that we can begin to construct a better version of that future. Otherwise we are likely to face a bleak version of that future in which decent middle-class jobs continue to dry up and intense competition for the remaining jobs drives wages down and drives a growing share of would-be workers out of the active labor market. A better future of less work would ensure a wide distribution of decent work (albeit less of it), more free time, and adequate material resources. That points us toward a fairly settled menu of strategy options: creating, preserving, and distributing work; spreading work through reduced hours per worker; or replacing work with non-work-based income. Or maybe all of the above.

5
Three Big Ideas (and Some Big Concerns)

Automation arouses both hopes and fears, threatening job losses while promising enormous gains in productivity, efficiency, and more. The question is how to ensure that the gains are distributed widely rather than overwhelmingly to the creators and owners of the technology. I've argued that we should judge policy proposals for a future of less work on their ability to ensure wide access to decent paid work, adequate material resources, and more time for life outside of paid work. Those are three dimensions of a good life that are at stake—either at greater risk or within closer reach—in a more automated future.

Each of those dimensions points to one of three basic public policy strategies for dealing with job losses: creating work, supplying non-work-based income or benefits, or spreading work by reducing hours per worker. Whenever and for whatever reason we face a job deficit, variations on those three options dominate the policy menu. We saw that during the Great Depression and more recently in the wake of the COVID-19 collapse: In both of those periods of mass unemployment, policy makers in the United States and elsewhere deployed all three of those strategies, sometimes in combination.[1] For there is no incompatibility among those basic strategies of job creation, income support, and work spreading.

Each of those three strategies has also been sculpted into a high-profile Big Idea: universal basic income (UBI), a federal job guarantee, and shorter working hours. Each of those Big Ideas is animated by one of the three goods we are aiming for—adequate income, decent work for all, or more free time; and each is touted by some proponents as an all-embracing solution to a range of societal problems, including future job scarcity. Each of those ideas has also been thoroughly vetted elsewhere. This chapter aims to add value by putting those Big Ideas in conversation with each other in light of Chapter 4's account of goals.

One point that emerges is that the Three Big Ideas, unlike the underlying strategies they embody, are not all compatible with each other. In particular,

Automation Anxiety. Cynthia Estlund, Oxford University Press. © Cynthia Estlund 2021.
DOI: 10.1093/oso/9780197566107.003.0005

UBI is incompatible with the JG in ways I'll explore here. That incompatibility is problematic because none of the Three Big Ideas by itself can deliver on all three goals of income, leisure, and work. Each takes aim squarely at one of those goals, and would at least incidentally advance a second one; but each falls short on a third goal. By way of preview:

- A full-scale UBI would guarantee adequate income, and would support more free time (on the broad definition used here) for those who choose to rely on that income; yet it falls short on ensuring wide access to paid work in a future of job scarcity.
- A job guarantee would ensure wide access to decent paid work, as well as adequate income from that work; but it would entrench the current norm of full-time work and miss the opportunity to distribute more free time in a more automated economy.
- A shorter standard work week takes square aim at expanding free time, and would more-than-incidentally spread available work to more people; standing alone, however, shorter working hours would fail to ensure adequate incomes for all.

In short, each of the Three Big Ideas meets two out of the three goals, while missing a third.

I don't mean to elevate geometric symmetry over solid analysis here. For one thing, a shorter work week is more compatible with alternative strategies than UBI or the JG is with each other. By juxtaposing the Three Big Ideas with each other and with our three basic goals, this chapter will lay the groundwork for the next two chapters and their three-dimensional prescription for a future of less work—one that aims to widely distribute adequate income, more free time, *and* decent work.

A. Universal Basic Income and the Perils of Decentering Work

Universal Basic Income, or UBI, in its contemporary form has several defining features: it is a cash grant that is universal, unconditional, individual, and regular.[2] The grant need not be large enough for an individual to live on to count as UBI, but that added feature generates many of the benefits claimed for UBI by its proponents, and that is part of what makes UBI a Big Idea for a future of less work.

The idea of a basic guaranteed income for all has a long history that runs through utopian thought as well as radical, progressive, and libertarian political programs.[3] But it has never come close to being adopted in the United States.[4] Perhaps that will change as rising anxiety about automation and future job losses draws interest to UBI ideas. Heads turned in the labor community in 2016 when Andy Stern, former head of the Service Employees International Union, emerged from a deep dive into the future of work as a strong proponent of UBI.[5] He came to that view mainly through discussions with people in Silicon Valley whose work with emerging technologies led them to believe that, in the foreseeable future, a shrinking share of the population would be able to find decent paid work. Andrew Yang's 2020 presidential run on a platform centered on UBI helped to put the concept into popular discourse.[6]

A full-scale subsistence-level UBI would have many virtues: It would effectively eliminate poverty and its debilitating burdens on adults and especially children.[7] (That might be reason enough to embrace UBI; but there are other less costly ways to combat poverty.) For those who lack other savings or family resources, a UBI would also allow people to leave a bad job or a bad domestic relationship; to search for a better job or train for one; to launch a new enterprise; or to take time off work for parenting, volunteering, or other valuable but unremunerated activities. Crucially, UBI could curb employer domination by underwriting workers' ability to quit a job or to exit the wage labor market altogether without falling into poverty.[8] UBI's creation of instant bargaining power for workers in the form of a "walk-away option" is one of its greatest virtues for some proponents.[9] Some proponents argue that UBI would make some employment regulations, even the minimum wage, unnecessary by alleviating the bare economic compulsion to work;[10] others disagree.[11]

Support for UBI runs from the far left, where it is seen as ushering in a post-capitalist future by freeing individuals from the need to sell their labor;[12] and the feminist left, where some see it as compensating otherwise-unpaid domestic work;[13] to the libertarian left, where it is seen as a market-friendly bulwark against employer domination;[14] and the libertarian right, where it is seen as an antidote to a bloated welfare state bureaucracy.[15] The concept of UBI also meets harsh criticism across the entire political spectrum.[16] Some on the left see UBI as propping up rather than undermining late capitalism,[17] as sapping solidarity at its source in shared work,[18] as reinforcing the gendered division of domestic labor by subsidizing the choice to stay home,[19] or as a Trojan horse that would lead to dismantling social welfare programs and leaving poor people worse off.[20] Others criticize UBI for giving "handouts" to able-bodied people, for the massive tax hikes it would require, and for the inflation it would supposedly generate.[21] Across the whole political spectrum, the idea of sending cash to Jeff Bezos (and millions of others who simply don't need it) provokes puzzlement or ridicule.[22]

Much of the debate centers on the cost of UBI. Two intertwined design issues largely determine its cost in any given society: the size of the basic grant, and whether it would replace or supplement existing social programs.[23] Here I'll hypothesize a full, subsistence-level UBI—enough for an individual to live on above the poverty threshold—that would count as income for existing means-tested programs (thus drastically shrinking those programs while leaving nobody worse off[24]). In the United States that is a little over $1,000 per month,[25] which is about the level suggested by many UBI proponents.[26] (On most versions of UBI, children would receive a smaller grant until adulthood.[27]) That is what it would take to secure the benefits cited by many UBI proponents—for example, to end poverty or to allow those without other resources to reject or quit a bad job. And that is what it would take for a UBI to supply adequate incomes to those displaced by automation. That, in short, is what qualifies UBI as a Big Idea as opposed to one of many possible social welfare reforms.

The feasibility of funding a full UBI is much debated.[28] On the one hand, given the outrageous fortunes that are flowing to those who create or own automating technology, there should be some combination of taxes on income, capital, or wealth that could foot the bill.[29] On the other, it is clear that a full UBI would absorb a sizable share of national wealth, even given savings on existing programs,[30] and that the tax bill would not only hit the wealthy.[31] Leading proponents Van Parijs and Vanderborght concede that a full-scale UBI is too costly to be politically feasible in the United States or other rich countries in the near or medium term; they propose instead a partial UBI—below the individual poverty level—that they hope will pave the way eventually for a full UBI.[32] That creates a dilemma. As one UBI critic argues, "to deliver the benefits its supporters hold out for it, the income must be substantial," and probably "too great for a society like ours to afford"; yet a more feasible partial UBI "would deliver few of the promised benefits yet still cost enough to present a serious hurdle."[33]

The cost of a full UBI would also foreclose other policy options. In particular, UBI is a rival, not a complement, to the federal job guarantee, and perhaps to any large-scale jobs program.[34] The incompatibility of UBI and a JG goes beyond cost. On the political plane, it is hard to imagine selling the public on the idea of granting and funding unconditional basic income for individuals who could, but chose not to, secure a guaranteed job at a living wage. Indeed, why *should* the public subsidize individuals' choice to opt out of paid work if that clearly is a choice—if a job is guaranteed at public expense? It isn't just politics but political morality that would force a choice between these two approaches to rebalancing the economy.

That brings us to a more basic critique of a full subsistence-level UBI: By design, it would replace paid work for some who are fully able to work. It would deliver a check—enough to live on and with no strings attached—to some people who otherwise could and would seek work.

We shouldn't exaggerate the work-replacing nature of UBI.[35] Most people with marketable skills would still seek paid work to supplement the basic grant. And unlike existing means-tested programs, a UBI would not actively discourage poor beneficiaries from working, for benefits would not drop as earned income rose.[36] The effect of a UBI on beneficiaries' activities is an empirical question, and it is a very difficult and expensive one to study.[37] (Not surprisingly, no existing studies fairly test the impact of universal subsistence-level UBI in a wealthy society.[38]) But plainly, and by design, subsistence-level individual grants would alleviate the need to work for many who could work. Indeed, several adults in one household could pool their individual grants and live well above poverty level without any of them working for pay. That in itself is not necessarily a knock on UBI.[39] But the virtue of ensuring adequate non-work-based income for all (and more-than-adequate income for many) is also its central flaw: UBI fails on the metric of ensuring the centrality of paid work for most adults for most of their lives.

UBI's subsidizing of individuals' choice to forego work raises two kinds of fairness concerns: fairness to the taxpayers who support it, and fairness to UBI recipients. Jon Elster expresses the first: It is simply "unfair for able-bodied people to live off the labour of others."[40] UBI is at odds with the idea that all members of a society who can do so have a moral obligation to support themselves and contribute to the well-being of the community and the society. Van Parijs calls this the "Malibu Surfer problem."[41]

Can one justify taxing non-rich working people to subsidize the Malibu surfer (or the suburban gamer) who chooses to live off taxpayer-funded UBI rather than working? Van Parijs offers an answer grounded in economics and liberal theory.[42] To brutally condense his elegant argument: In modern economies, partly due to conscious policy choices, labor markets do not clear; that is, some individuals who are willing and able to work are unemployed because wages do not fall to the level at which some employer is willing to hire them. That being so, those who *are* employed realize more by way of income and other rewards to work than they would in a market-clearing economy. It is fair, says Van Parijs, to tax part of that surplus to fund basic income for those who are left without a job. True, some of them could find work if they tried, but they would merely displace someone else; some number of would-be workers are left without work due to deliberate societal choices.[43] UBI, he argues, would fairly redistribute some of the burdens and benefits of those choices. Van Parijs's argument is at its strongest, he recognizes, in "affluent societies with high rates of unemployment."[44] As it happens, that describes not only much of Europe over the past half-century but also the future that automation might bring about in the developed world.

Even if we accept that response to the first fairness objection to UBI, however, it does not meet a second fairness objection grounded in Michael Sandel's idea of "contributive justice"—that is, the idea that society should ensure a fair distribution of the opportunity to contribute to the greater social good through work.[45] UBI fails on that dimension of social justice and even undercuts it by draining social resources that could be devoted to job creation; by subsidizing the choice not to work; and by communicating a societal judgment that many individuals' contributions are simply not needed.

These arguments about the *morality* of replacing work with guaranteed income begin to point to the troubling *consequences* of doing so. Decent work is worth much more to individuals and society than the income it generates. I have emphasized the social and political benefits of having most people engaged for most of their adult lives in productive work and working relationships, and especially the social ties that arise out of shared work and workplace associations in diverse workplaces. Some of the intangible gains from work would be lost in a UBI world in which workers' attachment to not-great but still decent jobs would be more tenuous. Some individuals with lesser but still marketable skills, or with the capacity to develop those skills, would drop out of the labor market and subsist on UBI, especially in a future of less work for those with ordinary skills. Freed from the need to show up and cooperate with others to earn a living, some would fall into social isolation, depression, or addictions.[46] UBI might also tilt the calculus of discontented workers toward exit and away from sticking it out and joining with co-workers in demanding better conditions.[47]

If individuals are going to be displaced by technology and ejected from the labor force, clearly it's better that they are able to feed, clothe, and house themselves. Just as clearly, we need to do more to bolster incomes at the bottom of the income distribution, especially in a future of less work. But guaranteed basic income is not the only option. Individuals, communities, and the whole polity will be stronger and healthier if work—though perhaps less of it—remains central to people's livelihoods, and if we steer public policy deliberately in that direction. Even if many people would genuinely prefer UBI to working for a living, the society has good reasons to favor work, at least to the point of putting public resources into job creation versus UBI. And even if it were fair to tax workers to subsidize others' choice not to work, it would not serve society's profound interest in promoting social integration and cohesion, especially across social divisions.

As Brishen Rogers puts it, "basic income is a simple and elegant way to redistribute resources. But there are no simple, elegant solutions to complex political and economic challenges."[48] A partial UBI might be part of the solution—not a "magic bullet," but more compatible than a full UBI with other strategies that center work.[49] And if we eventually face the tsunami of job destruction that some in the tech world foresee, a work-centered strategy might become unsustainable, and a full UBI might become the best path forward. For the foreseeable future, however, we should strive to keep decent work at the foundation of most people's livelihoods.

B. A Federal Job Guarantee: Doubling Down on Full-Time Full Employment

The pro-work case against UBI seems to point squarely toward the competing Big Idea of a federal job guarantee, which would afford both adequate income and the non-material individual and social benefits of work as a matter of right. The protean idea of a "right to work" has resonated throughout much of the world at least since the French Revolution, and especially in times of high unemployment.[50] The idea of a job guarantee has a lot more history in the United States than UBI, and it's worth briefly reviewing that history.

During the Depression, some populists called for a right to a job.[51] The goal of full employment became a central plank of the New Deal, and spawned the Civilian Conservation Corps and the Works Progress Administration but not a job guarantee.[52] World War II then brought full employment as a collateral consequence. But after the war and with a new conservative coalition in Congress, the cause of full employment suffered a more-than-symbolic defeat when the so-called "Full Employment Act" of 1945 was pointedly renamed the "Employment Act," and all of its binding provisions were stripped out.[53]

Over the next two decades, the political commitment to full employment and its Keynesian underpinnings lost ground to a new orthodoxy that prioritized fighting inflation. But in the late 1960s, with unemployment running twice as high for Black workers as for white workers, the Reverend Martin Luther King, Jr., called for an "economic bill of rights" that "would guarantee a job to all people who want to work and are able to work."[54] After his death, Coretta Scott King and other civil rights leaders campaigned vigorously for a federal commitment to full employment, culminating in the Humphrey-Hawkins Full Employment Act of 1978. The original bill provided an enforceable right to a job; but once again, that provision was stripped out before enactment.[55] Then the election of Ronald Reagan ushered in a new pro-market, anti-government ideology. For the next four decades there was barely a whisper in the United States of a "right to work" in the form of a job guarantee.

More recently, however, the JG idea has regained traction on the left. Senator Bernie Sanders proposed "a federal jobs guarantee program," in which "the US government would guarantee a job with a living wage and good benefits to any resident who wants or needs one."[56] In 2019, proponents of a Green New Deal incorporated a job guarantee into their program to combat both economic inequality and environmental degradation.[57] Although it does not appear to have made it onto the Biden administration's agenda,[58] the JG concept has struck a chord in the American electorate that UBI thus far has not.[59]

The two most developed proposals in circulation in the United States come from the Center on Budget and Policy Priorities (CBPP) and the Levy Economics Institute (LEI).[60] Both would pay well above the current federal minimum wage: either a uniform $15 per hour (LEI),[61] or a minimum wage of $11.83 per hour and average wage of $15.63 per hour, depending on skill level and local cost of living.[62] Both proposals would offer a fairly generous benefits package as well as job security—protection against discharge without cause—which is currently rare for US private sector workers.[63] I will focus here on the CBPP proposal.[64]

Any JG program would greatly expand the federal government's involvement in the labor market (which animates conservative critiques of the JG).[65] The main point is to employ those who are unemployed, underemployed, or discouraged from seeking work. No less important, however, would be the impact on non-JG jobs. As the CBPP puts it, "Make no mistake, this is a policy to transform the US labor market."[66] Because any worker could get a job with at least the minimum JG package of pay and benefits, that would effectively become the floor on wages and benefits in the private sector.[67] Employers who offered less would presumably lose their workers to JG jobs, making the JG a far more effective enforcement mechanism than now exists for minimum wage violations. As with any large minimum wage increase, there's a risk that some existing jobs would disappear (a risk that the LEI proposal assumes away).[68] But job losses would translate not into joblessness but into a bigger JG program, which would expand to absorb those workers.

In effect, the CBPP proposal (like the LEI proposal) would couple a JG with a big increase in the minimum wage and benefit package across the labor market. It would be possible, of course, to separate the two, and guarantee a job at the existing minimum wage, whatever it might be in the relevant jurisdiction.[69] That would make the JG a genuine fallback option, with lower participation levels and costs, and would neither dislocate nor transform the private sector labor market. But without also substantially raising the low minimum wage rate that prevails in much of the United States, that sort of JG would not afford anything like a decent income to participants. Standing alone, it wouldn't quite be the Big Idea pitched by JG proponents. So let's stick with the higher-wage JG concept for now.

Much of the debate over the JG, as with UBI, revolves around cost and financing. The CBPP estimates 9.7 million participants and an annual cost of about $543 billion (offset by large reductions in existing programs for the working poor and the unemployed—Medicaid, unemployment benefits, food stamps, for example).[70] But that estimate was from 2018, with its historically-low jobless rates. Both participation and costs would rise in an economic downturn. The resulting countercyclical stimulus is one point of a public job *guarantee* versus a conventional jobs program; but the size and manageability of such an open-ended program raises other concerns. The program would also grow steadily, and not just cyclically, in case of escalating job losses due to automation, a point to which we'll return.

As for how to pay for a JG, some proponents, including those at the LEI, think the question is misplaced. As adherents of "modern monetary theory" (MMT), they reject the orthodox premise that governments must pay for new programs through additional taxes or cuts elsewhere. MMT treats government debt as something like a fiction for a country like the United States that issues its own currency.[71] I'll return to MMT briefly in Chapter 8, but here I'll sidestep that controversy. My question here is this: Even assuming it would be possible to fund a JG with (or without) some combination of new taxes on income, capital, wealth, or consumption, would a JG be the right way to respond to a predicted future of less work?

The benefits of a *successful* job guarantee could be dazzling. Millions of workers would get a job or a sizable raise or both. Their additional purchasing power could help revive poor communities where job opportunities have been scarce.[72] There would also be less-tangible gains in public health and overall well-being, especially in economically moribund communities in the Rust Belt and elsewhere that have long been plagued by high levels of joblessness. According to the CBPP, it would bring about "the elimination of involuntary unemployment," "a true floor in the labor market"; "the elimination of working poverty"; "the restoration of local and state tax bases"; "macroeconomic stabilization"; and "the provision of socially useful goods and services" by JG workers.[73] And that is apart from the social and political benefits of wider engagement in paid work. All in all, a job guarantee—*if it could be successfully implemented*—would seem better along many dimensions than UBI. ("Both of the above" is not an option. The JG is incompatible with a full-scale UBI on grounds of sheer cost, political palatability, and normative underpinnings.[74])

Unfortunately, the sheer magnitude of a JG program raises doubts—from the labor-friendly Economic Policy Institute, no less—as to whether there is enough "public sector managerial capacity" to administer it.[75] The Progressive Policy Institute calls the JG "too big to succeed."[76] And those judgments were rendered at a time of historically low unemployment. The problem of administrability would loom larger now, and ever-larger in a future of less work.

Moreover, if the future is one of steady technological "task encroachment," then a JG runs into three additional objections. First, it would require bridging an ever-wider job gap—beyond normal cyclical downturns—at an ever-mounting cost and an ever-growing federal share of the labor market. Second, an ever-growing share of those guaranteed jobs would be "make-work" at least in the sense that they could be done better or more cheaply by machines. Third, entrenching a twentieth-century ideal of full-time full employment through a job guarantee would bypass a historic opportunity to reduce (without zeroing out) the portion of most people's lives that must be devoted to work.

The problem is not with a public jobs program as such. Nearly all the worries about a JG flow directly from the *guarantee* feature, while most of its benefits accumulate job by job, and do not hinge on the guarantee. For one thing, a JG must peg job creation to whatever skills applicants have.[77] There is a lot of work that needs doing in our society, from physical infrastructure construction and maintenance to green energy generation and conservation to social services, health care, child care, and early education. But most of that work requires vetting, training, and experience—demands that are out of sync with the concept of a job guarantee.[78] A JG seems unlikely to deliver high-quality public services and public goods. A JG also raises another nagging concern: If young people know the government will guarantee them a job with good wages and benefits—no matter how little they do to acquire useful skills—how will that affect their motivation to invest in training and education?[79]

The more profound question is this: If we face a future of less work, does the answer really lie in committing to maintain full-time full employment? Work itself has social and psychic value beyond the income it produces. Still, the work most people do is less rewarding and more draining than is mine and that of many readers. Putting aside the income trade-off, they might reasonably wish for less work rather than guaranteed full-time work. This might seem like an easy problem to fix (and both JG programs discussed here would offer a part-time option). But the JG's promise of adequate incomes is founded on the assumption of full-time employment. A shorter hours version of the JG, standing alone, would fall short on the metric of providing adequate incomes (unless wages were raised to a level that would probably be unsustainable).

At bottom, the JG concept rests on an assumption that the job deficit will remain within historical bounds, with a cyclical component and a fairly stable structural component, both of which could be brought to heel with a job guarantee. But if we are facing a future of declining overall demand for human labor—or for the kinds of labor most humans can muster—then an open-ended job guarantee is the wrong solution.

A JG would double down on the norm of full-time employment at a time when that might become increasingly difficult to achieve *and* when shorter working hours and more free time might become realistic aspirations. It would address two crucial dimensions of a balanced life and an equitable economy of less work—work and income—but would fall short on the third dimension: It would fail to reap and distribute the potential dividends that automation could yield in the form of time for family, friends, recreation, volunteer work, and everything else that makes up a good life outside of work. Better answers might emerge if we start by seeing an opportunity, not just as a threat, in declining demand for human labor.

C. Reviving the Shorter Hours Movement?

If we do face a future of scarce job opportunities, why not spread the work that remains, and increase time for the rest of life, by reducing hours per worker—for example, by shortening the work week?[80] Provided that could be done without reducing incomes at the bottom of the labor market—a crucial proviso—it would enable people to live lives less dominated by work and more congenial to other life pursuits without sacrificing the socially integrative role of work. In recent years, shorter working hours have been touted by historian Benjamin Hunnicutt as "the forgotten American dream,"[81] by law professor Matthew Dimick as "better than basic income,"[82]and by sociologist Jamie McCallum as "a bridge to larger political change," and an ideal rallying cry for a reenergized labor movement.[83] A recent report from the UK's Labour Party, "The Shorter Work Week: A Radical and Pragmatic Proposal," proposes a thirty-hour work week as the remedy for a range of social and economic ailments, including expected job losses from automation.[84]

In the current wave of automation anxiety, the strategy of reducing working hours has been overshadowed, at least in the United States, by its two flashier rivals, UBI and the JG. Historically, however, the quest for progressively shorter working hours was a central focus of the US labor movement and labor reformers, who helped reduce actual working time (in manufacturing) from an average of sixty-eight hours per week in 1850 to forty hours per week by 1950.[85] Shorter working hours is not just a Big Idea; it was a big success story of the first century of industrialization and organized labor in the United States.

The movement for shorter hours was only episodically focused on the goal of work spreading, which will take center stage in my own prescriptions for a future of less work. My main critique of the shorter hours strategy is that, by itself, it can't ensure adequate incomes at the bottom of the wage scale. I'll get to that. But first I want to briefly retell the history of the movement for shorter hours and its demise, relying on a leading chronicler, Benjamin Hunnicutt; for that history is studded with lessons for a future of less work.[86]

1. The Rise and Fall of the Shorter Hours Movement in the United States

Once capital and its managers won control of production through the factory system in the early 1800s, working hours became a major site of political and industrial conflict. For a good part of a century, the labor movement fought for its Ten-Hour System against managers' efforts to exact twelve or more hours a day out of workers—typically for six days a week—and then for the eight-hour day under the slogan "Eight hours for work, eight hours for rest, and eight hours for what you will."[87] The case for shorter hours was multifaceted. Workers sought relief from their exhausting physical labors, and more time for the rest of what life offered, including intellectual, cultural, and political pursuits once reserved to the propertied classes.[88] The struggle for shorter hours was central to organized labor's efforts to reconfigure the concept of "free labor" for the industrial age and to equip workers for active participation in the republican project of self-governance.[89] Some arguments for shorter hours were congenial to pragmatic capitalists: workers would be more productive with a shorter work day. And as the consumer economy began to take shape, some commentators argued that workers needed more leisure time in order to be good consumers.[90]

The case for shorter hours also drew support from the expectation that machines would gradually supplant human labor in the productive process. Many late nineteenth and early twentieth-century observers foresaw, as Marx had, the emergence of a technologically advanced economy that could meet the material needs of the citizenry with only a small fraction of the human labor that was currently employed.[91] Shorter hours would help to spread scarce work and wages and avert mass unemployment and immiseration. Indeed, if both labor inputs and the outputs of a highly automated and productive economy could be fairly distributed, then humanity could transcend scarcity and competition, and democratize the pursuit of humanistic and artistic aims that Walt Whitman called "higher progress."[92]

The aspiration to "higher progress" reflected in part critiques of capitalism. For some of its proponents, the quest for shorter hours was a strategy for peaceful and gradual retreat from capitalism as humans spent a shrinking part of their lives under the domination of employers and in the production of goods and services for market.[93] That was hardly an argument calculated to win over capitalism's defenders to the cause of shorter hours. But in the depths of the Great Depression, the future of capitalism seemed up for grabs.

John Maynard Keynes sought to square the circle by postponing the reckoning. He argued in 1930 that the problem of scarcity would be with us, and the prodigious growth machine of capitalism would still be needed, for many more decades. But he predicted that "our grandchildren" a century hence—that is, in 2030—would need to work no more than *fifteen hours per week* to meet their material needs. Then, "*for the first time since his creation man will be faced with his real, his permanent problem—how to use his freedom from pressing economic cares, how to occupy the leisure, which science and compound interest will have won for him, to live wisely and agreeably and well.*"[94] As it turned out, though, Keynes was writing near the end of the historic movement for shorter hours. What happened?

Before the New Deal, the shorter hours movement engaged a broad coalition that included both those who hoped to preserve capitalism in the face of growing skepticism about its viability and many of the skeptics themselves. That movement also tapped into both the fears and the hopes arising from the prospect of machines replacing human labor. Once the eight-hour day was an accomplished fact, however, and the shorter hours camp set its sights on a thirty-hour work week, the case for shorter hours had lost some pillars of its support. Some of the most broadly appealing arguments for shorter hours—such as those based on workers' physical health—began to fade, leaving more controversial aspirations—toward "higher progress," away from the endless pursuit of material abundance, and gradually away from capitalism itself—standing alone.

The shorter hours camp squared off against the proponents of "full-time, full-employment" during the Depression, and came tantalizing close in 1933 to winning congressional enactment of a thirty-hour work week (despite then-formidable constitutional hurdles). But the weight of opinion among New Dealers shifted toward revving up the engines of production and committing to the goal of full-time, full employment.[95] Some New Dealers doubted that most people could, or would, or even should replace productive work with salutary "higher" pursuits.[96] And they questioned whether the American economy was indeed close to meeting the people's material needs.[97] After all, parts of the country still lacked access to electricity. In the meantime, many workers themselves, having gained a modicum of leisure, aspired to higher incomes and the security and comforts they could buy; their unions followed course.

Congress's enactment of the Fair Labor Standards Act of 1938 (FLSA)[98] represented the culmination of the shorter hours movement in the United States. But it was far from a crowning achievement. The FLSA established the standard forty-hour work week, as well as a national minimum wage, for many private sector workers; yet it excluded many workers at both the high and low ends of the labor market from its protections. The "white collar exemptions" from the law's overtime provisions for salaried managers, administrators, and professionals helped to foster a "long hours" work culture that is still with us.[99] And the exclusions of domestic and agricultural workers—later narrowed but not eliminated[100]—relegated most Black workers in the Jim Crow South to near-feudal conditions.[101]

Even for the workers it covered, the FLSA did not cap working hours but instead "taxed" them with a time-and-a-half wage premium for overtime—that is, hours beyond forty per week. The shift in regulatory strategy is a bit surprising. Organized labor had long sought maximum hours laws; the Supreme Court had just opened the constitutional door to those laws in 1937; and labor's political clout was then at high tide.[102] Perhaps the overtime premium—a softer, more flexible form of regulation than a cap on hours—seemed more practical once regulation of hours was extended to white-collar occupations that prior working-time laws had never reached. But the overtime premium also encouraged workers to seek overtime even as it modestly discouraged employers from demanding it.

The movement for shorter hours soon began to fade. The war made full-time full employment a national imperative; after the war, pent-up consumer demand helped fuel a drive for material prosperity. Some labor leaders, especially the few women among them, sought to keep the shorter hours movement alive,[103] and some unions successfully bargained for shorter hours.[104] But most unions put their clout instead behind higher incomes—bolstered in part by more overtime—that would support a stay-at-home wife and a house in the suburbs for their overwhelmingly male members.[105] In the meantime, the rise of anti-Communism lent an almost un-American ring to the goal of "higher progress" versus material abundance (not to mention the goal of peacefully overturning capitalism). In the Cold-War battle for hearts and minds across the world, America advertised capitalism as a path to prosperity; and at home, consumption took on an almost-patriotic tinge, while increasingly sophisticated advertising campaigns fueled consumer appetites for comforts, luxuries, and status goods.[106]

From World War II until the 1970s, ordinary workers—those fortunate to have decent jobs with stable firms—drew their dividends from growing productivity in the form of higher wages rather than more leisure. Then most workers ceased drawing those dividends in any form at all.[107] As wages stagnated, workers began to pile up debt, and to scramble for more hours and even multiple jobs to make ends meet.[108] The dividends from economic growth flowed increasingly to the top, but still in the form of income versus free time.

Since the 1970s, growing economic inequality has tended to push toward longer hours at both the top and the bottom of the income scale. Low-wage workers seek longer hours, multiple jobs, or side gigs just to make ends meet. At the top, long hours are super rewarded, and are the price for gaining or retaining one's position and for climbing up the steep income slope from merely rich to very rich.[109] For perhaps the first time in the history of the world, high-income workers now work longer hours on average than lower-income workers, and those longer hours widen the growing income gap between rich and poor.[110] Overall, actual working hours per person in the United States increased from 1,687 hours annually in 1979 to 1,868 in 2007.[111] The ideal of shorter hours for all has largely faded from memory, lost in the scramble to rise to the top or to keep from falling to the bottom of the income distribution.

2. Work-Life Balance and the Prospects for a Revival of the Shorter Hours Movement

Women's mass migration into the labor market starting in the 1970s has revived and recast the debate over working hours. That migration was driven in part by sheer economic necessity, especially for growing numbers of single mothers, but also for two-parent families that could no longer make ends meet on one income in the era of wage stagnation and rising debt.[112] For college-educated women, the shift into paid work also reflected aspirations for a richer life, a wider role in the world, and a measure of economic independence and equality[113]—not to mention bigger homes, fancier schools for their children, and more lavish vacations.

Women's growing presence in the labor market helped to drive up average working hours per person since 1969. Indeed, "virtually all of the increase in families' hours of market work has come from increases in women's hours."[114] That trend in turn helped to generate growing criticism of "long hours" culture and demands for time away from work. Most women who worked outside the home (including those who worked in other people's homes) continued to perform the bulk of unpaid work at home as well (except for what they could afford to pay others to do).[115] The rise of the so-called "double-shift" led to demands for better work-life balance through parental leaves and part-time options, and to critiques of workplace cultures that require long hours and 24/7 availability as a condition of advancement if not survival. Working mothers have led the charge, but others have joined the call for a more balanced life.

What those developments have thus far failed to yield, at least in the United States, is a revival of popular demands for a shorter standard work week. That might change if job losses begin to mount. While the contemporary movement for work-life balance might look like a rather pallid echo of the turbulent historical movement for shorter hours, it might hold the key to a better future of less work—provided it comes with adequate incomes. And there's the rub.

Given widespread wage stagnation and economic insecurity, the kind of across-the-board reductions in working hours that workers won in the past, and that many had hoped would continue with technological progress, do not look like a solution to the problems of ordinary workers and their families. Nor will it look like a better solution in the future if automation continues to destroy more decent middle-skill jobs than it creates, and pits those with merely ordinary, widely-distributed human skills against each other in the competition for decent paid work. Unlike either UBI or the JG, a program of shorter working hours by itself does not promise to ensure adequate incomes. And unless workers can be confident incomes will not decline, they are unlikely to coalesce around a goal of shorter hours and work spreading.

Then again, shorter working hours was never seen as a complete answer to workers' economic struggles. In its heyday, the shorter hours movement went hand in hand with demands for higher hourly wages. Workers fought for a fair share of the productivity gains from technological progress in the form of both more leisure *and* higher standards of living. And incomes and living standards indeed rose even as weekly working hours fell in the late nineteenth and early twentieth century.[116] That was how "creative destruction" worked in an expanding industrial economy with a vibrant labor movement. Since the 1970s, however, workers' bargaining power has eroded, unions have lost ground, and wage gains ceased to mirror economy-wide productivity gains.

Unless we make a dramatic course correction, the divergence between productivity gains and median wages is likely to grow, and workers' bargaining power to decline further, as emerging technologies destroy decent jobs and depress wages for most workers. That makes the Big Idea of work spreading through shorter working hours, standing alone, an incomplete response to a future of less work: it could better distribute the work that remains and increase "time affluence," but it would fall short on the third goal of ensuring adequate incomes.

* * * * *

The UBI and the JG represent bold and sharply divergent strategies for averting a dystopic future of less work. The UBI would replace work, at least for some, with cash and freedom from work. But that prescription faces prohibitive political hurdles in the United States, given a broad and deep cultural attachment to work; and that attachment is worth cultivating, given the social and political value of shared work. The JG, by contrast, gains normative and political appeal in its coupling of income and work, broadly accessible to all. But if automation continues to destroy mid-skill jobs, and especially if it yields net job losses, a JG risks swelling to unmanageable proportions, and to put a growing number of people to work at taxpayer expense doing things that machines can do better and more cheaply. Besides, if that is where we are heading—if we can produce the goods and services that we need with less human labor—does it make sense to spend trillions of dollars to guarantee full-time, full employment? Shouldn't we instead be aiming to distribute more time, and a better balance between work and life, as one of the dividends of automation?

Shorter working hours promises that better balance—and without any eye-popping public price tag. But the idea of shorter working hours operates on a different plane than UBI or the JG. Far from foreclosing other strategies such as job creation or income support, the shorter hours strategy only works in tandem with some strategy for increasing incomes at the bottom of the distribution. Otherwise, shorter hours portend a decline in living standards.

Each of these Three Big Ideas, standing alone, falls short on one of the three dimensions of a good livelihood that are at stake in a future of less work: decent work for those who are able, adequate incomes, and more time for life beyond work. All three ought to be achievable across the whole society if "this time is different." But that will require a three-dimensional strategy that simultaneously pursues all three of those goals. Let us now consider what a three-dimensional strategy for a future of less work might look like.

6

Creating and Conserving Work

At least since the Great Recession, growing recognition of the damage that economic inequality and insecurity are inflicting on individual lives, communities, and democratic politics are making big and bold ideas thinkable and speakable again after a long period of cynicism about the capacity of government to improve people's lives. COVID-19 further boosted the political appetite and felt need for major policy interventions. If and when a future of less work comes into sharper public view, that might help to catalyze political efforts to channel some of the prodigious gains from super-smart machines—currently flowing mostly to their creators and owners (and their financiers)—toward those who are being sidelined by those machines. Big and bold ideas are clearly needed. But big and bold ideas need not come in a single neat package like UBI or a job guarantee.

Let's imagine for now that we somehow emerge on the other side of this benighted political era with a functioning representative government and a durable governing majority committed to improving the lives of ordinary working people. Imagining that better political state of affairs might require a willful suspension of disbelief. Creating it will require a heroic leap of imagination, faith in democracy and decency, and a lot of inspired political organizing (aspects of which I will discuss in the final chapter). But it will also require a vision of the future that we want to create and of potential pathways to that future. At the level of goals, I've argued that we should be simultaneously pursuing decent standards of living, a wide distribution of paid work, and more time for life outside of work. In this chapter and the next, I will sketch several components of a strategy for pursuing those three goals.

This chapter is focused chiefly on the goal of maintaining a wide distribution of paid work by creating and conserving jobs. As suggested in Chapter 5, job creation should be largely incidental to meeting public needs—public goods, public services, and basic social entitlements—that markets chronically fail to meet. Supplying needed public goods and services—that is, living up to the mission of government in a humane and prosperous society—will

Automation Anxiety. Cynthia Estlund, Oxford University Press. © Cynthia Estlund 2021.
DOI: 10.1093/oso/9780197566107.003.0006

incidentally generate decent and meaningful jobs as well as adequate incomes for those who do that work.

Now and for the foreseeable future, however, most workers will be employed (or self-employed) in the private sector. (Some readers might be disappointed in that concession to a market economy, but that is my working premise.) So we should also be looking to conserve decent private sector jobs—or to avoid their unnecessary destruction. Modestly slowing job losses would buy some time for the raft of adjustments, including work spreading and job training, that a future of less work will require of both individuals and the society. We can do that—and we can do it without degrading the quality of work or defeating the potential gains from automation—by re-engineering entitlements that are, or could be, but need not be linked to employment.

I'll begin briefly with public job creation, but my main focus is on the project of conserving decent private-sector jobs. That is not because it is more important than public job creation but because it is a more novel proposal, and is more closely intertwined with the law of work, where I can add greater value to the debate. This is where we'll return to some of the features of employment law discussed in Chapter 3. I'll postpone to the next chapter my proposals for spreading work and improving lives through regulation of working time.

A. Creating Public Jobs by Meeting Public Needs

There's plenty of work that needs doing in our society, and that needs doing (or funding) by government. That should be the main impetus and focal point for job-creating public investments. A more deliberate focus on job creation may be needed for some groups—those who live in chronically depressed regions, youth, and older workers. But we should start by creating and funding the work that most needs doing.

1. Expanding Basic Entitlements

If we were to ensure free or genuinely affordable and high-quality health care, child care, and education from pre-school through higher education and vocational training, we'd be a better and healthier society in ways and for reasons that have nothing to do with future job losses. For one thing, children's life prospects would not be so decisively shaped by their parents' wealth. That would be a huge gain for social and economic justice. This is standard progressive fare, and I will leave most of the questions it raises for others to untangle.[1] But I do want to underscore three points about expanding basic social entitlements in a future of less work.

First, expanding those basic entitlements will also create decent jobs, which would boost wage levels throughout the labor market, offset expected job and income losses from automation, and reduce the amount of work spreading to be done. *Second*, if the society provided more by way of universal entitlements and public goods, people would need less income (from work or otherwise); those investments would narrow the income gaps left by declining demand for human labor. *Third*, in deciding how to pay for new or existing social entitlements that accrue to individual workers or their families—health insurance and child care, for example—dilemmas await. The choice between funding from payroll taxes versus general revenues has both policy and political implications that I'll discuss briefly in this chapter, and in greater detail in Chapter 8, for the dilemma arises as to both existing entitlements and some new entitlements that I'll propose in the next chapter in connection with work spreading.

2. Creating Public Goods and Meeting Sustainability Challenges

Public investments in roads and bridges, public transportation and communication infrastructure, a cleaner and more sustainable environment, and even public support for the arts will also contribute, albeit less tangibly, to standards of living and overall well-being. Those investments would pay large societal dividends for generations, and are worthwhile regardless of the impact of automation or the outlook for jobs or incomes. But they will also help generate decent jobs (and incomes) at a range of skill levels.

High on the roster of work that needs doing is putting the society on a path to sustainability. Cleaner air and water, clean energy generation, carbon sequestration, and more sustainable modes of construction, transportation, and food production will yield gains in public health as well as decent jobs. For example, retrofitting commercial buildings for energy efficiency alone could create over 800,000 new "job years" across a range of skill levels.[2] Some "green jobs" will arise in the private sector, partly in response to stricter climate-sensitive environmental regulations;[3] but others will be public or publicly funded. Some of those jobs will be forward looking and sustainability enhancing, while others will mitigate or prepare for the effects of climate change that is already in motion. Rising seas and more severe flooding and storms, for example, will require massive projects of relocation (for those living in coastal areas now unsuitable for human habitation) and reclamation (to transform those coastal zones into buffers for communities further inland). The growing frequency and severity of fires will demand similar efforts in arid zones like California. We'll need more "first responders" who are trained to deal with fires, floods, severe storms, and other climate-related emergencies. In particular, the United States cannot continue to rely so heavily on volunteer firefighters (and prisoners) to cope with longer and more intense fire seasons.[4]

The growing need for those workers reflects formidable and frightening environmental challenges. At the brilliant core of the Green New Deal is the recognition that creating a more sustainable society will also generate decent jobs for people who need them. The inclusion of a job *guarantee* in the program, however, weighs down the commitment to decent green jobs with a host of practical and administrative challenges and an eye-popping price tag. For reasons explored in Chapter 5, a wholesale federal job guarantee is "too big to succeed" even without the threat of steady job losses, and in any case is not the best strategy for a future of less work.[5] By dropping the wholesale job guarantee, we could save the heart of the Green New Deal; create millions of decent jobs in clean and renewable energy, energy efficiency, carbon sequestration, and climate remediation; and advance toward a more sustainable future.

3. Serving Depressed Communities, Youth, and Older Workers

While job creation should be largely a byproduct of meeting public needs, a few groups call for special attention: residents of chronically depressed parts of the country, youth, and older workers, all of whom are likely to suffer disproportionately in a more automated economy.

Depressed regions: Parts of the country have been left out of economic growth for a long time, and are likely to fall further behind due to the skewed geography of automation-based job losses and gains.[6] If we relied entirely on people moving from depressed areas to denser and more dynamic ones, that would ensure rampant dislocation of families and destruction of communities (if people do leave their social networks behind) or continued stagnation (if they are not willing or able to do that).[7] Spreading out already-scarce work in those communities won't help much either. Jobs are needed. Those depressed communities are likely, of course, to have plenty of public work that needs doing—social problems that require public resources and human labor. But a more deliberate focus on employing the unemployed might be called for in those depressed areas. That might take the form of a priority in siting public projects, or even a smaller, targeted job guarantee for areas with chronically high unemployment—say, zip codes with four consecutive quarters above 150 percent of the national U-6 unemployment rate.[8] Either way, those depressed communities will benefit from the influx of decent public jobs, and from the public goods and economic stimulus they will create.

Youth: Young *workers*—those currently lacking a path to higher education—have long suffered high jobless rates and, partly as a consequence, high rates of drug use and mostly minor criminality, arrest, and incarceration; all of those add up to long-term scarring of life and employment prospects.[9] The problem of youth unemployment is likely to worsen in a more automated economy. An ideal approach for this group—with high up-front costs but large and lasting benefits—would integrate support for high school completion, further education or vocational training, and employment, as in a proposal by Georgetown Law School's Center on Poverty and Inequality.[10] One element of the Georgetown program—access to national service opportunities—is worth pursuing independently and more broadly.

Existing non-military service programs—including branches of AmeriCorps and the Peace Corps—offer a modest living allowance and sometimes a small grant for subsequent education.[11] Those programs already draw three to five times as many applicants as there are positions available.[12] Expanding and consolidating those programs would tap into aspirations to service that are widespread and worth cultivating. Especially for young people who are not otherwise headed to college, a year or two of national service could help them negotiate a period of scarce job prospects, build skills and work experience, and take a step toward further education or training.[13] But the case for a national youth service program is not only based on job readiness.

A recent Brookings report grounds a case for "universal national service" above all in the need to "rebuild our civic bridges."[14] Universal does not mean compulsory, but rather "an *expectation and opportunity* that young people as they come of age perform a year or more of military or civilian national service."[15] A program of voluntary versus compulsory national service would ensure that all participants from the outset share at least a willingness to devote themselves to serving public needs. The Brookings authors note:

> Such service would bring young people from different backgrounds, income levels, races, ethnicities, and areas of the country together in shared experiences to solve public challenges as they form their attitudes and habits early in life. Many would discover that they are leaders—the kind of leaders who could work across differences to get things done.[16]

This case for national service obviously resonates with Chapter 4's case for the social value of paid work—the value of working together over time and across differences in a diverse society. The societal benefits of even a year or two of work in modestly-paid national service would be amplified by the participants' youth and their shared commitment to serving public needs.

To turn away the large majority of those who seek these opportunities, as we do now, is a senseless waste of talent, energy, and civic spirit; and it would be even more senseless in a likely future of less work. An expanded National Youth Service Corps should offer opportunities for one or two years of public service to all individuals aged 18 to 25 who are willing to serve (and who meet basic eligibility criteria). Participants should earn, in addition to a modest living allowance, support for subsequent education or training.[17] They might also earn credits toward a few years of basic income—not universal basic income but earned basic income. (Tying an entitlement to basic income to periods of national civic service is a larger idea that deserves and gets fuller treatment elsewhere.[18])

A national service program that aims to engage all young people who are willing to serve bears an obvious resemblance to a job guarantee, albeit only a two-year age-restricted job guarantee. Like a JG program, it would presumably expand as unemployment levels rose, and would absorb some of the youth unemployment that otherwise depresses wages at the bottom of the labor market. But this narrower program would not be pitched or designed mainly to employ the unemployed but rather to draw a broad cross-section of public-spirited youth—whatever their future plans and prospects—into the mission of national and community service.

Older workers: Longer life expectancies—perhaps heading toward a century within several decades—are likely to lead to longer working lives. It will simply take more years of productive and remunerative work for most workers, and for Social Security and other pension systems, to build up enough savings and contributions to generate decent retirement incomes. (We could—and might have to—pour more societal resources into supporting retired senior citizens; but a lot of other social needs are competing for those additional resources; longer working lives will almost certainly be a necessary part of the response.) Unfortunately, older workers already face labor market hurdles—discriminatory and otherwise—and those are likely to grow in a more automated, fast-changing, and tech-infused economy.

One partial solution echoes the youth service proposal. The existing AmeriCorps Seniors program places volunteers over age 55 in part-time service positions tailored to the strengths (and weaknesses) of older workers—for example, tutoring, mentoring, and supporting students in and outside the classroom, companionship and light support for other seniors, help for veterans seeking jobs, or tax preparation help.[19] The program currently pays little or nothing to the 200,000 or so volunteers placed each year. But a larger program that included modest stipends might allow some low-income seniors to postpone drawing down retirement income. It would also keep them engaged in their communities, with prodigious benefits to physical and mental health.[20] This kind of program is most easily tailored to relatively educated (and obviously healthy) seniors from white-collar, non-physical occupations; it would take an overhaul, and a rethinking of the kinds of work less-educated seniors could do, to help the workers who are most in need of help on the pension front. Plainly we'll need other solutions, and almost certainly additional societal resources, for an aging population.

All told, public investments in social services, public health, education, infrastructure, and sustainability would create both decent jobs and needed public goods and services. Keying a job creation program in the first instance to the work that needs doing instead of the people who need work will produce both better, more meaningful jobs *and* better public services. And if there is still a gap between the supply of (ordinarily skilled) labor and the demand for that labor—as there is likely to be—then work spreading is a better way to address that gap than is an open-ended and expanding job guarantee, for work spreading has the virtue of increasing access to free time, or time for life outside of work. (More on work spreading in the next chapter.)

B. Conserving Private Sector Jobs by Unburdening Employment

For well over a century, the public stake in private sector jobs has been mainly expressed through legislation establishing minimum wages and labor standards, employee rights, and benefits for employees and structures of collective bargaining. From the beginning, opponents of those interventions claimed they would hurt their intended beneficiaries by destroying jobs. But for some New Deal proponents of higher labor standards, their tendency to displace workers was a feature, not a bug.[21] Higher labor standards would drive out low-road employers, and drive both consumer demand and labor supply toward more efficient producers who could afford to pay decent wages. And that more or less worked until the 1970s: higher labor standards did spur substitution of capital for labor and destroyed some jobs; but the resulting productivity gains helped to generate better jobs and higher pay. Maybe the past is prologue, but it is more likely that this time is different. Both globalization and automation have already spurred job polarization through the destruction of decent middle-skill jobs. Reducing the law's "tax" on labor would modestly curb firms' incentive to either outsource or automate work. The challenge is to do that without degrading the quality of work. The beginning of a solution lies in recognizing that not all of the trade-offs canvased in Chapter 3 are inescapable.

Let's start by separating the question of what workers are entitled to from the question of where the costs should fall. I'll mostly sidestep the first question by deferring to the evolving societal standard of decent work embodied in existing employment law. Workers' existing entitlements all reflect hard political and legal struggles; and those struggles continue over new entitlements such as paid sick leave and parental leave, fair scheduling laws, some of which I'll advocate in the next chapter. Concerns about automation-based job losses are not irrelevant to debates over new or existing entitlements. But rather than either folding in the face of those concerns or ignoring them, we can address them by rethinking who should bear the costs of workers' entitlements. Sometimes that has to be their employers, but sometimes it doesn't. Some of those costs could be shifted in whole or in part onto the public fisc. Where that is possible, we should look for practical and politically viable ways to do that.

1. Employee Entitlements That Require Employer Duties and Liabilities

Many employee rights and protections necessarily entail burdens or liabilities on those who employ them. Take, for example, the right to a safe workplace. Laws regulating workplace health and safety and ensuring compensation for work-related illnesses and injuries necessarily impose costs on employers for compliance and compensation. Employers decide what equipment or chemicals to use, how much to invest in maintenance or modernization or training, and what safety practices to adopt. Requiring employers to ensure a safe workplace and to bear the tangible costs of occupational injuries and illnesses encourages them to avoid those losses. To be sure, there might be less burdensome ways to ensure workers' health and safety; and there are certainly better ways.[22] Many state workers' comp laws are too stingy and poorly designed to promote safety.[23] OSHA inspections are too rare and penalties too low.[24] Effectively ensuring worker safety might cost more, but there is no way around imposing those costs on employers. That is how the law does its job. And if the cost of ensuring worker safety tips employers' calculus toward using robots in some dangerous jobs, so be it; that's an upside of automation and a desirable consequence of regulation.

The same is true for laws that regulate working time and scheduling, which employers typically control: The FLSA's overtime premium encourages employers to avoid excess hours by raising their cost. Local fair scheduling laws constrain onerous and "just-in-time" scheduling.[25] Those laws surely increase the costs of employing people in some jobs—relative, that is, to a baseline of unfettered employer discretion using the latest technology—and might conceivably tip the balance toward robots. But if those laws are justified, employers will have to bear whatever burdens they entail. There is no other way to regulate hours and scheduling.

So, too, for protections against discrimination and retaliation. Even if we could imagine rights and remedies that didn't entail employer liability—say, a public compensation scheme—they would make no sense. Employer liability for past harms is the law's main mechanism for deterring future wrongdoing and encouraging better practices. Laws against discrimination and retaliation, like workplace safety laws, could surely work better; but they could not work at all without imposing on employers the costs of respecting workers' rights and remedying wrongs.

By the same logic, if the United States were to make the leap from prohibiting particular unjust dismissals to requiring justification for dismissal, the corresponding costs—both compliance and enforcement costs—would similarly have to fall on employers. Much ink has been spilled on the costs, benefits, and economic consequences of unjust dismissal protections, both in theory and in fact; and I'll return to them in Chapter 7. For now the point is that the costs of unjust dismissal protections would have to fall largely on employers, for that is how the law works—how it discourages unjustified dismissal.

In short, lots of employment laws necessarily impose costs on employers, and make it a little more likely that they will replace workers with machines. But some trade-offs between the number of jobs and their quality are plainly justified. Debates over workers' rights and minimum labor standards are about *what jobs are worth having at all.* If we define a decent job as one that is safe and free from discrimination, for example, then employers have to bear whatever burdens correspond to those entitlements, for that is how the law works. And if protecting those entitlements requires joint employer liability that runs up the supply chain to lead firms, then so be it, even if some jobs might be lost.

2. Employee Entitlements That Can Be Detached from Employer Mandates

Not all entitlements that are or could be attached to employment address harms that are caused or preventable by the employer; they don't aim to change employer behavior. They might support crucial worker interests, but charging their cost to the employer is not necessary to do that. On the contrary, those charges function as taxes on the use of human labor; they distort firms' demand toward substituting capital for labor. It makes more sense as a policy matter to put those costs elsewhere, and to *unburden employment.*[26] Four quick examples—health insurance, paid leaves, higher incomes for low-wage workers, and pensions—will illustrate the strategy and some of its limitations.

Health Insurance is a big-ticket item for many US employers, partly because of the uniquely high cost of US health care.[27] Clearly employees (indeed, humans) need health insurance. But should its cost fall on their employers? Apart from occupational illness and injuries, which the law sensibly treats separately, employers bear little or no causal responsibility for the health-care needs of workers or their families. Requiring them to pay a large share of employees' health insurance costs, as the pay-or-play mandate of the Affordable Care Act (ACA) does, encourages no salutary change in employer behavior.

On the contrary, if the ACA does change employer behavior, it is mainly by reducing employment. Employers can avoid the costs of the ACA by employing fewer than fifty workers (the threshold for *employer* coverage) or by keeping employees' hours below thirty per week (the threshold for *employee* coverage).[28] Not surprisingly, some employers have cut workers' hours in response to the mandate.[29] One study estimated that the ACA mandate accounted for nearly one-third of involuntary part-time employment among workers without a college degree.[30] Another found an "extraordinary jump in the employment percentage of [firms] with less than fifty employees" after the ACA, and estimated a loss of some 250,000 positions from businesses seeking to stay below the ACA threshold.[31]

In short, putting much of the cost of employees' health insurance on employers tilts in favor of replacing full-time employees with part-timers, with contractors who are not covered by the mandate, or with machines.[32] We could extend the mandate to require firms to make pro rata contributions for their independent contractors; that would expand coverage while reducing the incentive to replace employees with contractors—all to the good.[33] But any costly mandate that is tied to the use of human labor will still tend to tilt the users' calculus toward the exit option of automation when that is feasible. And it is getting more feasible all the time.

Let's be clear: The ACA made crucial progress in expanding access to health care. The United States has long been an outlier among developed countries in its failure to ensure universal health coverage.[34] Apart from Medicaid for the poor and Medicare for the elderly, the United States had long relied on voluntary employer provision of health benefits (subsidized by the tax system). That left many people out in the cold, but it worked well enough for middle class and unionized workers to divert those crucial constituencies from the goal of enacting more inclusive public programs for the rest of the twentieth century.[35] It worked well enough, that is, in a growing economy dominated by vertically integrated firms with strong internal labor markets and a sizable union sector.[36] But in an age of shrinking unions, rampant fissuring, precarious work, and shorter job tenures, growing gaps in coverage put the issue of health coverage back on the political front burner in the mid-2000s.[37] The ACA extended coverage by imposing an employer mandate, along with a now-defunct individual mandate for those still left without coverage. But it still puts a sizable tax on the employment of human labor.[38]

We need a better way of ensuring access to health care that does not hinge on full-time employment *and* does not tax the use of human labor versus machines. Ideally that would be some form of universal single-payer health care, with either a single government provider (like the UK's system) or multiple and mostly private providers (like Canada's).[39] That would detach both the entitlement to health care and its cost from the employment platform; and that makes sense, as there is no logical link between employment and the need for health care. Achieving universal and affordable health coverage without accelerating firms' replacement of humans with machines calls for shifting some or all of the *cost* of health coverage off payrolls and onto general revenues. Of course, that is easier said than done. The details are devilish and the politics perilous, as seen in the controversies around "Medicare for All" in the 2020 US presidential campaign.[40] But ensuring workers' access to affordable health care does not dictate putting its cost on those who hire them. Politics aside for now, the policy logic of unburdening employment grows stronger as machines get cheaper and more capable.

Paid Leaves: The United States is also an outlier among developed countries in failing to guarantee new parents the right to take a reasonable period of time off work without losing their job or their income.[41] Several US states do guarantee paid family leave,[42] and some of those laws also allow self-employed individuals to opt in.[43] Moreover, some employers voluntarily offer paid leaves. But most US workers—especially lower-wage workers who can least afford it—still lack that entitlement. Paid family leave benefits employees and their families, and it can promote gender equality if done right, as we'll see a little later.[44] Paid family leave, unlike health insurance, does have a logical link to employment, or at least to paid work; only those working for pay need to be paid for time off work. But what about the costs?

Note first that guaranteed paid leave combines two entitlements: the right to take time off and return to the job—already modestly protected by the Family and Medical Leave Act[45]—and the right to be paid during the time off. The costs of the first entitlement must be borne by the employer, but they are modest and at least partly offset by higher employee retention.[46] The costs of the second entitlement are much higher, and they don't have to be borne by the employer. Far from trying to change employer behavior, we're trying to avoid doing that. If employers were required to pay the cost of each leave directly, they would be tempted to discriminate against likely leave-takers, such as women of childbearing age.[47] That is why existing paid leave mandates in the United States use a payroll tax, which spreads the cost across the entire workforce.[48] But that raises the cost of employing anybody, and that cost can be avoided by automating work where feasible.[49] Funding mandatory paid family leave through a payroll tax adds to the law's cumulative tax on employment.[50]

Of course, much turns on the particulars. Existing state paid leave mandates are modest, providing four to six weeks of partial salary replacement, up to a fairly low cap.[51] At those levels, the cost is quite small, wherever it falls.[52] But suppose we raised our sights and joined the rest of the developed world in guaranteeing paid parental leave of three or four months or longer—as well as paid sick days, an annual paid vacation of at least three or four weeks, and some number of paid holidays.[53] A payroll tax sufficient to fund those paid leaves would significantly raise the tax on employment and, with it, firms' incentive to offload employees through fissuring or automation. Robots don't take parental leaves or vacations.

This is a dilemma, but not an unavoidable one. We could grant those benefits but fund them in whole or in part through public funds (with the public share capped so that it flowed mainly to those with modest incomes). The main point would be to reduce the tax on the use of human labor; but it would also modestly redistribute income from the winners to the rest in a more polarized economy.

Some employer mandates usefully shape employer behavior by forcing them to internalize the costs of socially harmful conduct. But others are politically expedient off-budget ways to finance social entitlements that bear no necessary relation to employment. Political expedience is nothing to be sneezed at in an era of political polarization and gridlock. Still, we should be clear about policy aims even if political compromise might be in the cards.

Higher Incomes for Low-Wage Workers: Our go-to strategy for raising incomes at the bottom of the labor market is raising the minimum wage. That makes sense up to a point. But large minimum wage increases can lead to job losses, at least over time and especially where work is highly automatable.[54] Can we avoid that dilemma by separating the question of what workers should be entitled to by way of income from the question of how to pay for it?

Suppose we agree that workers ought to make at least a local "living wage"—enough for a single full-time worker to meet basic material needs for housing, food, clothing, personal care, and health insurance without public assistance. The current federal minimum of $7.25 per hour falls far short of that even in poor and low-cost places like Holmes County, Mississippi (estimated living wage of $10.35), and more so in cities like Atlanta ($13.62).[55] Even the higher minimum wages enacted by some states and cities may fall short of a living wage. In Manhattan, where the local minimum wage was $11.10 as of 2020, a living wage is estimated at $17.99.[56] Ensuring a living wage across the country would require either large locally targeted increases across the country or a very large increase in the federal minimum. And if we defined a living wage as one that allowed a full-time worker to support, say, two children, that would be $23.56 in Holmes County and $42.95 in Manhattan. Raising the minimum wage to those levels would inevitably destroy jobs and harm low-wage workers, especially over time and especially in highly automatable sectors like food services.

Low-wage workers plainly need and deserve higher incomes. But can we put some of that money into workers' pockets without raising the price and depressing the demand for labor? Indeed we can. The federal Earned Income Tax Credit (EITC), which is funded from general revenues in the form of a "tax expenditure," already does that for over 25 million low-income tax filers to the tune of nearly $2,500 per filer (in 2019).[57] It takes household income and size into account; it does not reflect local cost-of-living differences, but it could.[58] (It also covers self-employed workers.[59]) Many economists prefer the EITC to any minimum wage because it is better targeted at low-income households and does not tax employment.[60] Others see the two as complementary.[61] One catch is that workers get EITC benefits in a lump sum after filing their federal tax returns; many eligible workers don't know about these benefits and fail to file for them.[62]

Another way to increase incomes without taxing employment is through "wage subsidies" that low-wage workers receive with each paycheck.[63] If we cared less about rewarding work, we could turn instead to a negative income tax at low-income levels (or to guaranteed basic income).[64] Any of these devices could be combined with minimum wage increases. All of them effectively separate the question of what workers need or deserve to earn from what their employers should be required to pay them. They raise incomes for low-wage workers without dampening demand for human labor, and they redistribute income by tapping into general revenues and relatively progressive tax structures.

Many worker advocates prefer to rely on minimum wage hikes, at least implicitly on the premise that *employers deserve to pay whatever workers deserve to earn as a return on their labor*. Indeed, using public funds to supplement low wages instead of raising those wages might seem to "provide . . . a subsidy for unconscionable employers," as the Supreme Court put it in first upholding the constitutionality of a minimum wage law in 1937.[65] But if we are looking to approximate living wages without accelerating the loss of low-skill jobs, it makes sense to shift part of the cost off the employment platform and onto the public fisc.

Retirement Security: The US system of retirement security includes both employment-based pension plans—voluntary or collectively bargained—and individual savings plans, both subsidized by the public through favorable tax treatment. But those plans sit atop a universal, publicly administered Social Security system, which supplies basic old-age pensions for all and the only retirement income for about half of all private sector workers.[66] Social Security is funded by mandatory payroll taxes shared between employers and employees.

We don't need to know more than that to recognize that the logic of unburdening employment applies here: Putting much of the cost of funding basic pensions on employers adds to the cost of employing humans and the incentive to replace them with machines. Tapping into general revenues would both reduce the tax on human labor and allow for more redistribution from rich to poor than payroll-based funding allows.[67] (There is some redistribution within Social Security, but it is limited by the funding mechanism.)

It would clearly be possible to fund basic retirement benefits directly out of general revenues rather than from payroll taxes. (It would not make sense to publicly fund higher benefits for higher earners, as the current system does by tying contributions to wage levels.) After all, the *need* for basic income in old age is universal, not limited to those who were once employed; and the *rationale* for requiring one's past, even long-past, employers to fund that future income is at least debatable. Yet the logic of unburdening employment here is in tension with the perception of pensions as deferred compensation that is earned over one's career and that vests as a form of employee property. The *earned-and-owned* quality of Social Security benefits, and the payroll-based funding model that underpins it, have given Social Security a remarkable degree of political resilience even at times when other social programs are on the chopping block.

A lot needs fixing in our patchy and fraying system of retirement security.[68] But we should probably be looking to build on—or at least learn from—the strongest pillar of the system rather than dismantling it. The case of Social Security suggests a potential constraint on the unburdening strategy—and one that reaches beyond retirement income. Or maybe it suggests that we should look for ways to *both* unburden employment *and* emulate the earned-and-owned aura of Social Security. I'll take a closer look at funding mechanisms—at *how* to unburden employment—in Chapter 8. But first there is more to say about *why* and how much to do so.

C. Why Unburden Employment?

The unburdening strategy aims to modestly slow the pace of job destruction through automation. But automation will also produce new jobs that are safer, less tedious, and perhaps more satisfying; and it can produce productivity gains that could be redistributed in the form of income and free time for ordinary workers. It's very hard to say how much slowing of automation makes sense given the potential for both serious losses and impressive gains. But unburdening employment—that is, countering the burden of some public mandates without further subsidizing employment—should yield the right *kind* of slowing. It will also yield gains in liberty and equality in a changing world of work, whether or not net job losses are in the offing.

1. The Economic Virtues of Unburdening Employment

The strategy outlined here would reduce a subset of law-related labor costs that need not fall on employers in order to protect the underlying worker entitlements. Those costs *distort* demand for labor, and *inefficiently* tilt firms toward substituting capital for labor.[69] Efficiency isn't everything, but it is something. If we can protect workers' entitlements without inefficiently and artificially speeding job losses, we should do so.

The unburdening strategy would also have its greatest impact on the type of automation decisions that should most concern us—that is, those that mainly *substitute* for labor rather than those that complement labor, and those that are driven chiefly by *labor costs* rather than gains in quality, reliability, safety, or the like. Obviously, the same technology can both replace some workers and enhance others' productivity; and the same technology can both reduce labor costs and improve product quality. Still, the more heavily labor costs and labor substitution weigh in a decision about automation, the more that decision will be affected by reducing the excess tax on employment. Firms' pursuit of other gains from automation—quality, safety, and reliability, for example—would be left comparatively unaffected.

The unburdening strategy in some ways mirrors a recent proposal by Daron Acemoglu, Andrea Manera, and Pascual Restrepo to discourage "excessive automation,"[70] or what they call "so-so technologies" that replace workers with little gain in productivity. A significant driver of excessive automation, they argue, is the tax system's strong skew in favor of capital versus labor. They estimate that firms' use of capital is taxed at 5 percent versus 25 percent for labor.[71] They would attack the capital side of that asymmetry, ideally with an automation tax on those "so-so technologies." But they concede it is probably too hard to identify those particular technologies, and argue for symmetrical tax treatment of labor and capital as a second-best solution.

The unburdening strategy addresses the other side of the ledger by reducing the tax on labor, and it might achieve some of the targeting that an "automation tax" would do in theory but that is hard to achieve in practice. That is, it should have the biggest effect on automation decisions that are driven mainly by labor cost savings, and should have relatively little effect on those that would achieve meaningful gains in productivity, quality, safety, or reliability.

Given the potential gains from automation, including both productivity gains and the potential for expanding time outside of paid work, we should be looking to avoid either artificially speeding up job losses or artificially slowing them down. The unburdening strategy aims to hit that golden mean. It won't stop job losses, but that's not the goal. Unburdening employment has to be coupled with other strategies to create work, spread work, and ensure adequate incomes in a more automated economy.

2. Advances for Liberty and Equality

The strategy of unburdening employment meets skepticism from many worker advocates, who have devoted themselves to shoring up and embellishing the fortress of employment. That worthy effort is tinged with irony. Nineteenth-century artisans and early labor activists fought desperately to resist the wage labor relationship—which they called "wage slavery"—and the subordination and dependency it entailed.[72] Eventually most workers and their unions resigned themselves to the subordinate role of employee, and redirected their struggles toward winning an array of rights, minimum labor standards, and structures for collective representation—all to the end of transforming "wage slavery" into a decent way of economic life for ordinary workers. Yet even thus civilized, the fortress of employment is hardly an ideal to defend at all costs.

In any case, the fortress is now crumbling. Firms are finding ways through fissuring and automation to escape their end of the deal embodied in the standard employment relationship, and workers are either fleeing or being ejected from the constraints and protections of that relationship. We do need to improve and enforce employee rights and labor standards—those that are necessarily tethered to employment. But we also need to furnish the growing domain that lies beyond employment with the basic material requisites of a decent life for those who choose a more independent economic existence and those who cannot get into the fortress. As Alain Supiot presciently observed in 1999, "the employee subject to full-time, open-ended subordination is surely not the only model for working life. Another figure can be discerned on the horizon: a worker who can reconcile security and freedom."[73]

To reach that horizon, we need a new social model that supports many modes of working life, and that works better for all of those who work for a living. Even if automation is destined to take its toll not on the number of jobs but on job quality and inequality, it makes sense to construct a broader and more inclusive foundation for the more varied working lives that are likely in the labor markets of the future. Shifting the locus and costs of some crucial entitlements off the platform of employment and onto a broader base can begin to do that. To be sure, the strategy of socializing or subsidizing some entitlements faces political and practical challenges, given powerful anti-tax and anti-redistributive impulses even among some prospective beneficiaries. We shouldn't start dismantling the fortress of employment, creaky and flawed though it is, unless and until a better system is at hand. But we do need a better system.

For decades now, and especially since Supiot's 1999 report to the European Commission,[74] labor scholars have been questioning the viability of the employment contract as "the 'platform' for delivering rights and benefits."[75] That platform has been undermined by the rise of contingent and precarious work, self-employment, and other forms of fissuring, as well as automation. Extending basic social entitlements beyond employment and in some cases beyond paid work, and redistributing their costs, would help both to preserve decent jobs and to better protect those who no longer have (or never had) those jobs. That would serve both liberty and equality in a changing economy.

Uncoupling social benefits from the employment relationship would enhance liberty by freeing up some individuals to *choose* the greater autonomy and flexibility of self-employment or freelancing. The realm of self-employment, or freelancing within the "gig" or "sharing" economy, is often touted as a domain of economic freedom.[76] That rosy depiction rings hollow to those who would prefer to have a real job and the greater security and benefits that go with it.[77] Yet freelance and platform-based work is not just a sham or a last resort for those who can't get a full-time job. Many of those workers—including some Uber drivers—genuinely value freedom from direct supervision and the ability to determine their own work schedule, both of which they might lose if they were employees.[78] More individuals might choose independent work if they could count on basic social benefits like health insurance, pensions, and others. Uncoupling basic benefits from employment would begin to create that more secure baseline.

That broader benefit structure would also combat economic inequality in two ways. First, it would counter growing disparities between insiders and outsiders—between the well-provisioned employees of leading firms and those who are left largely to their own devices, whether formally employed or not. It would help to ensure that all workers and their families enjoy some basic requisites of a decent and healthy life even if they cannot or do not enter the fortress of full-time stable employment. Second, as I've already emphasized, shifting the cost of social benefits onto a more progressively-structured tax base would redistribute some of the outsized gains at the top of the income distribution to those whose living standards have fallen or stagnated.

Some of the biggest winners in our economy are tech-centric firms like Microsoft, Apple, and Alphabet (Google's parent) that employ relatively few workers compared with the corporate titans of the twentieth century. Those firms have helped drive both automation and the economic polarization it has wrought, and they have been on the winning end of both; yet they contribute comparatively little to the basic social benefits that are supported by payroll taxes. It is fair to tax those firms—along with their well-paid managers, lawyers, consultants, and financiers—more heavily and to redistribute some of the gains to those who have been on the losing end of technological progress.

* * * * *

Creating and conserving decent work has an obvious logic as we face a future of less work. But doing so in the ways prescribed here has other virtues. Keying public job creation, in the main, to public needs will create both better jobs and better public goods and services. Unburdening employment can preserve or extend workers' hard-won entitlements while conserving decent public jobs. But there is still the question of how to secure for workers the time dividends they deserve in a more automated economy—how to spread work from those with too much of it to those with too little—while maintaining adequate incomes. That is the agenda for Chapter 7.

7

Spreading Work and Supporting Incomes

Beyond creating and conserving work, we should also aim to capture some of the gains from automation in the form of more time for life outside of paid work. Indeed, we might merge two of our three goals—work and free time—into one: *a better work-life balance.* In contemporary parlance, work-life balance is mostly about satisfying individual preferences for less work and more time for the rest of life. Work-life balance as used here, however, is not just about satisfying individual preferences but about achieving a more balanced distribution of work and free time across the society. In a future of less work, achieving a better work-life balance calls for *spreading both work and free time*—that is, reducing weekly hours and annual weeks of work for many full-time or more than full-time workers, and pushing some of that labor demand down to those who are underemployed or even unemployed.

Work spreading would capture a big upside of automation—more time for life outside of paid work—and alleviate one of its biggest downsides—rising unemployment and underemployment. That is the "why" of work spreading, but most of this chapter will concern the "how," for the project of work spreading is bursting with complications that intersect with the law of work. In particular, we will be looking for ways to spread work while maintaining adequate incomes at the bottom of the labor market.

Not all the proposals advanced here will make sense until a future of less work is in sight or even upon us. But most of them make sense here and now, entirely apart from the prospect of net job losses. Already job polarization and growing inequality are producing problems of both overwork and underemployment. Most workers would benefit from a better *societal* work-life balance—more and steadier work for unemployed, underemployed, and precarious workers, and less work for overworked salaried white-collar workers all the way up the ladder.

Automation Anxiety. Cynthia Estlund, Oxford University Press. © Cynthia Estlund 2021.
DOI: 10.1093/oso/9780197566107.003.0007

A. Balancing Work and Life through Work Spreading: A Tour of the Terrain

Since the New Deal, we have tended to think about the regulation of working hours—if we think about it at all—as protecting workers from the evils of long hours or compensating workers who are saddled with them. The function of spreading available work to more people has largely receded from public consciousness. But that is changing, at least in Europe, where shorter work weeks are gaining traction.[1] During the COVID-19 crisis, several EU countries turned to temporary "short-time work schemes" to spread work and avoid layoffs, with public funds making up part of the income lost.[2] Indeed, much of Europe is far ahead of even the most worker-friendly US jurisdictions at nearly every point where public policy could improve both individual and societal work-life balance. European labor policies reflect wider skepticism about labor markets and a greater willingness to regulate them. We will often find ourselves looking across the Atlantic for ideas about how to improve work-life balance.

While the point of work-life balance in a future of less work is not only to accommodate individual preferences for a less-consuming work life, the two goals overlap. Apart from bettering the lives of workers and their families, some work spreading can also be achieved by accommodating preferences for shorter hours and temporary leaves from work. It is perverse, if it is avoidable, for some individuals to be working much more than they want while others are left with little or no decent work. Accommodating individual preferences for less work during their working lives is relatively low-hanging fruit in this policy landscape, though not without its challenges.

Enabling workers to choose a better work-life balance for themselves—worthwhile as it is—won't do enough to head off the prospect of growing numbers of workers getting squeezed out of the active labor market. And it will do little to counter either long working hours by choice (or apparent choice) in high-end jobs, or employers' penchant for splintering less-skilled jobs into part-time and just-in-time slivers or gigs that keep workers off-balance and insecure. The trick is to simultaneously counter both problems—too much work for some, too little work for others.

The challenges to work-life balance differ at the bottom, middle, and top of the wage scale, partly in how they map onto existing law. Lower-wage workers—roughly the bottom 40 percent of wage earners[3]—have problems of not enough work and too much: precarious gigs and involuntary part-time work; and lack of access to paid vacations, sick leaves, and family leaves. (They also face unlawful off-the-clock work demands and other forms of "wage theft"; but I'll leave enforcement problems for another venue.[4]) Many workers in the middle—say, from the 40th to the 90th percentile in income—are salaried white-collar workers who are or might be exempt from the FLSA's overtime provisions (because their salaries top $36,000).[5] Many of those workers face demands for extra work without extra pay; and much of that work could be spread to less skilled workers. Workers in the top decile—which runs from the comfortable to the ultra-rich—are mostly exempt from overtime laws, and many work very long hours. Some would prefer to work less even if it meant lower pay, but others would not.

The lucrative exchange of long hours for high pay at the top might seem like an esoteric rich people's problem. But some workers' willingness to work sixty or more hours a week on a regular basis, and to be available 24/7, deprives others of decent work opportunities they might otherwise have. (It also pressures co-workers to work longer hours.) Employers deploy sticks as well as carrots to induce a limited number of workers to offer up a virtually unlimited portion of their lives to their jobs rather than hiring more workers. And achieving work-life balance in a future of less work will require reducing long hours for some whose high pay makes those extra hours worthwhile. That is a tough regulatory challenge, and it will hit some upper limits; some work is so rarified and some skills are so scarce that it won't be practicable to spread that work to a wider group of workers. But if we value broad access to decent work, especially in a future of less work, we'll have to explore ways to constrain long hours for the sake of work spreading.

Take the case of lawyers at major law firms: mid-level associates can expect to earn around $360,000 including bonuses.[6] That reflects both a very high implicit hourly wage and very long hours of work—an average of 60 hours a week.[7] On the one hand, many of those lawyers and their counterparts in business and finance are quite willing to work long hours in exchange for outsized incomes and all they can buy—a house in the Hamptons, elite private schools for their children, a retinue of housekeepers and nannies, and lavish vacations when they manage to escape the office. On the other hand, some of those lawyers would prefer to work less, and they might be willing to take a *pro rata* pay cut to do so. But even if firms offer such choices, their tournament-like structure and culture discourage and penalize their use.[8] It would be all to the good if individuals were able to improve their own work-life balance through shorter hours or longer leaves without derailing their careers.

Any regulatory effort to reduce long hours and boundless availability in those high-end jobs will confront vigorous objections: Firms will argue that the work is indivisible and the skills scarce, and that the quality of services will suffer. Individuals will defend their freedom to work long hours in pursuit of wealth and advancement. The point for now is that the choice to work very long hours—even if it is well-compensated—has spillover consequences that may justify public intervention. In a future of less work, we should be looking for ways to restrain long hours at the top not only to promote a better work-life balance for those individuals but also to expand access to good jobs.

The project of work spreading is complicated, not only at the top but across the income scale, by the non-linear relationship between hours per worker and output. Sometimes the same work can get done by the same workers in less time; that might reflect productivity gains, which in turn might reflect either more focused, alert, and engaged workers or simply a more intensive work pace.[9] Either way, no work spreading and no new hiring would be expected.[10] Even if more hours are needed to get the work done, employers have reasons to exact those extra hours out of their current workforce rather than hiring more workers. There are fixed or quasi-fixed per-worker costs (such as office space, onboarding, and training) and uncertainty about new hires' productivity or "fit" with co-workers.[11] Especially at higher skill levels, employers often willingly pay a premium for long hours—whether or not the law requires it—instead of hiring more workers. In short, it might take a pretty heavy (and clever) regulatory thumb on the scale to induce employers to hire more workers versus exacting more hours or more effort per worker.

B. Spreading Work for a Better Work-Life Balance

We've already glimpsed several general approaches to improving work-life balance through work spreading:

- First, raise the floor on decent work through some familiar regulatory tools: guaranteeing more paid time off work for vacations, sick leaves, and family and medical leaves; restricting abusive scheduling practices and on-call demands; and expanding the reach of overtime laws.

- Second, put a societal thumb on the scale in favor of individual choices to work less than the full-time norm—that is, fewer hours per week or fewer weeks per year.
- Third, find ways to discourage very long hours in many high-end jobs.
- Fourth, reduce the standard work week.

Crucially, nearly all of this makes sense here and now. Whether or not we are facing a net loss of jobs, these measures would improve lives at work and outside work, and would counter the already-pronounced hollowing out of the labor market. Also crucially—given our polarized and nearly paralyzed Congress—nearly all of this could be, and some of it already has been, implemented at the state or even local level.

A few caveats are also in order. First, some of what is proposed here will raise the cost of human labor relative to machines. (Hoist with her own petard!, you might be thinking.) But once we are on our way, through work spreading, toward modestly less work for most instead of little or no work for many, then shrinking demand for labor will be less worrisome, even welcome (provided we can also maintain adequate incomes).

Second, some of these work-spreading proposals might seem anachronistic given the rise of remote work—work that takes place outside the "workplace" and often at home.[12] On the one hand, the rise of telework—which spiked during the COVID crisis but is sure to outlast it—clearly disrupts the terrain of working time regulation, at least for many white-collar workers. On the other hand, a great deal of remote work is done through electronic devices in ways that could be and often is monitored. The beginning of a solution might lie in redefining the object of regulation and of work spreading: Instead of restricting working time, perhaps we should be *protecting non-working time*. The idea would be to designate certain time periods—hours, days, weeks, or even months in the case of longer leaves—as non-working time free from all employer demands. That could be backed up, as is the existing US approach to working hours, with an overtime premium or penalty for incursions on that non-working time. That is mostly a conceptual reframing of existing approaches to working time and leaves, but it might also require some changes in how the law operates. I'll leave those issues for another venue.

Here I'll identify major challenges and dilemmas and point toward possible solutions. I want to stay out of the weeds while getting beyond the generalities sketched so far. To that end, I'll focus here on how the challenges of work spreading will play out in the United States against the background of current US law. Existing law will have to change, but it will also shape both the challenges and the options going forward. We do not write on a blank slate.

1. Raising the Floor on Decent Work: Expanding Overtime, Regulating Abusive Scheduling, and Guaranteeing Paid Leaves and Respites

Some problems of too little work and too much work are best addressed through new minimum labor standards. Take, for example, just-in-time scheduling practices, which splinter what could be decent jobs into shards of precarious work. Technology is enabling employers to squeeze out the paid downtime or breathing room between tasks or customers that used to be par for the course in routine service jobs. (And workers without a union are unable to push back.)[13] That problem will get worse as the technology gets better unless we intervene. Fair scheduling laws require decent advance notice of schedules and restrict some very short or onerous work shifts. They put some of the "risk" of downtime back onto employers and enable workers to plan their lives. Fair scheduling ought to be part of the federal definition of decent work (and, failing that, part of state or local law). And some aspects of fair scheduling—at least advance notice requirements—should be extended to gig workers, as a recent EU directive does in Europe.[14]

The problem of precarious dribs and drabs of on-demand work might be an early indicator of a future of less work. In any case, that problem points to the need for work spreading here and now: Reducing the work hours of some more-than-full-time workers (while also putting up hurdles to fractured part-time schedules) can increase demand for workers just below them in the skills ladder and should help to turn more of that precarious work into decent jobs.

That takes us from the problem of too little work to that of too much work. Even in the age of precarity, most US workers work full-time, and most of them work long hours by international standards, often including nights and weekends.[15] Part of the problem stems from work calls and emails outside of normal working hours and without compensation—common not only in high-end jobs (where it raises harder issues to be discussed), but in lower-level jobs as well. A European-style "right to disconnect" might address that kind of too-much-work problem.[16] Alternatively, at least the actual time spent on those calls, and sometimes the on-call time itself, should qualify as compensable working time and might trigger overtime rates (which should apply to a larger category of workers). Either would help combat the colonization of non-work time by employers' work demands, and might have a modest work-spreading effect by closing off the option of getting free or cheap work out of existing workers.

Long working hours partly reflect the fact that so many US workers are exempt from the FLSA's overtime "tax" on long hours. Time-and-a-half for excess hours is guaranteed for most hourly workers, but salaried workers with some administrative or supervisory duties can be exempt from overtime laws if they make more than $35,568 per year. They are very likely in any case to be treated by their employers as exempt, for the subjective legal criteria that apply to those workers are easier to game than to parse with any precision.[17] Workers can be exempt even if much of their working time is spent on "non-exempt" or routine duties—cleaning up, restocking shelves, or the like. If employers had to pay more of those workers time-and-a-half rates for extra hours, they would have some incentive to staff up—to hire more workers at a lower hourly rate to carry out those routine tasks. Those are potentially decent jobs that would exist but for employers' ability to exact extra hours from salaried workers.

A large hike in the salary threshold for white-collar exemptions—to $70,000 or more—would ensure that many more white-collar workers would be eligible for overtime. That would promote some work spreading and improve the lives of some white-collar workers. (Yes, at the margin it might tilt toward automating those mid-level jobs; but again, progress toward work spreading would make that less worrisome.) Some of those workers would still perform those extra duties, but at overtime rates that might raise their total compensation. ("Might" because basic salaries might fall if they didn't include extra hours of work.) Other workers would find their returns in free time, albeit at lower salaries.[18] Some of those previously exempt workers might object.[19] But many workers report that they would be willing to take a significant pay cut in exchange for lower or more stable working hours.[20] Employers' ability to exact extra hours without extra pay from low- to mid-level salaried workers invites opportunism and understaffing, and makes even less sense in a foreseeable future of job scarcity.

One reason US workers put in more total hours of work than most Europeans is that the latter are guaranteed a paid annual leave or vacation of at least four weeks, as well as numerous paid holidays.[21] In "No-Vacation

Nation USA," workers cannot count on any of those respites. European workers are also guaranteed paid leaves for sickness and medical care, childbirth, and recovery, and the occasional short-term needs of children or elderly parents, as well as longer fully- or partially-paid parental leaves of several months.[22] Most US workers, and especially low-wage and part-time workers, can't count on any of that. Bringing US laws up to par on these matters would be a relatively simple (if not easy) step toward a better work-life balance and work spreading.[23]

Ordinary workers should draw dividends from automation in the form of more time away from work without the loss of income that would otherwise entail. Guaranteeing paid leaves and respites from work is one way to spread both decent work and more free time while maintaining adequate incomes. It also recalls the question, raised in Chapter 6, of who should pay for those paid leaves and respites. Shifting at least part of the cost of those entitlements off payrolls and onto a broader tax base will avoid speeding up job losses and will permit some redistribution, especially in the bottom half of the labor market where job losses are most concerning and the need for redistribution is most compelling. Chapter 8 will return to these issues.

A final point deserves mention: Granting basic entitlements to workers as a matter of right does not ensure they will get them. You might have a legal right to take vacation, but can you be sure your job will be there when you get back? That you'll still be considered for promotion? Employees might reasonably fear retaliation even if the law prohibits it, and might accede to unlawful employer demands. Workers' rights are especially precarious in an at-will environment, for employers' power to fire workers without justification gives them the practical power to discriminate or retaliate or impose onerous conditions on continued employment.[24] Count this as one more reason to join the rest of the developed world in ensuring job security through protections against unjustified dismissal, a point to which we'll return below.

2. Accommodating Workers Who Choose to Work Less

However we define the standard work week and the basic entitlement to paid time off, some workers will want to work less—to take a longer leave or work shorter hours—even if it comes with a proportional pay cut. That might be for parenting or other family responsibilities, or for health reasons, or perhaps for study, travel, hobbies, activism, or whatever else in life beckons. At least in a world of job scarcity, public policy should weigh in on the side of workers' choice to work less (presumably with a pro rata pay cut) for at least some of these reasons.

The most compelling reasons for working less could be accommodated as a matter of right. In Sweden, for example, parents of children under the age of seven have had the right to choose a reduced work schedule (with reduced pay) since 1978.[25] Alternatively, the law might require firms to grant reasonable requests for such accommodations. US law already does that in principle for workers with a disability, but it could expand and strengthen the right to reasonable accommodations in the form of reduced working hours.[26] Similarly, the law could require employers to grant reasonable requests for job-sharing arrangements between co-workers. That is a very tangible kind of work spreading but one that is too circumstance specific to be mandated.[27] The law should also require at least pro rata benefit coverage for part-timers as EU law does; that contributes to higher rates of voluntary part-time work in Europe than in the United States.[28]

Making it easier for individuals to choose to work less than a normal schedule—whether fewer weeks per year or fewer hours per week—will *tend* to promote work spreading. Some employers will have to hire more workers to make up for lower average hours of work per worker. (To be sure, employers—especially small employers—might deal with a worker's parental leave by requiring co-workers to pick up the slack through longer hours. But a broader and more reliable wage premium for those longer hours should help to tip the scales toward hiring more workers versus exacting more hours per worker.) Especially—though not only—when job scarcity looms, we should use public policy levers to enable individuals to pursue their own less work-centered vision of life. That in turn can promote a better societal work-life balance by spreading work.

Still, there are dilemmas in sight, especially in the case of policies that accommodate family responsibilities. The problem has a familiar name: the "mommy track": In heterosexual couples, mothers are more likely than fathers to take advantage of opportunities to work less and travel less, and that often pulls them off the path to promotions and partnerships.[29] It's not just about women's choices; some women are pushed off the fast track because stereotypes about mothers clash with expectations of boundless dedication, hours, and availability in some jobs.[30] One way or another, even gender-neutral "family-friendly" policies can reinforce gender disparities—both at home and at work—if they are used mostly by women.[31] Those policies tend to enable women to remain employed and in their chosen field of work, but not necessarily to rise to the top jobs.[32]

Nudging fathers to take even a short period of parental leave after childbirth yields a big bang for the buck: Research indicates that fathers who do so spend more time on child care and childrearing long thereafter.[33] But policy levers are sparse. In much of Europe, which has long guaranteed relatively long paid *maternity* leaves, progress has been made through so-called "use it or lose it" policies, which allocate some period of paid parental leave solely to the father, to be lost unless the father takes the leave.[34] Given US law's stricter limits on gender discrimination, any paid parental leave mandate that extended beyond the period of physical recovery from childbirth would presumably be available to new mothers and fathers alike; fathers who didn't use paid leave would necessarily lose it.[35] That still wouldn't ensure that fathers will take the leave they're entitled to. Part of the problem is men's higher average salaries; if salary replacement is partial, capped, or both—as it is under most existing state paid leave laws—fathers tend to take a bigger economic hit than mothers. But gendered stereotypes about family responsibilities also play a role in discouraging men from taking more-than-nominal parental leaves; those who do so are reportedly stigmatized and penalized even more than women are.[36]

Beyond both choice and stereotyping, however, is a bigger impediment to both work-life balance and gender parity: that is, the tournament-like nature of many organizations, whose steep bonus structures and narrow partnership tracks foster intense competition to reach the top. The result is a long-hours culture in which workers not only work very hard but must constantly show they are working very hard through lots of "face time" and late-night communications.[37] The next section turns to the challenge of countering the long-hours culture that prevails in many high-end jobs and professions. For now, just note that accommodating workers' preferences to work less might take a toll on gender equality whatever its other benefits.

One response to the gendered uptake of family-friendly options at work, and another step toward work spreading, would be to make similar options available for a wider array of activities. (One activity—mid-career retraining and education—has less to do with work-spreading or facilitating workers' choices and more to do with building in-demand skills; I'll turn to this point later.) Workers of any gender might choose to take unpaid leave for an extra-long vacation, or to work on a political campaign or a volunteer project, or to work part-time for partial pay to devote more hours per week to their favored hobbies. (Think of it as a small step toward Marx's vision of workers who could "hunt in the morning, fish in the afternoon, rear cattle in the evening, criticise after dinner, just as I have a mind . . ."[38]) If we are facing a future of less work, and if we are aiming for *both* wide access to paid work *and* lives less dominated by work, there would seem to be nothing but upside to the idea of accommodating individual workers' preferences for such a life.

To be sure, the choice to work less for lower pay—whether for family time or fishing trips—would be more viable for workers with high incomes (or high-income spouses or parents) who can better afford to take a pay cut. We could do more for lower-income workers and for work spreading by subsidizing those choices at the bottom of the income scale. Imagine, for example, a social insurance fund, with contributions from workers, firms, and the public, to support ordinary workers who want to take a partially paid "sabbatical" of sorts.[39] The idea of using public funds to subsidize time off work for hobbies or volunteer work will strike some readers as a bridge too far. It is one of the work-spreading proposals whose appeal might hinge on a clear and present danger of net job losses. But at least in a future of both less work and more total social wealth, publicly subsidizing leaves for a range of purposes would both promote work spreading and replace some of the income lost by working less. And it would make time off more affordable to ordinary workers and more likely to be taken by all genders.

Accommodating and subsidizing the choice to work less than full-time would yield real benefits for workers and their families, and is a normatively appealing way to achieve some work spreading. But it would probably still leave the upper levels of major organizations, and the levers of power and richest rewards within those organizations and beyond, in the hands of those who choose to work all out, with long hours, boundless availability, and no long respites. That may be among the reasons not to lean too heavily on accommodating workers' choices as a work-spreading strategy.

3. Taking on Long-Hours Culture in Tournament-Like Workplaces

The next piece of the work-spreading project—pressing down long hours for high pay at the top—is a harder nut to crack, partly because both firms and workers have reasons to resist or evade regulatory interventions. To be sure, some workers "choose" long hours for high rewards only because they are surrounded by others who choose that deal, or who seem to choose it. They are immersed in a long-hours culture that punishes the choice to work less even if it is formally available, and even if many workers would prefer to work less for lower pay.[40] The second and third pieces of work spreading—accommodating the choice to work less and discouraging long hours even by choice—are thus mutually reinforcing: Anything that normalizes the choice to work less will counter a long-hours culture, and anything that counters a long-hours culture will make it easier for workers to exercise options to work less, including those afforded by law.

Work spreading is another good reason to push back against these apparently consensual long-hours arrangements. It might seem unlikely that reducing hours of law firm lawyers, for example, would do anything for the less-skilled workers who are most at risk of ending up with too little work; the skills gap is just too great. But that discounts the potential ripple effects of drawing some middle-skilled workers up into higher level jobs, if there were more of them to be had. For example, a meaningful reduction in the very long hours of high-end lawyers—if that were achievable—might induce firms to hire more lawyers at lower but still-high salaries, or to push more of the work down to contract attorneys or paralegals (. . . or to algorithms. But the work of high-end long-hours lawyers is still among the least automatable work in the economy.) It might also encourage firms to train their own mid-skill workers to do some of the higher-skilled work that trickles down as top workers work less.

There are also egalitarian reasons to intervene. Long hours in fields like law, business, and finance are one major barrier to the advancement of women, who make up about half of entry-level hires in those fields but only a small fraction of those who make it to the top.[41] If we care about gender equality in those top jobs—indeed, if firms themselves cared as much about gender equality as they claim to—that will require not just "family-friendly" options but a change in the underlying norm of long hours that make those options so costly for individuals to exercise.

Long hours are also a major contributor to the growth in top incomes, and thus to income inequality.[42] That is, longer hours and much higher implicit hourly rates together have produced the steep increase in the incomes of the top 1 percent. Automation is already partly to blame for polarization of both hours and incomes, and both will get worse in a world of less work, especially if we leave those high-end workers out of societal efforts to spread available work. Much more good than bad can come from the modestly egalitarian agenda of reducing long hours among high earners if it's done right.

Let's first ask what drives long-hours work cultures from both sides—workers and firms. Economist Claudia Goldin has observed that law is among the fields in which firms super-reward long hours; their pay structure is "convex," meaning that longer hours garner more-than-proportionately higher pay.[43] That reward structure motivates workers, but what motivates firms to create those reward structures? We've flagged some generic reasons why employers prefer to extract more hours out of a smaller workforce than to hire more workers. Those reasons are magnified for highly skilled workers, especially if long hours are episodic. "Crunch times" like trial prep, tax time, or major business deals are common in many high-end jobs. It is also easier for those handing out bonuses and promotions in these fields to observe who is putting in long hours than to discern who is producing the best work—which makes long hours an obvious way for workers to compete for those prizes. In short, there are reasons why firms encourage long hours among their highly skilled professionals and managers, especially in "winner-take-all" occupations like law, business, or consulting, in which employees are under pressure to meet clients' needs 24/7.

Some factors might cut the other way for firms themselves. Chronically long hours can undermine productivity in tangible and intangible ways.[44] And they can repel or drive out sought-after talent, especially but not only women, as we've seen. Many young lawyers, for example, say they would prefer a more balanced life even if it came with a salary cut.[45] All that being so, one might expect some firms to cater to those preferences by offering a more humane work schedule and modestly lower salaries and bonuses. Yet no major law firms have pursued that path. Apparently work-life balance has its price for young lawyers, and it is one that firms are willing to pay. Fears of "adverse selection" might also deter firms from getting out in front of their competitors on work-life balance; they might not want to become the favored choice for those who don't want to work as hard as their peers. All this is to say that it will not be easy for the law to disrupt these patterns.

If firms were motivated to shift from a "convex" pay structure to a more "linear" one that puts less of a premium on long hours, they could start by "making their employees better substitutes for each other."[46] That is how firms in health care, banking, brokerage, and real estate have made that shift, according to Goldin: "When clients perceive there is a greater degree of substitutability among workers, a more linear payment schedule emerges."[47] (That is also how voluntary job-sharing arrangements can be made more feasible.) That doesn't mean we should mandate either linear pay structures or "making employees better substitutes for each other"; firms have to figure out for themselves how to do that. But the law could and should make it worth their while.

So how could the law help to push down long hours at the top? Let's first assume that working time is reasonably measurable and verifiable even for high-end cognitive workers. (That's a big assumption, but lawyers who routinely record their hours for billing purposes would be hard-pressed to deny that.) And let's take off the table the idea of imposing a hard cap on hours in those jobs; such a heavy-handed approach to working hours at the top has no precedent in developed market economies. In principle, we could extend the FLSA's tax-like overtime premium to reach high-end professionals and managers; but that would seem either perverse or pointless. Given the large amounts at stake, either the wage premium would tilt those workers' incentives even further toward putting in long hours, and enrich those who did so, or firms would reproduce current compensation and hours expectations with a bit of arithmetic legerdemain.

But what if an overtime premium were more like an actual tax—one that went into public coffers and dampened employers' incentive to demand long hours without encouraging workers to log those longer hours? Here's an idea: Employers can now reduce their corporate taxes by fully deducting employee compensation as an expense. But the deduction could be reduced pro rata for long-hours workers—say, any employee who is treated by the employer as exempt from overtime and who works more than 2,000 hours per year (that is, 40 hours per week, 50 weeks per year, on average). So for an employee who worked 3,000 hours (60 hours per week on average) and who was paid $400,000 in salary and bonuses, the employer might be allowed to deduct only two-thirds of that amount—in effect, the pro rata share of compensation that corresponds to the first 2,000 hours. Keying the penalty to *annual* hours would accommodate "crunch times"; the employer could recover the full deduction by giving the employee compensatory time off over the course of the year—shorter weekly hours or weeks off. (And if the whole year is "crunch time," the employer should staff up.)

Any part of the suggested formula could be tweaked, but the idea would be to create some incentive to scale back the long hours of highly paid employees and to hire more workers if more hours are needed.[48] The excess hours penalty, if we call it that, would be modest at the current corporate tax rate of 21 percent, but greater at the higher rate that some Democrats propose.[49]

Firms could obviously reduce the pay of affected employees to reflect their lower hours, higher net cost per hour, or both; but that would be a gain for income equality (and not a major hardship at those salary levels). Of course, firms could also absorb the penalty if employees' extra hours were valuable enough or their skills rare enough.

This idea for countering the incentives that drive long hours at the top is more of a thought experiment than a practical proposal; for one thing, as my colleagues in tax law point out, it would present serious enforcement challenges given the novelty of reporting employees' hours. A much simpler (though less cleverly targeted) way to discourage very long hours at the top would be to raise taxes on the highest incomes. Period.

The astronomical rise in top incomes *and* long hours at the top is partly due to the relatively low marginal tax rates that now apply to those high incomes. In 1960, the top marginal federal income tax rate was 91 percent.[50] That predictably dampened those workers' incentive to work harder for more money, and that came to be seen as a problem for economic vitality (not to mention for the wealthy themselves). Beginning in the 1960s, and especially under Reagan, those top tax rates were reduced dramatically, eventually down to 37 percent by 2020, after the Trump tax cuts.[51] High earners now get to keep much more of whatever added income they realize, directly or indirectly, by working long hours. (High earners also make a greater share of their income from labor than they did a century ago.[52]) That is apart from some wealthy workers' ability to take their pay in forms like "carried interest" or capital gains that are taxed at even lower rates. Lower taxes on high-income workers is only one factor in the explosion of top salaries in recent decades, but it is perhaps the easiest to fix if we have a collective mind to do so. That would have the more-than-incidental benefits of curbing the incentive to work very long hours and of modestly spreading work, not to mention the benefit of raising revenues.

4. Reducing the Standard Work Week

If we did all of the above—regulated abusive scheduling, extended overtime premiums and penalties, guaranteed paid vacations and leaves for all workers, supported individuals' ability to choose less-than-full-time work, and pushed back against long hours at the top—we'd improve the lives of most workers by affording them more time for life beyond work, and we'd reduce unemployment and underemployment through work spreading.

At some point in the process of "task encroachment" and declining demand for human labor—if that forecast were borne out—more would be needed. At least at that point we would do well to resume the march toward ever-shorter working hours—a popular cause before the New Deal but mostly forgotten since then. We might start by reducing weeks or months per year through additional time off work—whether for family, education and training, volunteer work, or even hobbies—with a public subsidy for of those activities. But eventually we should reduce the standard work week to, say, thirty hours or fewer. That would be the new measure of "full-time" work, and that would be the point at which overtime would begin to accrue for the larger swath of the labor market entitled to an overtime premium. To continue to reap the benefits of work spreading—more leisure for those with jobs and jobs for those who might otherwise have none—that standard work week could be "indexed" to reflect further declines in aggregate demand for human labor.

A shorter work week would have many benefits, as chronicled in a recent UK report that calls for moving toward a thirty-two-hour work week within a decade.[53] Some of the benefits have been well-aired before: Beyond improving work-life balance, both at the individual level and at the societal level through work spreading, there would be gains in happiness, health, and well-being, in productivity, and in gender equality. There might also be sustainability gains, at least in the form of fewer daily commutes, and in "lower ecological footprints, carbon footprints, and carbon dioxide emissions."[54] Moreover, a shorter work week would make it easier for people to extend their working lives—as they might need to do given longer life expectancies—by reducing the mental and physical wear and tear of full-time work.

It will clearly take an enormous exertion of political will and investment of social resources to spread shrinking demand for human labor across the labor market. Accomplishing all of this without also reducing incomes for most workers poses its own challenges to which we'll soon turn. But that is the key to reaching a fair and humane future of less work.

C. A Note on Training and Job Security in a Future of Less Work and Longer Working Lives

Every piece of the work-spreading strategy would be more successful if more workers could move up into the more-skilled jobs that automation is likely to create. Whatever technology does to the number of jobs, it is plainly changing the skills needed in those jobs, and it is doing so at an accelerating rate. Better education and training are not *the* answer to technological change at work, but they are a necessary part of the answer. Anything that equips more people to move up from the routine low- or mid-skill jobs that are most at risk from automation, and into the new higher-skill jobs that will be created, will reduce both labor shortages at the top of the skills ladder and labor surpluses and downward wage pressure below the top.

Undoubtedly we need better schools, from pre-K on up, to prepare children for a lifetime of learning.[55] What that will require is a question far beyond the scope of this book. But basic social justice demands that individuals' life chances not be stunted from a young age by avoidable deficiencies in early education. Institutions of higher education and training will also have to be reconfigured to enable adults to re-immerse themselves periodically over the course of a long career and to shift gears. The idea is not that everyone should become a techie. Humans will be in high demand for many jobs that require psychological insight and social and organizational skills.[56] In a world of shorter working hours, people will also want to develop aptitudes that may have nothing to do with paid work—to learn a new language or a musical instrument or to study history or literature for pure enjoyment or edification, for example. But let's focus here on how to enable people to acquire new skills that are in demand in the labor market.

Employers have some incentive to build up their employees' general skills—those that enhance productivity both inside and outside the particular firm—and some do so.[57] Indeed, some of the most effective training occurs on-the-job; compared to free-standing programs of training and credentialing, the skills are more likely to be job relevant and to lead to better jobs.[58] But without any assurance of job security—either by law, as in most of the world, or by union contract, or even by the informal norms that once prevailed in much of the economy—employers have less incentive to invest in training. Employees who can be fired at will are more likely to be treated as disposable and may be more inclined to switch jobs; and employers are less likely to garner long-term gains from investing in employees' skills if employees take those skills elsewhere, even to a competitor. (That has given rise to some creative but sometimes-abusive contractual arrangements requiring employees to repay training costs if they leave the job within some period of time.[59]) This is yet another argument for legal protections against unjust dismissal: They tend to encourage employers to invest in building up current employees' skills instead of shedding them in favor of already-credentialed new hires. Still, some training will have to take place outside firms.

Workers themselves might be expected to invest in building their general skills, but they might not be able to afford it, especially if it requires taking time off work. They might forego valuable training that would pay off over time because they can't afford the up-front investment of foregone income and tuition. (Potential third-party investors have responded with another dubious contractual innovation—"income share agreements" by which lenders "advance a certain amount of training on the condition that the borrower repay the lender at a predetermined percentage of the borrower's future earnings," sometimes amounting to several times the cost of training.[60])

These are some of the reasons to publicly subsidize *both* effective training and educational programs—including those that cater to adults switching careers—*and* the time off work that most people need in order to take advantage of those programs. Public stipends for periodic intervals of full-time immersion in training and educational programs, like paid vacations and family leaves, would contribute incidentally to work spreading; but the main point would be to enable individuals to acquire the skills that will be in demand in a more automated economy.

The importance of enabling people to retrain over the course of their careers will be all the greater as working lives are extended up into their seventies. In principle, earlier retirements could contribute to work spreading and a better overall work-life balance for both individuals and the society as a whole. Unfortunately, that runs headlong into the stark demographics of greater longevity.[61] We've already noted that longer life expectancies will likely lead to longer working lives for those who can, if only to build adequate retirement savings. (Even so, we might have to channel a growing share of societal resources into meeting the economic and health-care needs of seniors.) The prospect of longer working lives also underscores the importance of expanding training and retraining opportunities. Older workers already face doubts—based partly but not wholly on stereotypes—about their facility with changing workplace technologies and their ability to learn new, cutting-edge skills. They are especially likely to get squeezed out of a more teched-up and job-scarce economy. Better opportunities for serious mid-career retraining won't solve that problem, but they will help.

Older workers' need to work longer might be yet another argument for protecting job security—that is, for bringing US law on this score into line with the rest of the developed world.[62] Legally-protected job security would bolster workers' ability to enjoy or enforce other workplace rights—to take a legally guaranteed vacation or part-time option, for example—and would encourage employers to invest in incumbent workers' skills instead of shedding them or trading them in for a skilled new hire. And it would modestly slow the technological displacement of incumbent workers.

Legal restraints on dismissal might take some toll on new hiring, and to protect incumbent workers relative to new entrants to the labor market. Indeed, using my own terminology here, job security mandates tend to *burden* employment—to impose costs on employers that weigh incrementally in favor of automation or outsourcing. I've already observed (in Chapter 6) that whatever costs are associated with these protections must fall on employers in order to protect the underlying entitlement; they can't be fully socialized (though they could be offset through public funds; more on this to come). The much-debated question is whether the many virtues of an entitlement to job security outweigh its labor market vices.

The best evidence on this question comes from a large-scale empirical study of the impact of employment protection laws—those regulating dismissals and layoffs and the use of temporary workers—in 117 countries over several decades.[63] That gargantuan study, led by Simon Deakin at Cambridge University, found that those laws have a small but mostly positive long-run impact on national economic performance, including modestly lower unemployment levels and a higher labor share of national income. Deakin and others have suggested one possible explanation: public and private investments in worker training might mitigate the costs and mine the benefits of job security, at least at the societal level.[64] Specifically, job-security protections encourage employers to invest in workers' skills instead of treating them as disposable.

Even the World Bank has changed its tune. It had long taken the line that employment protections not only burdened firms but harmed workers and the economy as a whole.[65] But in view of mounting contrary evidence, the Bank reversed course in 2015, acknowledging in that year's *Doing Business Report* that "employment regulations are unquestionably necessary" and "benefit both workers and firms"; indeed, labor laws could impair national competitiveness and growth "not simply where they were 'excessive' but also where they were 'insufficient.'"[66]

American law's adherence to employment at will is virtually unique in the world, and has gone hand in hand with US employers' tendency to treat their lower- and mid-skilled workers as disposable. That position gives too little weight to the interests of workers and of the society as a whole in the security and stability of employment. It's high time to enact practical protections against unjustified dismissal.

D. Mind the Gaps: Supporting Incomes in a World of Less Work

Imagine now that we have cracked the very hard nut of work spreading, and figured out both how to spread work opportunities across the adult population and how to better prepare people to take up those opportunities. In that imagined future, nearly all who can work will have decent work, though less of it—less than what now counts as full-time—and more time for the rest of life. That would be a monumental accomplishment. It would stave off the dystopian worst-case scenarios for a more automated economy, and would bring real gains in well-being. Successful work spreading would also mitigate income inequality—bringing down some top incomes by reducing long hours at the top and pulling more workers up into those higher wage jobs. Successful work spreading, along with an array of basic social entitlements and public goods and services and the resulting public jobs, would get us nearly all the way to a much better future of less work. But there remains a problem of maintaining adequate incomes.

Work spreading is likely to reduce incomes for many who end up working less. We should not worry about the top earners; their outsized income gains in recent decades are part of the problem we're trying to address. Nor should we worry much about the lower incomes of those who choose to work less than the norm. We should try to mitigate the gendered skew to those choices; but it is fair to assume that those who voluntarily trade off income for time are better off, and their choices might benefit others in the form of work spreading.

We should worry, however, about lower incomes for a big swath of the working population that is already pressed to make ends meet. In particular, those now working full-time (or more) at below-median wages will likely make less money if they work less. Some of the work-spreading mechanisms proposed here—such as paid and publicly subsidized vacations and leaves—are designed to minimize income losses for those below-median workers. Beyond that point, however, and at least with a shorter standard work week, incomes are likely to go down unless hourly wages go up. In the first century of progressively shorter working hours, incomes still rose because productivity gains were passed on to ordinary workers. But that ended in the 1970s, and automation is expected to further squeeze wages at the bottom of the labor market. In short, work spreading, however cleverly it is done, is likely to leave income gaps. Ample public goods and universal basic benefits would narrow those gaps. But people will still need money in a market economy (and I'm assuming that's what we will still have).

Higher minimum wages are unlikely to fill the whole gap. Imagine that average hours of work fell to twenty hours per week or less, and that work-spreading techniques succeeded, against all odds, in keeping most people engaged in paid work for much of their adult lives at around that level. To guarantee a "living wage" at that point—that is, for twenty hours of work per week to fully support a decent living—would require huge increases in the minimum wage. For example, it would take about $33 per hour in today's dollars, on average across the United States, for two working adults to support themselves and two children on twenty hours of work per week.[67] That risks decimating the demand for ordinarily-skilled human labor, and making it even harder to maintain a wide distribution of paid work across the adult population. We should consider other ways to bridge the income gap—that is, to supply some non-work-based income to most workers.

A negative income tax or a UBI—one that expanded as median hours of work fell—would make more sense than relying on existing means-tested welfare benefits. That is partly because their administration costs are so high relative to direct benefits. More to the point, those programs were designed to supply a "safety net" for an unfortunate few who fell between the cracks of a labor market that fully supported most people in some fashion. But in a future of much less work, we would be aiming to supplement the shrinking work-based income of a wide and growing share of the population. Some combination of basic income and basic benefits will be needed in that future of much less work.

As automation continues to swell capital's share versus labor's share of national income, an alternative strategy for ensuring that workers get a fair share of the economic gains from automation is widely distributed ownership of capital.[68] "Who owns the robots owns the world," says economist Richard Freeman, a leading proponent; so "[l]et us own the robots."[69] Freeman, along with Joseph Blasi and Douglas Kruse, would build on existing policies that encourage (or in some cases even require) firms to compensate employees partly in the form of stock ownership, and that have swelled stock ownership by pension plans.[70] They also point to evidence that employee stock ownership is linked to higher profits.[71] If workers did own a growing corpus of capital, then automation would tend to increase its value and the income from that capital even as it depressed wages and demand for most labor. The worker ownership strategy, with its built-in indexing of non-work-based income to declines in the availability of work, is a smart strategy for supporting workers' incomes in a future of less work.

The worker ownership strategy faces a dilemma, however: If the goal is to improve firm performance and to engage workers in firm governance—as many proponents of worker ownership hope—then workers should own shares in the firm that employs them. But if the goal is to protect workers' economic security, especially in light of declining returns to labor versus capital, a more diversified portfolio would do that much better.[72] The latter goal seems more urgent in a more automated economy, but it is the former goal that has drawn firms themselves to the idea of employee stock ownership.[73]

That is one reason that a capital ownership strategy is unlikely to meet the larger problem of declining incomes in a future of less work—at least without some radical changes in the existing templates. Thus far, employee ownership schemes are based at the firm (or sometimes sectoral) level; and they mostly benefit current or past employees of relatively profitable and stable firms. They do not reach low-wage workers in less-profitable service and supplier sectors, precarious workers, or gig workers; and they would not reach the would-be workers who never get the decent jobs that robots or algorithms are doing instead. A much more ambitious mandatory scheme for redistributing capital ownership would be required to reach those vulnerable groups; I'll leave that project for others.[74] Still, fostering wider employee ownership, even based on existing templates, through some combination of regulation and subsidies might go some distance toward meeting the income gaps that are likely to open up in a future of less work.

* * * * *

At some point, as machines erode humans' comparative advantages and become the most cost-effective producers of a larger share of goods and services, including public goods and services, the labor market will have ceased to function as the primary mechanism for distributing income. At that point, if not sooner, the problem of affording adequate incomes will overwhelm the objective of ensuring work for all who can and want to work. In other words, if predictions of continual "task encroachment" are borne out, the possibility of a three-dimensional future, with work at the center, will eventually run out. But that will be a topic for other books. By the time that future is in sight, much more will be known about how technology, the economy, the government, the climate, and the political landscape have developed and where they are headed. The future is notoriously hard to predict, but it gets easier the closer it gets. So I will leave planning for that remote future to our children and grandchildren.

The best path forward, now and for the foreseeable future, lies in a strong public commitment to basic social benefits for all, to more and better public goods and services and the jobs required to deliver them, and to work spreading. Much of that prescription has been standard progressive dogma for generations. And it will require sizable public expenditures and significantly higher taxes, especially on the rich. While making the case for those commitments, I've postponed crucial questions about money and politics. The next chapter will briefly address two funding issues: how to structure the funding of new and existing entitlements and where to get the necessary revenues. The final chapter will address the difficult politics of getting from here to there.

8
Footing the Bill

Nearly everything that is prescribed here will help address problems we face today—growing inequality, economic polarization, and degradation in the quality and security of work—even if we are not facing a future of overall net job losses. That is not happenstance; those prescriptions were designed with an eye to uncertainty about a future of less work. I think more will eventually be needed—more by way of work spreading and more by way of supplementing incomes at the bottom—at some point in the process of "task encroachment" by machines on humans' comparative advantages. But even many of those who are not convinced on the last point should recognize the urgency of improving job quality and expanding access to leaves and respites from work, and the value of creating public goods and universal access to basic benefits such as health care, child care, and education. Much of this will cost money, and quite a lot of it.

I will not attempt to cost out these proposals here. (Humans still have comparative advantages, but that is not one of mine.) But they raise two questions that I have thus far postponed: how to pay for them and how to summon the political will to enact them. I will leave politics for the last chapter, and take on the first question here in two parts: how to *structure* the funding of new and existing entitlements in light of the dilemmas already flagged; and, more briefly, where to get the public monies that will be needed.

A. How to Structure the Funding of New and Existing Entitlements

The proposals in Chapters 6 and 7 fall into three buckets, each of which raises distinct funding questions. One bucket of proposals—new public goods and public job creation—will necessarily entail direct public expenditures and presumably new revenue sources; that will be the subject of the next part. A second bucket of proposals contains new minimum standards—that is, revisions to the decent work standard—whose costs will fall on employers.

Automation Anxiety. Cynthia Estlund, Oxford University Press. © Cynthia Estlund 2021.
DOI: 10.1093/oso/9780197566107.003.0008

That includes fair scheduling laws, broader overtime protections for salaried workers, guaranteed access to (paid) vacations and leaves of various kinds, and protections against unjustified dismissal. Apart from the "paid" part of paid vacations and leaves, any net burdens from those entitlements will be borne largely by employers, much like the costs of workplace safety or protections against discrimination. That doesn't mean we can ignore those costs; we might even decide to offset them to some degree, in ways I'll suggest later in the chapter. But otherwise these proposals don't present a separate question of funding.

This part addresses the knottier funding questions raised by a third bucket of proposals—that is, entitlements that accrue to individuals, and whose costs are, or could be, but need not be funded through payrolls and payroll taxes. That includes Social Security and health insurance, as well as the "paid" part of guaranteed paid vacations and leaves, and higher incomes for low-wage workers. It could also include additional benefits like subsidies for child care, training and education, transportation, or housing. We could fund a lot of this through employment mandates and payroll taxes. But we don't have to, and Chapter 6 offers several good policy reasons to socialize those entitlements and their costs, in whole or in part: We could conserve jobs by reducing an inefficient tax on the use of human labor; enhance workers' freedom to choose independent work; narrow economic disparities between those with steady, decent full-time jobs and those relegated to precarious work and gigs; and achieve more income redistribution than is possible with the rather regressive payroll tax.[1]

Yet payroll-based funding has significant political advantages. Payroll-funded benefits don't require direct public appropriations, and they are more readily seen as both *earned* and *owned* by their beneficiaries as opposed to taxpayer-supported "hand-outs." Payroll-based funding largely circumvents the political minefield through which overtly redistributive programs have to pass, and makes them more resistant to political attacks.[2] Social Security in particular has unique political virtues: It is essentially universal (versus targeted at the poor); and yet it achieves some under-the-radar redistribution from richer beneficiaries toward those who most need the support.[3] This is what political scientist Theda Skocpol calls "targeting within universalism."[4] All of these features together have made Social Security the crown jewel of US social programs—even the "third rail" of US politics—virtually untouchable even when other social programs are under attack.[5] The anti-Obama protesters whose signs read "Keep your government hands off my

Medicare!" suggest the same is true of that payroll-based program, which ensures health coverage to those over age sixty-five (though Medicare adds a twist, as we'll see).

All in all, there is a potent political logic to using the payroll-based model, along with "targeting within universalism," for a wider range of benefits. Unfortunately, that would further increase the tax on using human labor while sharply limiting the room for redistribution. In short, politics weighs in favor of payroll-based funding, while policy weighs against it.

A solution might lie in a hybrid funding mechanism that combines payroll-based funding with funding from general revenues. That could garner some of the political appeal and staying power of earned-and-owned benefits while reducing the tax on the use of human labor; and it could achieve "targeting within universalism," with more redistribution in favor of needier beneficiaries than a wholly payroll-tax-based program allows.

As it turns out, Medicare fits that mold: It is supported by payroll-based taxes, and plainly shares the earned-and-owned aura of Social Security. But Medicare, unlike Social Security, also gets a chunk of its funding from general revenues. That makes it a significant budget item and an occasional object of political wrangling; but that wrangling has to reckon with the sense of ownership that current and future beneficiaries—together, nearly all voters—feel toward Medicare. This mixed funding solution—putting aside for the moment the question of where the public moneys would come from—might offer a way out of the policy-versus-politics dilemma of how to fund many basic benefits.

One way to implement a mixed funding mechanism for the entitlements at issue here might be through wage subsidies. Wage subsidies can be directed either to employers or to employees (though in either case some of the benefits flow to the other). Wage subsidies to employees can be used, as we've noted, to supplement low wages. Wage subsidies to employers have been used to encourage employers to hire or retain particular categories of disadvantaged workers, such as younger, older, disabled, or long-term unemployed workers. Let's look first at the former.

Wage subsidies to employees can boost incomes of low-wage workers. Unlike minimum wage increases, and like the EITC, wage subsidies come from general revenues, and they don't tax employment by increasing the cost of labor. Unlike the EITC, however, wage subsidies go to workers in each paycheck and without the need for filing a tax return. The economics of wage subsidies are complex.[6] But Oren Cass, among others, argues that they are the best policy tool for supplementing low-wage workers' incomes, encouraging employment, and rewarding work and workers.[7] Some worker advocates are skeptical of wage subsidies on the ground that, even if they go directly to low-wage workers and increase their take-home pay, they effectively subsidize low-wage *employers* by lowering nominal wages—more than the EITC, and unlike minimum wage increases.[8] But maybe subsidizing low-wage employers is not such a bad idea when we are facing the prospect of growing job losses at the bottom and middle rungs of the skill ladder.

Indeed, wage subsidies—coupled with minimum wage increases—might offer a strategy for unburdening employment while capturing some of the earned-and-owned quality of payroll-based entitlements. If wage subsidies effectively channel general revenues to both low-wage employees and their employers, that would achieve *both* some redistribution to workers who most need it *and* some unburdening of employment at the bottom of the wage scale where that would be most helpful. That is precisely where the cost of employment mandates and payroll taxes is highest (relative to wages), most likely to fall on employers (instead of on employees through lower wages), and most likely to affect firms' decisions about deployment of capital versus labor. Wage subsidies might be a way to redistribute income and unburden employment while preserving the political advantages of payroll-based benefits.

Now let's switch our focus to wage subsidies that go directly to *employers*. Those have sometimes been used to encourage the employment of particular groups of workers with relatively low expected marginal productivity, such as older workers, young workers without work experience, disabled workers, or other marginalized workers whose long-term unemployment is both a signal and a cause of limited employability. Wage subsidies have had some success in helping those groups, though sometimes to the detriment of other groups rather than by increasing overall employment.[9] With that caveat, this use of wage subsidies could make sense in a future of less work for those same groups, who are at high risk of getting squeezed out of the active labor market in a more automated economy.

Broader-gauged wage subsidies (to employers) could also be used to offset the tax, literal and figurative, that some employment mandates inescapably impose on employment. Just as any wage subsidy that goes directly to employees will indirectly benefit employers to some degree, any wage subsidy to employers will confer some benefit on employees, mainly in the form of jobs that would not otherwise exist. Labor markets are slippery that way.[10])

For example, wage subsidies for new hires might help to counter whatever slowdown in new hiring follows from enacting employment protections for incumbent workers.

B. Where to Get the Revenue

Any strategy for injecting general revenues into funding of benefits linked to employment—whether through wage subsidies or otherwise—as well as new public benefits, public goods, and public jobs, will presumably require new revenues or budgetary savings elsewhere. Or at least that is the conventional wisdom. We should start by recognizing a strong counterpoint to that conventional wisdom in what is called Modern Monetary Theory (MMT). On the precepts of MMT, new government spending does not necessarily require new taxes or budgetary savings, and government debt is largely a fiction, in a country like the United States that issues, and can pay its debts, in its own currency:

> [G]overnment should never have to default so long as it's sovereign in its currency: that is, so long as it issues and controls the kind of money it taxes and spends. The US government . . . can't go bankrupt because that would mean it ran out of dollars to pay creditors; but it can't run out of dollars, because it is the only agency allowed to create dollars. It would be like a bowling alley running out of points to give players.[11]

The point is not that the government can simply print money to pay for programs. Spending is still constrained, but it is constrained by the risk of inflation, not by the availability of revenue.[12] That puts a premium on spending money in ways that support economic growth. In particular, job-creating investments in physical and social infrastructure are seen as effectively self-financing.[13] That is how some proponents of a federal job guarantee respond to the cost question.[14]

MMT has strong roots in Keynesian thought and a kinship with more conventional views about deficits and public spending, and it may be gaining converts.[15] But it remains controversial even on the left.[16] Rather than tethering my proposals to a highly contested theory of public finance, I'll assume here that new revenue sources will be needed to support much of what I have called for here.

Insofar as new taxes are required, they should obviously target the rich—and not only for the obvious reasons. Automation has already increased economic inequality—by boosting the returns to capital versus labor, by raising wages for the most skilled workers, and by depressing wages below the top—and those trends are expected to continue.[17] A lopsided share of the gains have accrued to tech-centric firms, which are creating and profiting from labor-displacing innovations, and most of which employ few workers and thus contribute relatively little to the payroll tax revenues that support basic entitlements for much of the population. Whether we harken to basic political morality or to the feared social consequences of an ever-more polarized economy, there is a strong case for redistributing income from the winners to those who have lost ground or are just scraping by.

Redistribution can be achieved and inequality countered through policy decisions on both the taxing and spending sides of the public ledger.[18] More egalitarian European countries, for example, rely heavily on consumption taxes (especially the value-added tax), which are fairly regressive; but they also tax more heavily overall, and spend more on programs that disproportionately benefit lower-income households.[19] Still, the net redistributive impact of these programs, and the impact on economic inequality, will depend on how they are financed—on the taxation side of the ledger.

A "robot tax," suggested by both Bill Gates and Elon Musk, might seem irresistible.[20] In principle, such a tax could simultaneously replace lost payroll tax revenues as payrolls shrink, redistribute income from those who make and own the robots to those whose jobs they are destroying or degrading, and slow down the replacement of people by robots. But most economists scoff at the idea of a robot tax.[21] There is the challenge of identifying a robot—they don't all look like C-3PO or R2-D2 from *Star Wars*[22]—as well as the arbitrariness of targeting robots versus non-robotic forms of automation.[23] And some argue that a robot tax would counterproductively depress (or drive overseas) innovation and productive capital investments, along with the good jobs that accompany both.[24]

Acemoglu and his colleagues, who support higher taxes on capital in principle, conclude that a robot tax sweeps both too broadly and too narrowly to do the trick. As noted in Chapter 6, they make a case in principle for an "automation tax" on what they call "so-so technologies"—those that replace labor but do little for productivity.[25] But they conclude that it is too hard for the tax code to distinguish between those technologies and good, productivity-enhancing technologies, and argue instead for simply correcting the generic asymmetry in the tax system's treatment of labor and capital:[26] "tax reforms that level the playing field between capital and labor can discourage so-so automation, stimulate employment and significantly improve welfare."[27] Raising the tax on capital might also raise some needed revenue and effectuate a bit of redistribution in the right direction.

Another potential source of revenue would be a higher corporate tax rate. But we might do better by keying the corporate tax rate to *the ratio of profits to number of employees*; the higher the ratio, the higher the tax rate. That would achieve some of what a robot tax or an automation tax is meant to do without having to identify robots or to distinguish good from "so-so" technologies. It would counter the tax system's current tilt in favor of capital versus labor, and would modestly counter the incentives both to automate *and* to contract out labor needs. And it would fall most heavily on some of the biggest winners and the biggest drivers in the ongoing wave of automation—that is, firms that are heavily automated, firms that create the underlying automation technologies, and firms in the financial sector, all of which tend to employ few workers relative to their revenues and therefore pay little in payroll taxes.

But maybe simplicity is the best policy here. The simplest way to fund new entitlements and public goods and to achieve some redistribution of income, at least in the United States, is to increase personal income tax rates and steepen their progressivity.[28] Higher marginal tax rates at the top would also indirectly contribute to work spreading and reduce inequality, as noted in Chapter 7, by dampening the incentive of very high-wage workers to work very long hours. No number crunching is required to recognize that there is some income tax rate structure that could fund everything proposed here—and without returning to the top marginal tax rates of 70 to 90 percent that we had from 1936 to 1980.[29]

We obviously do not need to identify a single source of revenue. A smaller increase in top income tax rates could be combined with a wealth tax,[30] a tax on financial transactions,[31] a meaningful estate or inheritance tax,[32] or a European-style consumption tax.[33] Each of these forms of taxation has advantages and disadvantages, all explored elsewhere.[34] Some of them raise serious problems of tax avoidance and evasion—through transnational machinations or restructuring of income flows or otherwise—but I will leave those complex issues to others.[35] The bottom line is that some combination of taxes on income from labor, capital, wealth, wealth transfers, financial transactions, and consumption could fund everything on our wish list while also redistributing some of the gains from galloping developments in automation technologies to those whose jobs and wages are most threatened.

* * * * *

There are ways and means, and enough wealth sloshing around in the US economy, to do all that is proposed here and to pave the way toward a more inclusive and humane future of less work. The biggest deficit we face is not budgetary or fiscal but political. From where we sit today, it might be hard to imagine the political sea change that it will take to enact and fund these proposals. In the Conclusion I hope to make that a bit more imaginable, or at least to sharpen the focus on the political hurdles ahead.

9

The Politics of Hope and Fear in a Future of Less Work

The claim that machines will make human labor obsolete has been often stated, and often overstated, since labor-saving machines first made their debut in the economy. It has surfaced periodically—often with the addendum that "this time is different"—only to be buried by the next wave of economic growth, driven by technological innovation and creative destruction. History offers solace to the enthusiasts of innovation and markets who reject predictions of a future of less work. Yet sometimes the future really is different from the past. Consider Malthus: At the close of the eighteenth century, he extrapolated from centuries of economic stagnation to predict that the society's essentially-fixed food supply would inevitably be exhausted by a growing population. Then came the Industrial Revolution, which proved him spectacularly wrong.[1]

We already face a foreseeable future of shrinking demand and falling wages for many workers whose heretofore-marketable skills are being replicated or surpassed or made irrelevant by ever-smarter and more cost-effective machines. That is a devastating prospect for the vast majority that depends on paid work for their livelihood and the material support of their dependents. And it is a profoundly unsettling prospect for a society in which paid work is not only a source of income but a primary locus of connectedness outside of families and friendships. For the foreseeable future, decent work for those who want and need it should have a central place in policy making around work and the economy.

Wide access to decent work is also an achievable aspiration, even as demand for ordinary human skills declines. Job creation and conservation is part of the answer. But over the long haul, the key lies in work spreading—less work for nearly all versus too much work for some and too little or none for others. I've proposed an array of work-spreading techniques, including but not beginning with a shorter standard work week. Work spreading, together with expanded social benefits and investments in public goods and

Automation Anxiety. Cynthia Estlund, Oxford University Press. © Cynthia Estlund 2021.
DOI: 10.1093/oso/9780197566107.003.0009

public jobs, can cushion the losses and spread the gains from the increasing automation of production.

Many of these proposals, though not all, will require sizable public expenditures and—in the United States—a renewed public commitment to redistribution. Although we might have made a start on the necessary political transformation in the wake of COVID (and Black Lives Matter, and Donald Trump), it is still fair to ask: How do we get there? I'll paint with broad strokes here, focusing mostly on how automation and the prospect of net job losses might intersect with the politics of redistribution, and on the potentially pivotal if not indispensable role of organized labor. I'll close by reflecting briefly on how a future of less work, together with the ambitious suite of policy responses proposed here, might intersect with the future of capitalism.

A. The Politics of Redistribution in a More Automated Future

Proposals abound on the left for regulating labor markets, investing in public goods, public services, public jobs, and universal benefits, and for taxing the rich to pay for those programs. All such proposals, like those offered here, will require new legislation and new appropriations. And all of them face daunting political challenges, including the outsized political power of the rich, anti-tax and anti-government attitudes that hold sway much further down the income scale, and simple skepticism about the efficacy of government. The last time the United States enacted an ambitious suite of redistributive programs—at least before Biden's bold opening moves in 2021—was during the mid-1960s as part of President Johnson's Great Society, a self-conscious effort to revive and complete the New Deal. As it happens, that was also a period of automation anxiety, especially for those pinning their economic hopes on manufacturing jobs.

In an extraordinary 1965 essay, famed civil rights leader Bayard Rustin warned that the country was "in the midst of a technological revolution [that was] altering the fundamental structure of the labor force, destroying unskilled and semi-skilled jobs—jobs in which Negroes [were] disproportionately concentrated."[2] He called for the civil rights movement to pivot from its nearly victorious campaign against Jim Crow toward the more challenging pursuit of economic justice in a changing economy. It was time, he wrote, "to propose alternatives to technological unemployment, urban decay, and the rest" and to call for "for public works and training, for national economic planning, for federal aid to education, for attractive public housing, all this on a sufficiently massive scale to make a difference." Rustin maintained that the struggle for economic justice would require alliances with trade unionists and other progressive actors. After all, white workers were facing many of the same economic challenges. And "[t]he labor movement, despite its obvious faults, has been the largest single organized force in this country pushing for progressive social legislation."[3]

For Rustin, LBJ's 1964 landslide victory—in which most white voters chose a desegregated Great Society over retrograde racial appeals—"proved . . . that economic interests are more fundamental than prejudice." That lesson, he said, "must be kept alive, for the civil rights movement will be advanced only to the degree that social and economic welfare gets to be inextricably entangled with civil rights."[4]

From our vantage point over a half-century later, it is almost heartbreaking to hear the optimism that shines through Rustin's assessment of his own time and of the challenges ahead. In early 1965, when Rustin wrote, the Voting Rights Act had not yet passed. Interracial marriage was still illegal across the South. Many Southern lawmakers were still overtly committed to white supremacy and "massive resistance" to court-ordered desegregation. Many good jobs were closed to Black workers regardless of qualifications. And the faults of the labor movement were obvious indeed, as many local unions were still committed to racist exclusion and segregation even if their national leadership was a crucial part of the civil rights coalition. How could it possibly be more challenging today than it seemed to Rustin in 1965 to build a cross-racial political coalition in support of economic justice and against the polarization of the economy into winners and losers?

Yet the challenges today do loom large. One is that, while the labor movement is far more integrated and thoroughly committed to racial justice than it was in 1965, it is also a lot smaller—and a smaller force in national politics. (We'll return to the political role of unions.) Other obvious challenges lie in the national political landscape. In 1965, it was plain that big positive changes were possible in both the legislatures and the courts. From where we sit today, the catalogue of major programs enacted by Congress just from 1964 to 1966—in civil rights, health care, community development, education, and the environment—is stunning.[5] Especially after the 1964 election, with the presidency and two-thirds majorities in both houses of Congress, even an internally divided Democratic Party was able to push through an extraordinary array of legislation, almost all of it tending, or at least intending, to promote the same progressive goals that still animate much of the American left.

This is not the place to chronicle our decades-long descent into political polarization and legislative paralysis.[6] But one factor—both cause and effect of political paralysis—is waning popular confidence in the efficacy of law, policy, and politics in achieving positive social change. In part that might reflect some Great Society failures and disappointments, as well as the sheer difficulty of the tasks at hand—much more difficult, as Rustin stressed in his 1965 essay, than desegregating lunch counters and buses. But it also reflects a methodical and concerted campaign on the right—with roots and branches in the academy, conservative political and legal circles, and the business community—to propound the virtues and vitality of markets as against redistributive and regulatory interventions by government.[7]

The market fundamentalists linked government in the public mind with bureaucratic rigidity, waste of taxpayer money, rent-seeking, and economic sclerosis. "Government is not the solution to our problem; government is the problem," as Ronald Reagan famously put it in 1981.[8] For several decades, popular beliefs about the appropriate relationship between government and the economy were refracted through that neoliberal prism, which shifted the political center of gravity to the right, emboldened opponents of redistribution and regulation, and clipped the wings of left-of-center reformers.[9]

The conservative countermovement targeted not only government but also organized labor, which represented a different kind of challenge to "free markets."[10] Anti-union crusaders never gave up their fight after the New Deal, and scored critical legislative and judicial victories in the 1940s on behalf of the so-called "right to work" and against labor's most effective organizing and bargaining tactics.[11] In terms of organizing the unorganized, unions began losing (and ceding) ground after 1950 for many reasons. One might have seen hope for a turnaround in a surge in grassroots union activism and strikes in the late 1960s and early 1970s. But the activism of unions' remobilized business-led adversaries proved more potent. That was seen in 1978 in the brilliantly choreographed filibuster and defeat of a union-backed labor law reform bill that had seemed destined for passage with the Democrats again holding the presidency and supermajorities in both houses of Congress.[12] The counterrevolution from the right had captured the center.

Even this very terse retelling of the rise of neoliberal market fundamentalism in the United States might seem like a misplaced digression in a book about automation. But the redistributive and regulatory policies that are needed to prepare for a more automated future will run smack into the political blockade that has stymied major progressive reforms since the 1970s unless there's a way around or through that blockade. Is there?

Market fundamentalism has taken a bit of a drubbing in the public mind since the Financial Crisis and the Great Recession exposed the colossal risks of underregulated financial markets, and both exacerbated and exposed the highest levels of economic inequality since the Gilded Age. In the meantime, however, the partly orchestrated resurgence of white racial and cultural resentments may have extended the life span of market fundamentalism. The Republican Party has become the home of both, so that white ethnonationalists fortify the electoral fortunes of market fundamentalists (and vice versa), even though the non-college-educated white voters targeted by the former have suffered mightily under the latter's reign. The election of Donald Trump in 2016 made it vividly clear that widespread economic distress and anger at elites and business-as-usual did not necessarily augur a leftward turn in American politics.

Then came 2020, and a series of shocks to the system—the COVID-19 pandemic, the disastrous government response, the attendant economic contraction, a new spate of police killings and the wave of Black Lives Matter protests—that highlighted long-festering injustices and racial disparities in lives, life expectancies, and livelihoods. In a less polarized political era, those serial blows to public confidence in the established order (not to mention revulsion over Trump's serial offenses to political decency) might have produced a wave of progressive electoral victories, much like the Great Depression did nearly a century ago. Instead, the 2020 election brought rather narrow victories for the Democrats amidst widespread refusal among Republican voters and elected officials to acknowledge that the Democrats had won at all.

President Biden in his first months sought to make the most of these narrow victories, and to reinvigorate the notion that an energetic and effective government is essential to a healthy society and must act to prevent or redress the casualties of economic dislocation. Readers will know more about the fate of these early forays than I do as of this writing. But one thing is certain: Political polarization is alive and well, and a small swing in the electorate could bring a big swing of the pendulum back to the right.

What might be the impact on this political landscape of growing fears about automation? Those fears were mostly swamped in 2020 by a cascade of other crises. But that might change. The COVID-19 pandemic and the resulting economic dislocation are bound to accelerate automation and attendant job losses. And those job losses—even if they are numerically offset by new jobs elsewhere—will fall especially hard on groups that are already overrepresented at the bottom of the economic pyramid, including workers of color. As the economy begins to dig out from COVID, we are likely to see both greater economic polarization—already painfully evident and well-documented in the pre-pandemic era of historically low unemployment—and a wave of permanent job losses to automation. We are also likely to see greater economic concentration, and gains in market share and market capitalization for Apple, Alphabet, Amazon and other tech-centric behemoths.

It might be years before the experts reach a consensus about whether and how this round of automation is different. Different swaths of the public might reach their own conclusions sooner or later, and more or less informed by the experts. Change will come not with a thunderclap but with a rising tide of concern, much like public views of climate change. And as with climate change, young people are likely to be the most affected and the most concerned. If a critical mass of the electorate comes to the view that they or their children are facing a future of less work, that is likely to alter the political landscape. But how?

Rising public concern about a future of less work will not necessarily tilt public opinion toward redistributive policies and higher taxes on the rich. On the contrary, deteriorating job opportunities and job quality might fuel anti-immigrant sentiment and a desire to tighten national borders. And if joblessness and economic distress lead to social disorder and rising crime, that might fuel support for more "law and order" and repressive and expensive criminal justice policies. Anxieties over crime and immigration reflect and potentially exacerbate racial cleavages and racist attitudes that have long divided the US working class and undercut the appeal of left-leaning political parties and policies.[13] Since the 1970s, and especially since 2008, historically high immigration levels and growing economic insecurity laid the groundwork for a populist turn in politics, especially among white rural and working-class voters.[14] And both ethnonationalist ideologues and partisan opportunists have worked mightily to bend that populist turn to the right with divisive narratives of us versus them, invasion and predation, and an embattled heartland of authentic citizens versus outsiders. Anxiety over automation-based job losses could feed those divisive narratives.

Sadly, a national consensus is too much to hope for at this benighted point in our political evolution. But finding our way to a humane and sustainable future of less work will require widening the band of public support for combating inequality and for redistributive policies and the taxes and expenditures they require. That, in turn, will require dampening the racial and ethnic divisions that would doom those policies. A progressive program centered on the goal of decent work for all—as opposed to, for example, one centered on basic income, universal or otherwise—has a better chance of garnering that wider support and narrowing those divisions. That is partly because of widely shared though frayed beliefs about the dignity of work and of earning one's livelihood. And it is partly because the goal of decent work for all potentially taps into a wide (if shallow and depleted) reservoir of connections with relatively diverse co-workers and the mostly-positive sentiments that shared work engenders.

The invocation, again, of the social and political value of working together might seem to lean too heavily and naively on faith in people's ability and propensity to transcend social divisions through work. So let me be clear: The reservoir of workplace connections and connectedness can be a resource in political coalition building, but it is a resource that needs to be actively cultivated and deepened. And that will require organizing and organizations. In particular, labor unions could play a crucial part in building the necessary coalition for an economically just redistribution of work and income through public policy.[15] That's another thing that Rustin was right about, and that speaks to the current political moment. But it requires some elaboration (not to mention some hope).[16]

What is needed to turn the political tide is a powerful counternarrative that appeals to working people's shared interests and solidarity across ethnic and racial lines. Trade unions are uniquely well-positioned—putting aside for the moment their shrunken state—to propound that counternarrative, both at work and in politics. That is because unions' and workers' material interests reinforce the moral case for cross-racial solidarity in several ways.

First, trade unions connect with workers at and through work, where people are comparatively likely to cooperate and find common cause with diverse others, and to experience shared economic grievances and aspirations. *Second*, trade unions that represent or seek to represent diverse workforces have a strong institutional self-interest in cultivating solidarity and combating divisions, for that is how they can win gains for workers and thrive as organizations. *Third*, trade unions can make a credible case to workers that their own economic interests are best served by intergroup solidarity. That pitch, especially if it helps workers win economic battles, is more likely to resonate with workers than abstract appeals to the values of equality and diversity. *Fourth*, unions have organizational roots and branches from the workplace level up to the plane of national politics; even now they are comparatively well-resourced national political actors, and practically the only ones that represent ordinary working people regardless of racial or ethnic identity. They are in a unique position to elevate and amplify sentiments of intergroup solidarity from the workplace level up into national electoral politics and policy debates.

Admittedly, that might sound more like an elegy for a dying order than a path to future progress. For even as unions have become more committed than ever to the message that "economic interests are more fundamental than prejudice," they have become less powerful messengers given their shrinking membership and weaker hold on working-class voters. Nearly every major trend in the world of work since the 1970s—deindustrialization, declining job tenures and rising precarity, fissuring of production and disintegration of internal labor markets, and the rise of "gig" work and remote work—has taken a toll on both the density and durability of co-worker ties and the power and reach of unions.[17] Common work has become less conducive to the sturdy co-worker bonds that can bridge racial and ethnic divisions, while unions have grown smaller, weaker, and less capable of nurturing those workplace bonds into forms of cross-racial solidarity that can carry into the political domain.

The fragmentation of work and the decline of unions have been devastating for workers' economic security and well-being. The impact on public discourse and the political landscape is more diffuse but profound. Trade unions' waning ability to propound a credible, racially inclusive, class-wide political message makes it more challenging to combat divisive ethnonationalist appeals and to build political support for pro-worker policies, including the policies proposed here.

Even so, one might find cause for hope on several fronts: a recent uptick in worker activism and strikes, including among workers and in sectors that have not historically been unionized;[18] the turn toward union organizing and bargaining "for the common good" alongside public constituencies;[19] the rise of organizing across firms and outside the traditional exclusive representation model, including the Fight for Fifteen;[20] the engagement of Black Lives Matter activists in union campaigns;[21] and the stunning pair of Democratic victories in the 2021 Georgia senatorial runoff elections, with unions—especially UNITE-HERE and SEIU—playing a surprisingly large role.[22] Unlikely as it might have seemed five years ago, Georgia's two senators will now be among the vocal proponents and reliable votes in the Senate for the rights of workers and unions.

If what we're looking for are signs of a resurgence of unions as such, we might miss a larger lesson: Nearly every one of those encouraging recent developments points toward the emergence of broader cross-racial coalitions, with or without unions at the center, in support of shared interests of ordinary working people both at work and beyond. The overlapping grievances and demands of low-income workers and people of color were vividly highlighted during the COVID crisis: many of the publicly-celebrated "essential workers" who were at greatest risk of infection and death were also among the worst-paid US workers, the least likely to enjoy either paid sick leave or health insurance, and disproportionately immigrants and workers of color.[23] Those overlapping grievances and demands were also reflected in the final report of the Harvard-based Clean Slate for Worker Power project, which proposes a "fundamental redesign of labor law" that is intended "to enable all working people—including those who have been excluded by systemic racism and sexism—to create the collective economic and political power necessary to build an equitable economy and politics."[24]

Labor unions and civil rights groups have long been allies, and have been at the heart of the "New Deal coalition" that sustained the Democratic Party for much of the twentieth century. But those groups' goals, programs, and constituencies have perhaps never been as intertwined as they are now, nor have they ever been as fully embraced by the Democratic Party. It took several decades, but the exodus of the anti-labor and racially retrograde "Dixiecrat" faction has helped to make the Democrats a more thoroughly progressive party—especially on race and workers' rights—than it has ever been.

Perhaps the converging crises of public health, unemployment, and police violence that marked 2020 will also instigate a more profound reckoning with the economic forces that reinforce racial stratification.[25] And perhaps it will draw attention to the decades-long hollowing out of labor markets and destruction of decent middle-class jobs, trends that are falling heavily on already-marginalized workers of color and that automation is bound to exacerbate. Powerful economic forces have converged with policy failings to undercut economic security and decent work for the bottom half of the income distribution across racial and ethnic lines; but workers of color are still heavily concentrated in that bottom half.

Enacting constructive policy responses to those trends along the lines developed here will require a broad cross-racial movement for economic justice. I think that will require a bigger and stronger labor movement. If that in turn depends on first achieving comprehensive labor law reform—a goal that has eluded the labor movement for many decades—then we might be facing a colossal chicken-and-egg problem that will frustrate progress on either front. Then again, in 1932—in the depths of the Great Depression and following a long period of union suppression and decline—union density was no higher than it is today.[26] It might have taken a spectacular leap of faith then to predict that the country was on the cusp of a transformative (if incomplete) New Deal in which organized labor would play a leading role.[27]

There's no question that the pursuit of progressive and redistributive policies would benefit enormously from better institutions for workers' collective representation from the workplace level up to the plane of national politics. Unions and collective labor law could also play a constructive role in shaping technological trends at work.[28] Given the stubborn hurdles to federal labor law reform, however, one virtue of the suite of proposals advanced here is that they mostly fall within the bailiwick of employment law, in which less-paralyzed and polarized state and local legislatures can act without the suffocating pall of federal labor preemption and without the ideological baggage that union-specific reforms carry even among some workers themselves. Even Congress has been less consistently deadlocked on employment legislation than on labor law reform. This is a program that labor unions, BLM activists, and progressives of all stripes could rally around and help to build the wider coalition that would be needed for major labor law reform.[29]

If today's depleted but newly-energized labor movement were to join forces with the resurgent movement for racial equality in support of economic justice for all, they might together relearn and reteach the lessons that Rustin drew from the 1964 election "that economic interests are more fundamental than prejudice," and that "the civil rights movement will be advanced only to the degree that social and economic welfare gets to be inextricably entangled with civil rights."[30] However difficult it will be in the present moment to build a cross-racial movement for economic justice, that is the only way to move our heterogeneous and fractious society toward a more humane and equitable version of capitalism.

B. Toward a Better Variety of Capitalism in a Future of Less Work

The three-dimensional vision of a future of less work that I have argued for here—a future of wide engagement in decent paid work, more time for the rest of life, and decent incomes and standards of living for all—will require big changes in law and social policy. Some readers will doubt that these changes are possible under capitalism, while others might doubt that a society thus transformed would still *be* capitalist. But there are varieties of capitalism, and some of them leave room for *both* the prodigiously innovative, energizing, and coordinating forces generated by markets for goods and services, labor, and capital, *and* the humanizing and rationalizing forces of regulation, redistribution, and democratization of economic life.[31]

Capitalism does not necessarily entail the hollowed-out state, stingy social benefits and underfunded services, and the poorly regulated labor markets that have become the calling card of American-style neoliberalism since the 1980s. Social democracy, for its part, is compatible with private ownership of the means of producing most goods and services, and with heavy reliance on markets for distributing most goods and services and most work and income. Since the fall of the Soviet Union, the term "socialism" itself has come to mean something quite different, for both fans and foes, than state ownership of the means of production and a planned economy in place of markets.[32] Some on the right will label as "socialist" any move to enlarge the social welfare state and the reach of regulation. But that might only burnish the appeal of socialism among Democrats and young people, many of whom already view it positively.[33] This is a contest that could be won by proponents of a socially inclusive, democratized, and democratically-regulated market economy.

The strategy advanced here—which fits squarely under the umbrella of social democracy—could be seen as another in a long line of progressive-minded efforts to save capitalism from itself, and from the social and political unrest that may follow if we stay the current course in the face of technological job destruction and growing economic insecurity. Randall Collins, a leading American sociologist, has argued that "the end of middle-class work" due to "technological displacement of labor . . . will generate the long-term and quite possibly terminal crisis of capitalism."[34] That is partly because job losses will depress purchasing power and stall the economy. But it is also because of the political consequences of widespread economic deprivation, which will lead, he posits, to either the end of capitalism or the end of democracy, or perhaps both.

At least for the foreseeable future, it seems preferable and possible to pursue a middle course—or what used to be called the "middle way" or the "third way" until the collapse of state socialism and the rise of neoliberalism relocated the middle several notches further to the right.[35] In a *socially democratic* market economy, markets would still drive much of the economy; but the government would play a larger role in the provision of public goods and a basic social minimum and in the regulation of markets and the mitigation of the "public bads" that market forces manifestly generate. In a *more-automated* socially democratic market economy, that will require a three-dimensional strategy that spreads work, free time, and material necessities more widely and equitably than our existing economic and political institutions will otherwise do. And in a socially *democratic* market economy, we will have to get there and stay there by democratic means—that is, by persuading a large majority of voters that it is the best path forward for them and their families. An increasingly vivid threat of job losses due to automation, and fears of a future of less work for themselves and their children, could help to nudge a critical mass of voters toward that conclusion.

Notes

Preface

1. Andrew Stern & Lee Kravitz, Raising the Floor (2016).
2. Two books in particular by Benjamin Kline Hunnicutt made an early impression: Free Time: The Forgotten American Dream, 148–53 (2013); and Work Without End: Abandoning Shorter Hours for the Right to Work (1988).

Chapter 1

1. John Markoff, *Computer Wins on 'Jeopardy!': Trivial, It's Not*, N.Y. Times (Feb. 16, 2011), http://www.nytimes.com/2011/02/17/science/17jeopardy-watson.html.
2. *See* Bruce Weber, *In Upset, Computer Beats Chess Champion*, N.Y. Times (Feb. 11, 1996), https://www.nytimes.com/1996/02/11/us/in-upset-computer-beats-chess-champion.html.
3. *See* Choe Sang-Hun, *Google's Computer Program Beats Lee Se-dol in Go Tournament*, N.Y. Times (Mar. 15, 2016), https://www.nytimes.com/2016/03/16/world/asia/korea-alphago-vs-lee-sedol-go.html.
4. *Id.*
5. *See* Matthew Hutson, *This Computer Program Can Beat Humans at Go—With No Human Instruction*, Science (Oct. 18, 2017, 1:00 p.m.), https://perma.cc/LCA9-M36M.
6. Jason Furman (then-chairman, Council of Econ. Advisors), Address at New York University: *Is This Time Different? The Opportunities and Challenges of Artificial Intelligence* 4 (July 7, 2016), https://perma.cc/VT7V-WQ8X.
7. *See* Sage Lazzaro, *Google Is Using Artificial Intelligence to Make a Huge Change to Its Translate Tool*, N.Y. Observer (Mar. 6, 2017, 3:04 p.m.), https://perma.cc/944Z-QF6U; Gideon Lewis-Kraus, *The Great A.I. Awakening*, N.Y. Times Mag. (Dec. 14, 2016), https://www.nytimes.com/2016/12/14/magazine/the-great-ai-awakening.html.
8. Bernard Marr, *Will Machine-Learning Make Human Translators an Endangered Species?*, Forbes (Aug. 24, 2018), https://perma.cc/58FQ-WDQF.
9. Mark Muro et al., *What Jobs Are Affected by AI?*, Brookings (Nov. 2019), https://perma.cc/WN9U-NQUF.
10. I am indebted to Brishen Rogers for emphasizing this point.

11. Theranos's breadbox-sized blood-testing machine was supposed to be able to run dozens of blood tests using a single drop of blood, while its ostensible results were in fact being produced—behind the curtain, as it were—by lab technicians using conventional methods. *See* JOHN CARREYOU, BAD BLOOD: SECRETS AND LIES IN A SILICON VALLEY STARTUP (2018).
12. *See* Ella Morton, *The Mechanical Chess Player That Unsettled the World*, SLATE (Aug. 20, 2015), https://slate.com/human-interest/2015/08/the-turk-a-chess-playing-robot-was-a-hoax-that-started-an-early-conversation-about-ai.html.
13. *See* Michael Simon et al., *Lola v. Skadden and the Automation of the Legal Profession*, 20 YALE J. L. & TECH. 234 (2018) [hereinafter Simon et al.].
14. *See id.* at 279–81.
15. *See* Julie Sobowale, *How Artificial Intelligence Is Transforming the Legal Profession*, ABA J. (Apr. 1, 2016), https://perma.cc/74DJ-DQW4; Asma Khalid, *From Post-It Notes to Algorithms: How Automation Is Changing Legal Work*, NPR (Nov. 7, 2017), https://perma.cc/8BF6-HUR7.
16. Daniel N. Kluttz & Deirdre K. Mulligan, *Automated Decision Support Technologies and the Legal Profession*, 34 BERKELEY TECH. L.J. 853, 863–64 (2019).
17. *See* RICHARD SUSSKIND, ONLINE COURTS AND THE FUTURE OF JUSTICE 37–38, 271–72 (2019) [hereinafter R. SUSSKIND]. For a more skeptical assessment, *see* Dana Remus & Frank Levy, *Can Robots Be Lawyers? Computers, Lawyers, and the Practice of Law*, 30 GEO. J. LEGAL ETHICS 501, 518–19 (2017).
18. Debra Cassens Weiss, *JPMorgan Chase Uses Tech to Save 360,000 Hours of Annual Work by Lawyers and Loan Officers*, ABA J. (Mar. 2, 2017), https://perma.cc/VXP8-26AB.
19. Lyle Moran, *Casetext Launches Automated Brief-Writing Product*, ABA J. (Feb. 25, 2020), https://www.abajournal.com/news/article/casetext-launches-automated-brief-writing-product.
20. *See* Kathryn D. Betts & Kyle R. Jaep, *The Dawn of Fully Automated Contract Drafting: Machine Learning Breathes New Life into A Decades-Old Promise*, 15 DUKE L. & TECH. REV. 216, 224–32 (2017).
21. Remus & Levy, *supra* note 17, at 539.
22. Kate Beioley, *Robots and AI Threaten to Mediate Disputes Better Than Lawyers*, FIN. TIMES (Aug. 13, 2019), https://www.ft.com/content/187525d2-9e6e-11e9-9c06-a4640c9feebb.
23. R. SUSSKIND, *supra* note 17, at 272. For a discussion of models and algorithms that outperform human experts in predicting outcomes of Supreme Court cases, *see* Matthew Hutson, *Artificial Intelligence Prevails at Predicting Supreme Court Decisions*, SCIENCE (May 2, 2017), https://perma.cc/KF3V-9R2U.
24. *See* R. SUSSKIND, *supra* note 17, at 277–92.
25. Remus & Levy, *supra* note 17, at 533–36.
26. *See* McKinsey Global Institute, *Jobs Lost, Jobs Gained: Workforce Transitions in a Time of Automation* 30, 102. MCKINSEY & CO. (Dec. 2017) [hereinafter MGI, *Jobs Lost, Jobs Gained*] https://perma.cc/F8TR-HEJS.

27. Bernie Monegain, *IBM Watson Pinpoints Rare Form of Leukemia After Doctors Misdiagnosed Patient*, HEALTHCARE IT NEWS (Aug. 8, 2016), https://www.healthcareitnews.com/news/ibm-watson-pinpoints-rare-form-leukemia-after-doctors-misdiagnosed-patient. On the benefits of AI for the health-care system, *see* ERIC TOPOL, DEEP MEDICINE: HOW ARTIFICIAL INTELLIGENCE CAN MAKE HEALTHCARE HUMAN AGAIN (2019).
28. *See, e.g.*, Cade Metz, *A.I. Shows Promise Assisting Physicians*, N.Y. TIMES (Feb. 11, 2019), https://www.nytimes.com/2019/02/11/health/artificial-intelligence-medical-diagnosis.html; Julia Belluz, *3 Ways AI Is Already Changing Medicine*, VOX (Mar. 15, 2019), https://www.vox.com/science-and-health/2019/3/15/18264314/ai-artificial-intelligence-deep-medicine-health-care.
29. Janet Morrissey, *Looking to Technology to Avoid Doctors' Offices and Emergency Rooms*, N.Y. TIMES (Feb. 21, 2019), https://perma.cc/FF2W-8KGM.
30. Denise Grady, *A.I. Is Learning to Read Mammograms*, N.Y. TIMES (Jan. 1, 2020) [hereinafter Grady, *A.I. Is Learning*], https://www.nytimes.com/2020/01/01/health/breast-cancer-mammogram-artificial-intelligence.html; Denise Grady, *A.I. Took a Test to Detect Lung Cancer. It Got an A.*, N.Y. TIMES (May. 20, 2019), https://perma.cc/T7ZE-JAFV.
31. Grady, *A.I. Is Learning*, *supra* note 30.
32. Lauren Silverman, *Scanning the Future, Radiologists See Their Jobs at Risk*, NPR (Sept. 4, 2017), https://perma.cc/G2J5-SMF2.
33. *See* Ajay Agrawal et al., *Artificial Intelligence: The Ambiguous Labor Market Impact of Automating Prediction* 14 (Nat'l Bureau of Econ. Research, Working Paper No. 25619, Feb. 2019), http://www.nber.org/papers/w25619.
34. *See* Casey Ross & Ike Swetlitz, *IBM Pitched Its Watson Supercomputer as a Revolution in Cancer Care. It's Nowhere Close*, STAT (Sept. 5, 2017), https://www.statnews.com/2017/09/05/watson-ibm-cancer/.
35. *See generally* FRANK PASQUALE, NEW LAWS OF ROBOTICS: DEFENDING HUMAN EXPERTISE IN THE AGE OF AI (2020).
36. *See* Steven Greenhouse, *Driverless Future?*, AM. PROSPECT (Mar. 21, 2017), https://prospect.org/economy/driverless-future/. For varying estimates, *compare* Exec. Office of the President, *Artificial Intelligence, Automation, and the Economy* 15 (2016), https://perma.cc/82SU-N48H (2.2 to 3.1 million driver jobs at risk), *with* Center for Global Policy Solutions, *Stick Shift: Autonomous Vehicles, Driving Jobs, and the Future of Work* (2017), https://perma.cc/G3NQ-967D (up to 4 million jobs at risk if transition is rapid).
37. *See, e.g.*, David Autor et al., *The Work of the Future: Shaping Technology and Institutions*, MIT WORK OF THE FUTURE TASK FORCE 33–34 (2019), https://perma.cc/S62A-GPCS; Kelsey Piper, *It's 2020. Where Are Our Self-Driving Cars?*, VOX (Feb. 28, 2020), https://www.vox.com/future-perfect/2020/2/14/21063487/self-driving-cars-autonomous-vehicles-waymo-cruise-uber.
38. *See Tesla Vehicle Safety Report*, TESLA, https://www.tesla.com/VehicleSafetyReport. By comparison, the general accident average nationally is one accident per 479,000 miles driven. *Id.* On the difficulty of measuring safety, *see* Emily Stewart,

Self-Driving Cars Have to Be Safer Than Regular Cars. The Question Is How Much, Vox (May 17, 2019), https://www.vox.com/recode/2019/5/17/18564501/self-driving-car-morals-safety-tesla-waymo.

39. *See* John J. Leonard et al., *Autonomous Vehicles, Mobility, and Employment Policy: The Roads Ahead*, MIT Work of the Future Taskforce (2020), https://perma.cc/W5DJ-SAVW.
40. *See* Theo Leggett, *How Sellafield's Radiation-Proof Robots Do Our Dirty Work*, B.B.C. (Aug. 11, 2015), https://www.bbc.com/news/business-33849026; Adam Satariano, *One Job the Robots Can Have: Cleaning Nuclear Waste*, Bloomberg (Feb. 16, 2017), https://perma.cc/ZCF8-DN3P; Martin Fackler, *Six Years After Fukushima, Robots Finally Find Reactors' Melted Uranium Fuel*, N.Y. Times (Nov. 19, 2017), https://perma.cc/78BY-264H.
41. *See* Peter Holley, *Firefighters Had a Secret Weapon When Notre Dame Caught Fire: A Robot Named 'Colossus,'* Wash. Post (Apr. 17, 2019), https://perma.cc/9PAY-K3CV.
42. *See* Wired Staff, *Search and Rescue: Squad Leaders Musters Robots to US Disaster Zones*, Wired (June 06, 2009), https://www.wired.com/2009/06/st-alphageek-3/; *Small, Unmanned Aircraft Search for Survivors in Katrina Wreckage*, Nat'l Sci. Found. (Sept. 14, 2005), https://www.nsf.gov/news/news_summ.jsp?cntn_id=104453.
43. *See* Jonathan Woetzel & Scott Nyquist, *How the Natural Resources Business Is Turning into a Technology Industry*, Harv. Bus. Rev. (June 2, 2017), https://hbr.org/2017/06/how-the-natural-resources-business-is-turning-into-a-technology-industry; Liz Hampton, *In US Gulf, Robots, Drones Take on Dangerous Offshore Oil Work*, Reuters (May 3, 2018), https://www.reuters.com/article/us-world-work-oildrones/in-u-s-gulf-robots-drones-take-on-dangerous-offshore-oil-work-idUSKBN1I4100.
44. *See* Tanya M. Anandan, *Robots to Extremes*, Robotics Indus. Ass'n (Jan. 25, 2019), https://perma.cc/J2H9-SVLL.
45. Daniel Susskind, A World Without Work 81–82 (2020).
46. *See* Asha Bharadwaj & Maximiliano A. Dvorkin, *The Rise of Automation: How Robots May Impact the US Labor Market*, Fed. Res. Bank of St. Louis (2019), https://perma.cc/6KV2-ZNB9. *See also* Mary Hallward-Driemeier & Gaurav Nayyar, *Have Robots Grounded the Flying Geese? Automation and Offshoring in the Manufacturing Sector*, Brookings (Feb. 6, 2020), https://perma.cc/YT6B-AYRM.
47. Kerwin Kofi Charles et al., *The Transformation of Manufacturing and the Decline in US Employment*, 1, 16 (Nat'l Bureau of Econ. Research, Working Paper No. 24468, Mar. 2018), https://www.nber.org/papers/w24468.
48. *See generally* Daron Acemoglu & Pascual Restrepo, *Robots & Jobs: Evidence from US Labor Markets* (Nat'l Bureau of Econ. Research, Working Paper No. 23285, Mar. 2018), http://www.nber.org/papers/w23285.
49. Will Knight, *China Is Building a Robot Army of Model Workers*, MIT Tech. Rev. (Apr. 26, 2016), https://www.technologyreview.com/s/601215/china-is-building-a-robot-army-of-model-workers/.
50. Joshua Hunt, *This Company's Robots Are Making Everything—and Reshaping the World*, Bloomberg Businessweek (Oct. 18, 2017), https://perma.cc/BU8C-VWHS;

Austin Weber, *Lights-Out Automation: Fact or Fiction?*, ASSEMBLY MAG. (May 9, 2019), https://perma.cc/J9YC-E67M.

51. *See 10 Most Amazing Robots in the World*, VENTURE PACT (Nov. 11, 2016), https://perma.cc/AYZ6-YKDG.
52. Noam Scheiber, *Inside an Amazon Warehouse, Robots' Ways Rub Off on Humans*, N.Y. TIMES (July 3, 2019), https://www.nytimes.com/2019/07/03/business/economy/amazon-warehouse-labor-robots.html; Eugene Kim, *Amazon's $775 Million Deal for Robotics Company Kiva Is Starting to Look Really Smart*, BUS. INSIDER (June 15, 2016, 4:02 p.m.), https://perma.cc/S2NY-7VS5.
53. Donna Tam, *Meet Amazon's Busiest Employee—The Kiva Robot*, CNET (Nov. 30, 2014, 9:01 PM PST), https://perma.cc/FSY7-N9NB.
54. *Id.*
55. David H. Autor, *Why Are There Still So Many Jobs? The History and Future of Workplace Automation*, 29 J. ECON. PERSP. 3, 23–24 (2015).
56. Adam Satariano & Cade Metz, *A Warehouse Robot Learns to Sort Out the Tricky Stuff*, N.Y. TIMES (Jan. 29, 2020), https://www.nytimes.com/2020/01/29/technology/warehouse-robot.html.
57. *Id.*
58. *Id.*
59. Stuart Dredge, *Robear: The Bear-Shaped Nursing Robot Who'll Look After You When You Get Old*, GUARDIAN (Feb. 27, 2015), https://www.theguardian.com/technology/2015/feb/27/robear-bear-shaped-nursing-care-robot.
60. Maggie Jackson, *Would You Let a Robot Take Care of Your Mother?*, N.Y. TIMES (Dec. 13, 2019), https://www.nytimes.com/2019/12/13/opinion/robot-caregiver-aging.html.
61. Stephy Chung, *Meet Sophia: The Robot Who Laughs, Smiles, and Frowns Just Like Us*, CNN (Nov. 2, 2018), https://www.cnn.com/style/article/sophia-robot-artificial-intelligence-smart-creativity/index.html. To view Sophia's facial expressions and ability to emote in response to an interview, *see Meet Sophia—The Robot with 50 Facial Expressions*, B.B.C. (Mar. 12, 2019), https://www.bbc.com/news/av/world-africa-47544105/meet-sophia-the-robot-with-50-facial-expressions.
62. Joelle Renstrom, *Will Care-Bots Cure the Loneliness of Nursing Homes?*, DAILY BEAST (May 1, 2019), https://www.thedailybeast.com/will-care-bots-cure-the-loneliness-of-nursing-homes?ref=scroll. Not all care robots mimic humans. Paro, a robotic baby seal, is being used in over thirty countries to help comfort elderly persons, especially those with dementia. *See, e.g.*, Amy Harmon, *A Soft Spot for Circuitry*, N.Y. TIMES (July 4, 2010), https://www.nytimes.com/2010/07/05/science/05robot.html; Rowan Moore, *Hello, Robot Review—Where Human and Machine Don't Quite Meet*, GUARDIAN (Nov. 9, 2019), https://www.theguardian.com/artanddesign/2019/nov/09/hello-robot-v-and-a-dundee-review.
63. Adam Satariano et al., *Meet Zora, the Robot Caregiver*, N.Y. TIMES (Nov. 23, 2018), https://www.nytimes.com/interactive/2018/11/23/technology/robot-nurse-zora.html.
64. *See* Corinne Purtill, *Stop Me if You've Heard This One: A Robot and a Team of Irish Scientists Walk Into a Senior Living Home*, TIME (Oct. 4, 2019), https://time.com/

longform/senior-care-robot/; Gabriella Mulligan, *Is Robotics a Solution to the Growing Needs of the Elderly?*, B.B.C. (Mar. 17, 2017), https://www.bbc.com/news/business-39255244.

65. Daniel Hurst, *Japan Lays Groundwork for Boom in Robot Carers*, GUARDIAN (Feb. 5, 2018), https://www.theguardian.com/world/2018/feb/06/japan-robots-will-care-for-80-of-elderly-by-2020.
66. Jared Spataro, *2 Years of Digital Transformation in 2 Months*, MICROSOFT BLOG (Apr. 30, 2020), https://perma.cc/43ZR-8H3S (quoting CEO Satya Nadella).
67. *See, e.g.*, Carl Benedikt Frey, *Covid Will Only Increase Automation Anxiety*, FIN. TIMES (Apr. 21, 2020), https://www.ft.com/content/817228a2-82e1-11ea-b6e9-a94cffd1d9bf; David Autor & Elisabeth Reynolds, *The Nature of Work after the COVID Crisis: Too Few Low-Wage Jobs*, HAMILTON PROJECT (2020), https://perma.cc/48XB-Q5NJ; Mark Muro et al., *The Robots Are Ready as the COVID-19 Recession Spreads*, BROOKINGS (Mar. 24, 2020), https://perma.cc/F59P-RRAG; McKinsey Global Inst., Susan Lund et al., *COVID-19 and Jobs: Monitoring the US Impact on People and Places*, MCKINSEY & COMPANY (Apr. 29, 2020), https://perma.cc/N9QJ-NVVL; A recent empirical study confirmed that the automation of automatable jobs sped up during the pandemic. Lei Ding & Julieth Saenz Molina, *"Forced Automation" by COVID-19? Early Trends from Current Population Survey Data*, Discussion paper, Federal Reserve Bank of Philadelphia, Sept. 2020, https://perma.cc/KQ2N-53UR.
68. *See* Brad Hershbein & Lisa B. Kahn, *Do Recessions Accelerate Routine-Biased Technological Change? Evidence from Vacancy Postings*, 108 AM. ECON. REV. 1737, 1762–67 (2019); Nir Jaimovich & Henry E. Siu, *Job Polarization and Jobless Recoveries*, 102 REV. OF ECON. & STATS. 129 (2020).
69. Jaimovich & Siu, *supra* note 68.
70. Similar dynamics follow minimum wage increases—another kind of economic shock; *see* Chapter 3.
71. *See* Hershbein & Kahn, *supra* note 68; Jaimovich & Siu, *supra* note 68.
72. *See* Erika Hayasaki, *Covid-19 Could Accelerate the Robot Takeover of Human Jobs*, MIT TECH. REV. (June 17, 2020), https://www.technologyreview.com/2020/06/17/1003328/covid-19-could-accelerate-the-robot-takeover-of-human-jobs/.
73. *Id.*
74. *See* Rich Blake, *In Coronavirus Fight, Robots Report For Disinfection Duty*, FORBES (Apr. 17, 2020), https://perma.cc/QGE7-74Q8; Kim Bo-gyung, *Robots Deployed to Help Fight Coronavirus Contagion*, KOREA HERALD (Mar. 13, 2020), https://perma.cc/NC4R-W88K; Jason Slotkin, *Meet 'Spot:' The Robot That Could Help Doctors Remotely Treat COVID-19 Patients*, NPR (Apr. 24, 2020), https://perma.cc/5PVT-JEAU.
75. *See* Amina Khan, *Meet Humanity's New Ally in the Coronavirus Fight: Robots*, LA TIMES (Apr. 11, 2020), https://www.latimes.com/science/story/2020-04-11/overcoming-coronavirus-with-help-of-robots.
76. *See* Frey, *supra* note 67; Zoe Thomas, *Will Covid-19 Speed Up the Use of Robots to Replace Human Workers?* B.B.C. (Apr. 19, 2020), https://www.bbc.com/news/technology-52340651.

77. Emily Pandise, *Which Big Names Have Filed for Bankruptcy Since the Coronavirus Pandemic Hit? Here's the List*, NBC News (Aug. 12, 2020), https://perma.cc/L4AE-TP87.
78. Autor & Reynolds, *supra* note 67, at 3.
79. That shift was dramatic during the pandemic, of course. *See* Patti Domm, *Terrible Retail Sales Report Shows Acceleration in Fates of Struggling and Thriving Retailers*, CNBC (May 15, 2020), https://perma.cc/G745-9F88.
80. Autor & Reynolds, *supra* note 67, at 2–4.
81. *Id.* at 3.
82. *See* Carl Benedikt Frey & Michael A. Osborne, *The Future of Employment: How Susceptible Are Jobs to Computerisation?*, 114 Tech. Forecasting & Soc. Change 254 (2017); and *A Future That Works: Automation, Employment, and Productivity*, McKinsey Global Inst., 109 https://perma.cc/X9BX-9RWQ.
83. *See, e.g.*, Steven Greenhouse, *Autonomous Vehicles Could Cost America 5 Million Jobs. What Should We Do About It?*, L.A. Times (Sept. 22, 2016, 4:00 a.m.), https://perma.cc/N49P-3ZE8; Casey Newton, *Uber Will Eventually Replace All Its Drivers with Self-Driving Cars*, Verge (May 28, 2014, 3:52 PM), https://perma.cc/QN7W-CBP9.
84. Jane Wakefield, *Foxconn Replaces '60,000 Factory Workers with Robots,'* BBC News (May 25, 2016), https://perma.cc/XQ3A-6DSG; Keith Bradsher, *A Robot Revolution, This Time in China*, N.Y. Times (May 12, 2017), https://www.nytimes.com/2017/05/12/business/a-robot-revolution-this-time-in-china.html.
85. *See* William Gallagher, *How Apple Learned Automation Can't Match Human Skill*, AI (2020), https://appleinsider.com/articles/20/06/04/how-apple-learned-automation-cant-match-human-skill.
86. *See* Kai-Fu Lee, *Kai-Fu Lee on How Covid Spurs China's Great Robotic Leap Forward*, Economist (June 25, 2020), https://perma.cc/FF2A-9LFJ.
87. *See* Erik Brynjolfsson & Andrew McAfee, Race Against the Machine (2012); Erik Brynjolfsson & Andrew McAfee, The Second Machine Age (2014); Martin Ford, Rise of the Robots (2015); Jerry Kaplan, Humans Need Not Apply (2015); Andrew Stern & Lee Kravitz, Raising the Floor (2016).
88. For example, the "grey goo" scenario, in which self-replicating nano-robots rapidly consume all organic matter on Earth. *See* K. Eric Drexler, Engines of Creation (1986).
89. *See, e.g.*, Ben Miller & Robert D. Atkinson, *Are Robots Taking Our Jobs, or Making Them?*, Info. Tech. & Innovation Found. 1 (Sept. 2013), https://perma.cc/XP76-QWXF.
90. For two famous examples, *see* Karl Marx, Capital (Ben Fowkes trans., Penguin Books 1976) (1867); and John Maynard Keynes, *Economic Possibilities for our Grandchildren* (1930), *in* Essays in Persuasion (1963).
91. Autor, *Why Are There Still So Many Jobs?*, *supra* note 55, at 10. Capitalism's dynamics of "creative destruction" were named and elucidated by Joseph Schumpeter. *See* Joseph A. Schumpeter, Capitalism, Socialism and Democracy 81–86 (3d ed. 1975).

92. A 2014 survey of economists found that 52 percent believed that technological advancement would not destroy more jobs than are created by 2025. Aaron Smith & Janna Anderson, *AI, Robotics, and the Future of Jobs*, PEW RESEARCH CTR. 5 (Aug. 6, 2014), https://perma.cc/PG4R-LHYK. A 2017 survey found that 78 percent of economists agreed that growing automation was "likely to create benefits large enough that they could be used to compensate those workers who are substantially negatively affected for their lost wages." *Robots and Artificial Intelligence*, IGM FORUM, CHI. BOOTH (Sept. 12, 2017), http://www.igmchicago.org/surveys/robots-and-artificial-intelligence-2/. Of course that begs the question whether they will be used to that end.
93. *See* Richard B. Freeman, *Who Owns the Robots Rules the World*, IZA WORLD LAB. 1, 9 (2015), https://perma.cc/V8R9-7PRX; Laura Tyson & Michael Spence, *Exploring the Effects of Technology on Income and Wealth Inequality*, *in* AFTER PIKETTY: THE AGENDA FOR ECONOMICS AND INEQUALITY 170 (Heather Boushey et al. eds., 2017); *see also* TYLER COWEN, AVERAGE IS OVER: POWERING AMERICA BEYOND THE AGE OF THE GREAT STAGNATION (2013).
94. Autor, Mindell & Reynolds, *supra* note 37, at 25–26.
95. Richard B. Freeman, *Ownership When AI Robots do More of the Work and Earn More of the Income*, 1 J. PARTICIPATION & EMP. OWNERSHIP 74, 79–80 (2018).
96. Freeman, *Who Owns the Robots*, *supra* note 93, at 4.
97. Daron Acemoglu et al., *Taxes, Automation, and the Future of Labor*, MIT WORK OF THE FUTURE TASK FORCE, 7 (2020), https://perma.cc/2YZX-WUTJ (citing Daron Acemoglu & Pascual Restrepo, "The Labor Share, Displacement and Wage Inequality," Mimeo, MIT (2020)).
98. *See* Randall Collins, *The End of Middle-Class Work: No More Escapes*, *in* IMMANUEL WALLERSTEIN ET AL., DOES CAPITALISM HAVE A FUTURE? (2013).
99. JOSEPH FISHKIN & WILLIAM FORBATH, THE ANTI-OLIGARCHY CONSTITUTION (forthcoming 2021).
100. David Autor, *The Faltering Escalator of Urban Opportunity*, MIT WORK OF THE FUTURE TASK FORCE 15–17 (2020), https://perma.cc/THM5-RAP8
101. Not all agree. Economists at the Economic Policy Institute argue that automation is a distraction, and that wage stagnation stems from globalization of trade and finance, declining union strength, and lagging enforcement of labor standards. Lawrence Mishel & Josh Bivens, *The Zombie Robot Argument Lurches On: There Is No Evidence That Automation Leads to Joblessness or Inequality*, ECON. POL'Y INST. (May 24, 2017), https://perma.cc/N6N5-DECE; John Schmitt et al., *Don't Blame the Robots: Assessing the Job Polarization Explanation of Growing Wage Inequality*, ECON. POL'Y INST. (Nov. 19, 2013), https://perma.cc/N5DV-MPRD.
102. *See, e.g.*, NICK SRNICEK & ALEX WILLIAMS, INVENTING THE FUTURE: POSTCAPITALISM AND A WORLD WITHOUT WORK 107–18 (2015).
103. H. W. Arthurs, *The New Economy and the New Legality: Industrial Citizenship and the Future of Labour Arbitration*, 7 CANADIAN LAB. & EMP. L.J. 45, 46 (1999); *see also* H. W. Arthurs, *Developing Industrial Citizenship: A Challenge for Canada's Second Century*, 45 CANADIAN B. REV. 786 (1967).

104. *See* David Charny, *The Employee Welfare State in Transition*, 74 TEX. L. REV. 1601, 1601 (1996); Katherine V. W. Stone, *A Fatal Mismatch: Employer-Centric Benefits in a Boundaryless World*, 11 LEWIS & CLARK L. REV. 451 (2007).
105. Elise Gould & Hilary Wething, *US Poverty Rates Higher, Safety Net Weaker Than in Peer Countries*, ECON. POL'Y INST., Issue Brief No. 339, 5–7 (2012), https://perma.cc/9C4K-Q6D8. "Social spending" in the United States is lower than the average of OECD countries (as a percentage of GDP), and much lower than in comparably rich developed countries in Western Europe. *See Social Spending*, OECD, https://perma.cc/HT68-Q439.
106. *See generally* CYNTHIA ESTLUND, WORKING TOGETHER: HOW WORKPLACE BONDS STRENGTHEN A DIVERSE DEMOCRACY (2003).
107. *E.g.*, Srnicek & Williams, *supra* note 102.
108. JEREMIAS PRASSL, HUMANS AS A SERVICE: THE PROMISE AND PERILS OF WORK IN THE GIG ECONOMY 55–58 (2018); Jeremias Adams-Prassl, *What if Your Boss Was an Algorithm? The Rise of Artificial Intelligence at Work* 41 COMP. LAB. L. & POL. J. 123 (2019), available at SSRN: https://ssrn.com/abstract=3661151.
109. IFEOMA AJUNWA, THE QUANTIFIED WORKER: LAW AND TECHNOLOGY IN THE MODERN WORKPLACE (forthcoming 2021).
110. *See* BRISHEN ROGERS, DATA AND DEMOCRACY AT WORK (forthcoming 2021); Brishen Rogers, *The Law and Political Economy of Workplace Technological Change*, 55 HARV. CIV. RIGHTS-CIV. LIBERTIES L. REV 531 (2020).
111. Valerio De Stefano, *'Master and Servers': Collective Labour Rights and Private Government in the Contemporary World of Work*, 36 INT'L J. OF COMP. LAB. L. & IND. REL. (2020), available at SSRN: https://ssrn.com/abstract=3675082.
112. Pegah Moradi & Karen Levy, *The Future of Work in the Age of AI: Displacement or Risk-Shifting?*, *in* OXFORD HANDBOOK OF ETHICS OF AI 271 (Markus Dubber et al., eds., 2020).
113. ROGERS, *supra* note 110.

Chapter 2

1. *See* ROBERT J. GORDON, THE RISE AND FALL OF AMERICAN GROWTH: THE U.S. STANDARD OF LIVING SINCE THE CIVIL WAR 595 (2016).
2. *Id.* at 62–93.
3. *Id.* at 94–95.
4. *Id.* at 566–604.
5. *See generally* THOMAS PIKETTY, CAPITAL IN THE TWENTY-FIRST CENTURY (Arthur Goldhammer trans., 2014).
6. *See* Emmanuel Saez, *Striking It Richer: The Evolution of Top Incomes in the United States* 10 (Feb. 2020), https://eml.berkeley.edu/~saez/saez-UStopincomes-2018.pdf.

7. Since 1978, CEO compensation has grown close to 1,000 percent since 1978, while a typical worker's pay has grown just 12 percent. Lawrence Mishel & Julia Wolfe, *CEO Compensation Has Grown 940% Since 1978*, Econ. Pol'y Inst. (Aug. 14, 2019), https://www.epi.org/publication/ceo-compensation-2018/.
8. *See* David Autor et al., *The Fall of the Labor Share and the Rise of Superstar Firms*, 135 Q. J. Econ 645 (2020), https://doi.org/10.1093/qje/qjaa004; Robert H. Frank & Philip J. Cook, The Winner-Take-All Society (1995).
9. The Editorial Board, *No, Robots Aren't Killing the American Dream*, N.Y. Times (Feb. 20, 2017), https://perma.cc/J36Y-ZGWN. The editorial cites data from the Economic Policy Institute; *see also* Lawrence Mishel & Josh Bivens, *The Zombie Robot Argument Lurches On: There Is No Evidence that Automation Leads to Joblessness or Inequality*, Econ. Pol'y Inst. (May 24, 2017), https://www.epi.org/publication/the-zombie-robot-argument-lurches-on-there-is-no-evidence-that-automation-leads-to-joblessness-or-inequality/.
10. Larry Summers, Former Dir., Nat'l Econ. Council, Remarks at the Brookings Institute's "Future of Work" Panel (Feb. 19, 2015) (partial transcript available at https://perma.cc/JN97-QS43).
11. *See* David Autor et al., *The Work of the Future: Shaping Technology and Institutions*, MIT Work of the Future Task Force 25–26 (2019) [hereinafter MIT Work of the Future 2019], https://workofthefuture.mit.edu/research-post/the-work-of-the-future-shaping-technology-and-institutions/ (discussing Daron Acemoglu & Pascual Restrepo, *Automation and New Tasks: How Technology Displaces and Reinstates Labor*, 33 J. Econ. Persp. 3 (2019)).
12. Erik Brynjolfsson et al., *The Productivity J-Curve: How Intangibles Complement General Purpose Technologies* (NBER, Working Paper No. 25148, Oct. 2018), https://www.nber.org/papers/w25148.
13. Tyler Cowen, *In a Robot Economy, All Humans Will Be Marketers*, Bloomberg View (July 26, 2017, 1:16 p.m.), https://perma.cc/Q9G5-KPJV.
14. *Id.*
15. David H. Autor, *Why Are There Still So Many Jobs? The History and Future of Workplace Automation*, 29 J. Econ. Persp. 3, 6–7 (2015) (citing James Bessen, Learning by Doing 107 (2015)). Parenthetically, bank teller employment did decline as a share of U.S. employment; Autor, *Why Are There Still so Many Jobs?*; and it was also boosted by a legal change that allowed banks to set up branches across state lines. Calum Chace, *"A World Without Work" by Daniel Susskind, A Book Review*, Forbes (Jan. 30, 2020), https://www.forbes.com/sites/cognitiveworld/2020/01/30/a-world-without-work-by-daniel-susskind-a-book-review - 4550fe96dd71.
16. Autor, *supra* note 15, at 7.
17. Cowen, *supra* note 13.
18. Binyamin Appelbaum, *Lack of Workers, Not Work, Weighs on the Nation's Economy*, N.Y. Times (May 21, 2017), https://www.nytimes.com/2017/05/21/us/politics/utah-economy-jobs.html.
19. *See* Gordon, *supra* note 1, at 250–53.

20. *The Long-Term Decline in Prime-Age Male Labor Force Participation*, White House Council Econ. Advisers 7 (June 2016), https://perma.cc/AZ76-5E95.
21. *Id.* at 2.
22. *See* Sandra E. Black et al., *The Recent Decline in Women's Labor Force Participation*, Brookings (Oct. 2017), https://perma.cc/4YTT-8M38.
23. *See* Audrey Breitwieser et al., *The Recent Rebound in Prime-Age Labor Force Participation*, Brookings (Aug. 2, 2018), https://www.brookings.edu/blog/up-front/2018/08/02/the-recent-rebound-in-prime-age-labor-force-participation/.
24. Marginally attached workers are neither working nor actively seeking work but who say they want and are available for a job and have looked for one within the past twelve months. US Bureau of Labor Statistics, Alternatives Measures of Labor Underutilization (2020), https://www.bls.gov/news.release/empsit.t15.htm.
25. *Id.*
26. US Bureau of Labor Statistics, Concepts and Definitions: Civilian Noninstitutional Population, https://www.bls.gov/cps/definitions.htm#population.
27. On total incarceration numbers, *see* Wendy Sawyer & Peter Wagner, Prison Pol'y Initiative, Mass Incarceration: The Whole Pie 2020 (Mar. 24, 2020), https://www.prisonpolicy.org/reports/pie2020.html. On the higher incarceration rate for young Black men, *see* The Urban Inst., A Matter of Time: The Cause and Consequences of Rising Time Served in America's Prisons 13 (July 2017), https://apps.urban.org/features/long-prison-terms/a_matter_of_time_print_version.pdf. On higher unemployment for that group, *see* US Bureau of Labor Statistics, Labor Force Statistics from the Current Population Survey: Unemployment Rates by Age, Sex, Race, and Hispanic or Latino Ethnicity, https://www.bls.gov/web/empsit/cpsee_e16.htm.
28. *See* Lucius Couloute & Daniel Kopf, Prison Pol'y Initiative, Out of Prison & Out of Work: Unemployment Among Formerly Incarcerated People (July 2018), https://www.prisonpolicy.org/reports/outofwork.html; Adam Looney & Nicholas Turner, The Brookings Inst., Work and Opportunity Before and After Incarceration 1 (Mar. 2018), https://www.brookings.edu/wp-content/uploads/2018/03/es_20180314_looneyincarceration_final.pdf.
29. On growing inequality since the 1970s, *see* Emmanuel Saez & Gabriel Zucman, *Wealth Inequality in the United States Since 1913: Evidence from Capitalized Income Tax Data*, 131 Q.J. Econ. 519, 520 (2016). On the rise of mass incarceration, *see* American Civil Liberties Union, Overcrowding and Overuse of Imprisonment in the United States: Submission to the Office of the High Commissioner for Human Rights 1 (2015), https://www.ohchr.org/Documents/Issues/RuleOfLaw/OverIncarceration/ACLU.pdf.
30. Some argue that incarceration "is used to regulate excess black unemployment." Robynn J. A. Cox, Economic Policy Institute, Where do we Go from Here? Mass Incarceration and the Struggle for Civil Rights 11 (Jan. 16, 2015), https://files.epi.org/2014/MassIncarceration Report.pdf.

31. Gordon, *supra* note 1, at 258–59. The decline before World War II mainly reflects the shorter work week and the advent of vacations; after World War II it reflects partly the entry of women into the workforce and the rise of part-time jobs. *Id.* at 259–60.
32. U.S. Bureau of Labor Statistics, U.S. Dep't of Labor, *The Employment Situation—February 2020* (Mar. 6, 2020), https://www.bls.gov/news.release/archives/empsit_03062020.htm.
33. *Compare, e.g.*, Carl Benedikt Frey & Michael A. Osborne, *The Future of Employment: How Susceptible Are Jobs to Computerisation?* 44 (Oxford Martin Sch., Working Paper, 2013), https://www .oxfordmartin.ox.ac.uk/downloads/academic/The_Future_of_Employment.pdf (finding nearly half of all jobs are at "high risk" of automation), *with* Melanie Arntz et al., *The Risk of Automation for Jobs in OECD Countries: A Comparative Analysis* 4 (OECD Soc., Emp. & Migration Working Papers No. 189, 2016), https://perma.cc/ZJU7-UGUD] (estimating that 9 percent of jobs in OECD countries are at risk). Differences depend partly on whether researchers focused on automatable tasks, automatable jobs (which include automatable and non-automatable tasks), or even automatable occupations.
34. McKinsey Global Inst., *A Future That Works: Automation, Employment, and Productivity*, 109 [hereinafter MGI, *A Future That Works*], https://perma.cc/X9BX-9RWQ. The MGI's headline estimate of automatability is virtually identical to the oft-cited Frey & Osborne study out of Oxford University, *supra* note 33. But I rely on the MGI study because it breaks down the data in especially useful ways, and because MGI followed up with a companion study of job creation, *see infra*, note 54.
35. MGI, *A Future That Works* at 35 exhibit 3.
36. *Id.* at 29, 35 exhibit 3, 72.
37. *Id.* at 6 exhibit E3, 7 exhibit E4.
38. *Id.* at 42 & exhibit 8.
39. *Id.*
40. *Id.* at 44 exhibit 9.
41. *Id.*
42. *Id.* at 5 exhibit E2.
43. *See generally* Mark Muro et al., *What Jobs Are Affected by AI?*, Brookings (Nov. 2019), https://www.brookings.edu/research/what-jobs-are-affected-by-ai-better-paid-better-educated-workers-face-the-most-exposure/.
44. *Id.* at 32. That estimate is nearly identical to that of the widely cited Oxford study; *see* Frey & Osborne, *supra* note 33, at 38, which estimated 47 percent automatability.
45. Autor, *supra* note 15, at 27.
46. *See* Callan Wienburg, *How to Stop Customer Service Automation from Annoying Your Customers*, Soliditech (May 13, 2016), https://perma.cc/P2TL-HRRV.
47. MGI, *A Future That Works*, *supra* note 34, at 114–15.
48. Steven Begley et al., *Automation in Retail: An Executive Overview for Getting Ready*, McKinsey & Company (May 2019), www.mckinsey.com/industries/retail/our-insights/automation-in-retail-an-executive-overview-for-getting-ready?referringSource=articleShare.

49. MGI, *A Future That Works*, *supra* note 34, at 10, 12, 40, 31, 53, 76–77, 80, 83, 95–96.
50. *Id.* at 67–70.
51. *Id.* at 7 exhibit E4, 68.
52. *Id.* at 109–16. *See also* Jason Furman, Address at New York University: *Is This Time Different? The Opportunities and Challenges of Artificial Intelligence* 4 (July 7, 2016), https://perma.cc/VT7V-WQ8X; Matthew Yglesias, *The Automation Myth*, Vox (July 27, 2015, 7:00 a.m.), http://www.vox.com/2015/7/27/9038829/automation-myth; http://perma.cc/Y7R6-BWTR.
53. *See* MGI, *A Future That Works*, *supra* note 34, at 90. Indeed, it is "vital that there be new demand for labor displaced by automation." *Id.* On automation's expected contribution to growth, *see id.* at 87–101.
54. McKinsey Global Institute, *Jobs Lost, Jobs Gained: Workforce Transitions in an Age of Automation*, https://www.mckinsey.com/featured-insights/future-of-work/jobs-lost-jobs-gained-what-the-future-of-work-will-mean-for-jobs-skills-and-wages#.
55. *Id.* at 7 (estimating 20–50 million new jobs in developing and deploying new technology by 2030). *Cf.* Daron Acemoglu & Pascual Restrepo, *Artificial Intelligence, Automation and Work* 10 (NBER, Working Paper No. 24196, 2018)[hereinafter, Acemoglu & Restrepo, *Artificial Intelligence*], https://www.nber.org/papers/w24196;
56. *See* Acemoglu & Restrepo, *Artificial Intelligence*, *supra* note 55, at 10.
57. MGI, *Jobs Lost, Jobs Gained*, *supra* note 54, at 70.
58. *Does the Past Predict the Future?*, Economist (Sept. 23, 2009) https://www.economist.com/free-exchange/2009/09/23/does-the-past-predict-the-future.
59. *See* Erik Sherman, *Automation Won't Create New Jobs Like Technology Did in the Past*, Forbes (Dec. 17, 2016), https://perma.cc/4R3M-RNZF.
60. MGI, *Jobs Lost, Jobs Gained*, *supra* note 54, at 14.
61. *Id.* at 6–8.
62. *Id.* at 102.
63. *Id.* at 6–8, 11.
64. The MGI researchers acknowledge the point. *See id.* at 65–85.
65. *Id.* at 6, 58.
66. The point is acknowledged in the MGI report at 87–88. *See* Josh Bivens & Lawrence Mishel, *Understanding the Historic Divergence Between Productivity and a Typical Worker's Pay*, Econ. Pol'y Inst. (Sept. 2, 2015), https://www.epi.org/publication/understanding-the-historic-divergence-between-productivity-and-a-typical-workers-pay-why-it-matters-and-why-its-real/. *See also* Richard B. Freeman, *Who Owns the Robots Rules the World*, IZA World Lab. 1, 4–7 (2015), https://wol.iza.org/uploads/articles/5/pdfs/who-owns-the-robots-rules-the-world.pdf.
67. *See* Acemoglu & Restrepo, *Artificial Intelligence*, *supra* note 55, at 33; *see also* Josh Zumbrun, *How Rich and Poor Spend (and Earn) Their Money*, Wall St. J. (Apr. 6, 2015, 12:38 p.m.), https://blogs.wsj.com/economics/2015/04/06/how-the-rich-and-poor-spend-and-earn-their-money.
68. *See* Daniel Susskind, A World Without Work 115–19 (2020) [hereinafter D. Susskind].

69. *See* Joanne Kimberlin, *"Full-Closet Effect" Puts Damper on Consumer Spending, Retail Consultant Says*, Knight-Ridder/Tribune Business News, Feb. 10, 2002, https://www.highbeam.com/doc/1G1-82735497.html.
70. *See* D. Susskind, *supra* note 68, at 29–44.
71. *Id.* at 27.
72. *Id.* at 35.
73. David Autor et al., *The Skill Content of Recent Technological Change: An Empirical Exploration*, 118 Q.J. Econ. 129 (2003); David Autor, *The Polarization of Job Opportunities in the U.S. Labor Market: Implications for Employment and Earning*, Hamilton Project & Ctr. for Am. Progress 4, 12 (Apr. 2010), https://economics.mit.edu/files/5554.
74. David Autor, *Polanyi's Paradox and the Shape of Employment Growth*, 7, 11 (NBER Working Paper No. 20485, 2014), https://www.nber.org/papers/w20485.pdf.
75. *See, e.g.*, MGI, *A Future That Works*, *supra* note 34; Int'l Monetary Fund, World Economic Outlook: Gaining Momentum? (2017); World Bank Group, World Development Report 2016: Digital Dividends 20–23, 120–28 (2016); Maarten Goos et al., *Explaining Job Polarization in Europe: The Roles of Technology, Globalization and Institutions* (Ctr. For Econ. Performance, CEP Discussion Paper No 1026, 2010), http://cep.lse.ac.uk/pubs/download/dp1026.pdf.
76. Acemoglu & Restrepo, *Artificial Intelligence, supra* note 55, at 6, 11. Another recent study found that investments in robots are associated with localized net job losses. Daron Acemoglu & Pascual Restrepo, *Robots and Jobs: Evidence from US Labor Markets* (Mar. 17, 2017), https://perma.cc/5A9C-8FU4.
77. Daron Acemoglu & Pascual Restrepo, *Automation and New Tasks: How Technology Displaces and Reinstates Labor*, 33 J. Econ. Persp. 3, 4 (2019).
78. *Id.* at 6.
79. *Id.* at 5–6.
80. MIT Work of the Future 2019, *supra* note 11, at 14 (citing Daron Acemoglu & David H. Autor, *Skills, Tasks and Technologies: Implications for Employment and Earnings*, *in* 4B Handbook of Labor Economics 1043 (Orley Ashenfelter & David Card eds., 2011)).
81. MIT Work of the Future 2019, *supra* note 11, at 22, 26.
82. *Id.* at 10.
83. *Id.* at 17.
84. *See generally* Lynda Gratton & Andrew Scott, The 100 Year Life (2016); Anne Alstott, *Law and the Hundred-Year Life*, 26 Elder L.J. 131 (2016)
85. For some illustrative scenarios, *see* Gratton & Scott, *supra* note 84, at 39–66. Our system of retirement security is already teetering, partly because people are living nearly twenty years longer than the 1930s when the Social Security Act was enacted. *See* Katherine Newman, Downhill from Here: Retirement Insecurity in the Age of Inequality (2019). On longer life expectancies, *see* Lauren Medina et al., *Living Longer: Historical and Projected Life Expectancy in the United States,*

1960 to 2060 (US Census, Current Population Rep. P25-1145, Feb. 2020), https://perma.cc/254P-7XLK.

86. Specifically, systems that promise *defined benefits* (like Social Security and many public sector pension plans) will need higher contribution levels, lower benefits, higher retirement ages, or perhaps all three. *Defined contribution* plans, which now dominate in the private sector, will require higher annual contributions by individuals and their employers, more years of contributions, or both to fund a decent retirement income.
87. *See* Leng Leng Thang, *Populating Aging, Older Workers, and Productivity Issues: The Case of Singapore*, 27 J. Comp. Soc. Welfare 17, 26–30 (2011); Shekhar Aiyar et al., *The Impact of Workforce Aging on European Productivity* 16–18 (IMF Working Paper 16/238, 2016).
88. *Attitudes About Aging: A Global Perspective*, Pew Res. Ctr. 22–32 (Jan. 2014), https://perma.cc/4YTE-RM49.
89. David Autor & Elizabeth Reynolds, *The Nature of Work After the COVID Crisis: Too Few Low Wage Jobs*, 2, Brookings (July 16, 2020), https://www.brookings.edu/research/the-nature-of-work-after-the-covid-crisis-too-few-low-wage-jobs/.
90. *See generally id.*
91. *See* David Autor, *Polanyi's Paradox and the Shape of Employment Growth*, *supra* note 74, https://economics.mit.edu/files/9835.
92. D. Susskind, *supra* note 68, at 44.
93. *Id.* at 53 (citing David Silver et al., *Mastering the Game of Go Without Human Knowledge*, 550 Nature 354 (2017)).
94. *Id.* at 45–59.
95. *Id.* at 78–79.
96. *Id.* at 5.
97. *Id.* at 3.
98. *See* Erik Brynjolfsson & Andrew McAfee, Race Against the Machine (2012).
99. *See* Robert Frank & Philip J. Cook, The Winner-Take-All Society (1996).
100. *See* Autor & Reynolds, *supra* note 89, at 4.
101. *See* Binyamin Appelbaum & Damon Winter, *One Job is Better Than Two*, N.Y. Times (Sept. 1, 2019), https://www.nytimes.com/2019/09/01/opinion/working-two-jobs.html. Current Population Survey (CPS) data show that the rate of multiple job holding has declined in the past two decades. US Dep't of Labor, *4.9 Percent of Workers Held More than One Job at the Same Time in 2017*, Bureau Lab. Stat: Econ. Daily (Jul. 19, 2018), https://www.bls.gov/opub/ted/2018/4-point-9-percent-of-workers-held-more-than-one-job-at-the-same-time-in-2017.htm. But those data exclude some self-employment, *see* Lawrence F. Katz & Alan B. Krueger, *Understanding Trends in Alternative Work Arrangements in the United States*, 15 (NBER Working Paper No. 25425, Jan. 2019), https://www.nber.org/papers/w25425, and informal work. *See* Katharine G. Abraham & Ashley Amaya, *Probing*

for Informal Work Activity (NBER, Working Paper No. 24880, Aug. 2018), https://www.nber.org/papers/w24880.

102. Jamie K. McCallum, Worked Over (2020).
103. The market-backed injunction to be entrepreneurial about one's own life and career is, for some critics, a signal feature of neoliberalism. *See* Wendy Brown, Undoing the Demos: Neoliberalism's Stealth Revolution 22 (2015).
104. Daniel Markovits, The Meritocracy Trap (2019).
105. Angus Deaton & Anne Case, Deaths of Despair and the Future of Capitalism (2020).
106. MIT Work of the Future 2019, *supra* note 11, at 36–40; MGI, *A Future that Works*, *supra* note 34, at 18–19, 113–16; MGI, *Jobs Lost, Jobs Gained*, *supra* note 544, at 77–90, 106–14, 123–28; Mark Muro et al., *Automation & Artificial Intelligence: How Machines are Affecting People and Places*, Brookings (Jan. 2019), available at https://www.brookings.edu/research/automation-and-artificial-intelligence-how-machines-affect-people-and-places/.
107. *See* Rucker C. Johnson & Robert F. Schoeni, *The Influence of Early-Life Events on Human Capital, Health Status, and Labor Market Outcomes Over the Life Course*, 11 B.E.J. Econ. Analysis & Pol'y 2521 (2011). For one thing, parents with limited resources cannot borrow against their child's future earnings to finance crucial investments in their future earning capacity. *See* Flavio Cunha & James Heckman, *The Technology of Skill Formation*, 97 Am. Econ. Rev. 31 (2007). Nor do we want them to be able to do so.
108. D. Susskind, *supra* note 68, at 5.
109. My terminology here unintentionally echoes Peter Frase, Four Futures: Life After Capitalism (2016). But his futures are more starkly futuristic than those sketched here.
110. *See* Gordon, *supra* note 1, at 593–604; Autor, *supra* note 15, at 9–14; *Robots Won't Take Your Job—They'll Help Make Room for Meaningful Work Instead*, Quartz (Mar. 15, 2017), https://perma.cc/V792-5D23.
111. *See* MGI, Jobs Lost, Jobs Gained, *supra* note 54, at 14.
112. *See generally* Frase, *supra* note 109 (offering a speculative portrait of what this future might entail).
113. For an early articulation of the tension between sustainability and economic growth, *see* Donella H. Meadows et al., The Limits to Growth (1972). For a recent overview and intervention, *see* Jeroen C. J. M. van den Bergh, *A Third Option for Climate Policy within Potential Limits to Growth*, Nature Climate Change (Feb. 1, 2017), https://www.nature.com/articles/nclimate3113.pdf.
114. Tony Judt, Ill Fares The Land 75 (2010). *See also* Peter Baldwin, The Politics of Social Solidarity 1875–1975 (1990); Gøsta Esping-Andersen: The Three Worlds of Welfare Capitalism (1990). Others have found lessons in European social democracy for the United States. *See, e.g.*, Lessons From Europe? (R. Daniel Kelemen ed., 2015); Lane Kenworthy, Social Democratic America (2015); Stephen Hill, Europe's Promise (2010).

Chapter 3

1. *E.g.*, Chad Stone et al., *A Guide to Statistics on Historical Trends in Income Inequality*, Ctr. on Budget & Pol'y Priorities (Jan. 13, 2020), https://www.cbpp.org/research/poverty-and-inequality/a-guide-to-statistics-on-historical-trends-in-income-inequality. *See generally* Thomas Piketty, Capital In The Twenty-First Century (Arthur Goldhammer trans., 2014); Joseph E. Stiglitz, The Price of Inequality (2012).
2. *See* David Weil, The Fissured Workplace (2017).
3. *See generally* Irving Bernstein, The Turbulent Years: A History of the American Worker, 1933–1940 (Haymarket Books 2010) (1970); William E. Forbath, Law and the Shaping of the American Labor Movement 59–97 (1991).
4. That is embodied in the Charter of the International Labor Organization (ILO), founded in 1919, and the ILO's 1998 *Declaration on Fundamental Principles and Rights at Work*. *See infra*, note 13, at xx.
5. On the economic, social, and legal changes transforming the world of work since the mid-1950s, *see generally* Katherine V.W. Stone, From Widgets to Digits: Employment Regulation for the Changing Workplace (2004); Paul C. Weiler, Governing the Workplace: The Future of Labor and Employment Law (1990).
6. US Dep't of Labor, Bureau of Labor Statistics, *Union Members Summary: Union Members 2019* (Jan. 22, 2020), https://www.bls.gov/news.release/union2.nr0.htm.
7. On the decline of collective bargaining and the rise of employment law, *see* Cynthia Estlund: Regoverning the Workplace: From Self-Regulation to Co-Regulation 52–74 (2010).
8. On the comparative point, *see* Mariya Aleksynska & Friederike Eberlein, *Coverage of Employment Protection Legislation*, ILO 5 (2016), https://perma.cc/KBP3-WLJD. For a philosophical take on at-will employment, *see* Elizabeth Anderson, Private Government: How Employers Rule Our Lives (and Why We Don't Talk About It) (2017).
9. Cynthia Estlund, *Wrongful Discharge Protections in an At-Will World*, 74 Tex. L. Rev. 1655 (1996).
10. Discussed further, *infra* notes 75–83, this chapter.
11. *See* Jonathan Timm, *Why Fair Scheduling Could Be Labor's Next Big Fight*, In These Times (Nov. 25, 2016), https://perma.cc/6VFV-XHJ6.
12. Though courts sometimes undercut those rights or enable employers to do so, as they have done in sanctioning mandatory arbitration agreements, imposed as a condition of employment, to foreclose litigation. *See* Cynthia Estlund, *The Black Hole of Mandatory Arbitration*, 96 N.C. L. Rev. 679 (2018).
13. See Int'l Labour Org. [ILO], *Declaration on Fundamental Principles and Rights at Work and its Follow-up*, Annex, Part II, § B (June 18, 1998, rev. June 15, 2010).
14. Those core labor standards are reflected, albeit with controversial gaps and flaws, in the 13th Amendment of the US Constitution, the NLRA, and other federal

statutes. As for gaps and flaws, *see* LANCE COMPA, HUMAN RIGHTS WATCH, UNFAIR ADVANTAGE: WORKERS' FREEDOM OF ASSOCIATION IN THE UNITED STATES UNDER INTERNATIONAL HUMAN RIGHTS STANDARDS (2002).

15. Those matters are left by the ILO to national judgments whether or not workers have a meaningful voice in those national judgments. *See* Philip Alston, *"Core Labour Standards" and the Transformation of the International Labour Rights Regime*, 15 EUR. J. INT'L L. 457, 488–90, 498 (2004).
16. In principle, private ordering takes place only above that legislated floor; but in practice, given weak enforcement and even pockets of informal employment, private ordering sometimes corrodes and undermines that floor.
17. *See* Katherine V.W. Stone, *A Fatal Mismatch: Employer-Centric Benefits in a Boundaryless World*, 11 LEWIS & CLARK L. REV. 451, 454–60 (2007). That stemmed partly from wartime wage controls in the 1940s, which steered collective bargaining into benefits, and partly from the so-called "Treaty of Detroit" between the United Auto Workers and General Motors in 1950. *See* NELSON LICHTENSTEIN, WALTER REUTHER: THE MOST DANGEROUS MAN IN DETROIT (1995).
18. *See* Peter Cappelli, *Changing Career Paths and their Implications*, *in* AMERICA AT WORK: CHOICES AND CHALLENGES 211, 212–14 (Edward E. Lawler & James O'Toole eds. 2006).
19. *See generally* WEIL, *supra* note 2. For a concise summary, *see* Heather Boushey, *Equitable Growth in Conversation: In Conversation with David Weil* (June 22, 2017), https://equitablegrowth.org/equitable-growth-in-conversation-david-weil/.
20. *See* Bruce Goldstein et al., *Enforcing Fair Labor Standards in the Modern American Sweatshop/Rediscovering the Statutory Definition of Employment*, 46 UCLA L. REV. 983 (1999); Matthew W. Finkin, *Beclouded Work, Beclouded Workers in Historical Perspective*, 37 COMP. LAB. L. & POL'Y J. 603 (2016).
21. *See* David Weil, *Income Inequality, Wage Determination, and the Fissured Workplace*, *in* AFTER PIKETTY: THE AGENDA FOR ECONOMICS AND INEQUALITY, 209, 224–27 (Heather Boushey, J. Bradford DeLong, & Marshall Steinbaum eds., 2017).
22. Lawrence Mishel & Jori Kandra, *CEO Compensation Surged 14% in 2019 to $21.3 Million*, ECON. POL'Y INST. (Aug. 18, 2020), https://perma.cc/QE8J-8XQ5.
23. Erling Barth et al., *It's Where You Work: Increases in Earnings Dispersion Across Establishments and Individuals in the U.S* (NBER Working Paper No. 20447, 2014), https://www.nber.org/papers/w20447; David Autor et al., *The Fall of the Labor Share and the Rise of Superstar Firms*, 135 Q. J. ECON. (forthcoming 2020), https://economics.mit.edu/files/12979. *See also* DANIEL SUSSKIND, A WORLD WITHOUT WORK 119 (2020) [hereinafter D. SUSSKIND].
24. *See Made in China?*, ECONOMIST (Mar. 12, 2015), https://perma.cc/FAW9-PQUK.
25. *India Tops 2016 Outsourcing Index*, HINDU BUS. LINE (Jan. 12, 2016), https://perma.cc/3TE5-LBWH.
26. *Amazon Mechanical Turk*. https://www.mturk.com.
27. The Bureau of Labor Statistics (BLS) found that self-employment actually declined from 7.4 percent in February 2005 to 6.9 percent in May 2017. See BLS, *Contingent and Alternative Employment Arrangements—May 2017*, US Dep't of Lab. 6 (June 7,

2018), https://perma.cc/7HK8-93US. Other studies have found modest increases. *See, e.g.*, Lawrence F. Katz & Alan B. Krueger, *Understanding Trends in Alternative Work Arrangements in the United States*, 10 (Nat'l Bureau of Econ. Research, Working Paper No. 25425, Jan. 2019), https://perma.cc/CSS8-ECGQ; Katherine Lim et al., *Independent Contractors in the US: New Trends from 15 Years of Administrative Tax Data* 2 (July 2019), https://perma.cc/QEY7-SERB; Lawrence Mishel, *Social Security Data Confirm Same Old Pattern*, ECON. POL'Y INST. 11 (June 28, 2018), https://perma.cc/SMB7-KNVY.

28. McKinsey Global Inst., *Independent Work: Choice, Necessity, and the Gig Economy*, MCKINSEY & COMPANY 26 (2016) [hereinafter MGI, *Study on Independent Work*] viii–ix, https://perma.cc/RE86-CFZ6.
29. One study found that most who engaged in "independent work" said they did so by choice, either for their primary income (30 percent) or for supplemental income (40 percent); others did so out of necessity, either as their primary income after failing to secure a "traditional job" (14 percent), or for needed supplemental income (16 percent). *Id.* at 7. For a sanguine view of a future of independent workers, see ARUN SUNDARARAJAN, THE SHARING ECONOMY (2016).
30. On the United States, *see generally* STONE, *supra* note 5; WEIL, *supra* note 2; Katherine V.W. Stone, *The New Psychological Contract: Implications of the Changing Workplace for Labor and Employment Law*, 48 UCLA L. REV. 519 (2001). On the rise of non-standard employment in the industrialized world, *see* ILO, NON-STANDARD EMPLOYMENT AROUND THE WORLD 47–110 (2016); Günther Schmid & Johannes Wagner, *Managing Social Risks of Non-Standard Employment in Europe*, ILO (Feb 20–21, 2018), https://perma.cc/B3H9-RMAX.
31. *See* WEIL, THE FISSURED WORKPLACE, *supra* note 2, at 54–58, 60–63, 167–74.
32. *See id.* at 60–63, 171–74.
33. On the transformative impact of container ships and bar codes on global supply chains, *see* Witold Rybcyznski, *Shipping News*, N.Y. REV. BOOKS (Aug. 10, 2006), https://perma.cc/23LB-CVU6.
34. Whether Uber can do so without being the legal employer of those drivers is a hotly contested issue, as discussed below. *See infra* notes 90–110 and accompanying text.
35. ROSALIND DIXON & RICHARD HOLDER, FAIR MARKETS: LIBERALISM AFTER COVID (forthcoming 2020), manuscript p. 103.
36. Some observers call the resulting economy "hypercapitalism." *See* Marina Vujnovic, *Hypercapitalism*, *in* 2 THE WILEY-BLACKWELL ENCYCLOPEDIA OF GLOBALIZATION 978 (George Ritzer ed., 2012).
37. For a cogent critique of the excesses of liberalization of trade and finance, *see* DANI RODRIK, THE GLOBALIZATION PARADOX: DEMOCRACY AND THE FUTURE OF THE WORLD ECONOMY (2011).
38. Steven Berkenfeld, Managing Dir., Barclays Capital, Opportunities and Challenges, Presentation at the US Department of Labor Conference on the Future of Work (Dec. 10, 2015) (transcript on file with author).
39. *Id.*
40. *Id.*

41. Olivier Garret, *How the Coming Wave of Job Automation Will Affect You and the US*, FORBES (Feb. 23, 2017), https://perma.cc/6KGV-AKLC.
42. *See, e.g.*, WEIL, *supra* note 2 [1].
43. RICHARD B. FREEMAN & JAMES L. MEDOFF, WHAT DO UNIONS DO? (1984).
44. *See* Jose Pagliery, *You Make $70k but Cost Your Boss $88k*, CNN MONEY (Feb. 28, 2013, 9:16 a.m. ET), https://perma.cc/RD5C-J4AH.
45. *See* Charlotte S. Alexander, *Legal Avoidance and the Restructuring of Work*, *in* THE STRUCTURE AND STRUCTURING OF WORK IN ORGANIZATIONS 311 (Lisa E. Cohen et al. eds., 2016).
46. *See* Ryan Abbott & Bret Bogenschneider, *Should Robots Pay Taxes? Tax Policy in the Age of Automation*, 12 HARV. L. & POL'Y REV. 145, 151–52, 163–68 (2018).
47. How much they spend is unclear. *See* Michael Hiltzik, *Labor Dept. Finally Closes a Loophole Favoring Union-Busters—After 57 Years*, L.A. TIMES (Mar. 24, 2016), https://perma.cc/GYT7-Z88C; Noam Scheiber, *Rules to Require Employers to Disclose Use of Anti-Union Consultants*, N.Y. TIMES (Mar. 23, 2016), https://perma.cc/6FU2-KFFX.
48. HSBC, for example, anticipated spending $3.3 billion on regulatory and compliance actions in 2017 alone. Richard Partington, *Banks Trimming Compliance Staff as $321 Billion in Fines Abate*, BLOOMBERG (Mar. 22, 2017), https://perma.cc/P784-NAHC.
49. *See* Alan B. Krueger & Uwe E. Reinhardt, *The Economics of Employer Versus Individual Mandates*, 13 HEALTH AFF. 34 (1994); Lawrence H. Summers, *What Can Economics Contribute to Social Policy?: Some Simple Economics of Mandated Benefits*, 79 AM. ECON. REV. 177, 180 (1989); John Olson, *What Are Payroll Taxes and Who Pays Them?*, TAX FOUND. (July 25, 2016), https://perma.cc/X4K3-W4G9.
50. For evidence that employers bear a large share of payroll taxes, *see* Daniel S. Hamermesh, *New Estimates of the Incidence of the Payroll Tax*, 45 S. ECON. J. 1208, 1217 (1979); Krueger & Reinhardt, *supra* note 49, at 43.
51. Summers, *supra* note 49, at 181.
52. TRUMAN F. BEWLEY, WHY WAGES DON'T FALL DURING A RECESSION 173–80 (1999).
53. *See* Hamermesh, *supra* note 50.
54. For just one prominent voice on this theme, *see* Alain Supiot, *Law and Labour: A World Market of Norms?*, 39 NEW LEFT REV. 109, 120 (May–June 2006)
55. *See* Christine Jolls, *Employment Law and the Labor Market* 2 (NBER Working Paper No. 13230, 2007), https://www.nber.org/papers/w13230.
56. *See* Zoe Adams et al., *The Economic Significance of Laws Relating to Employment Protection and Different Forms of Employment: Analysis of a Panel of 117 Countries, 1990–2013*, 158 INT'L LAB. REV. 1, 2 (2019). The point is discussed further in Chapter 7.
57. The "efficiency wage" theory in fact holds that higher-than-market wages can raise productivity. *See* Lawrence F. Katz, *Efficiency Wage Theories: A Partial Evaluation*, *in* 1 NBER MACROECONOMICS ANNUAL 1986, at 235, 248 (Stanley Fischer ed., 1986). But they are thought to do so by eliciting loyalty and extra effort, or by setting employers apart from competitors so they can attract better workers. Neither is likely to follow from across-the-board mandates. *See* Michael L. Wachter, *Neoclassical Labor*

Economics: Its Implications for Labor and Employment Law, *in* RESEARCH HANDBOOK ON THE ECONOMICS OF LABOR AND EMPLOYMENT LAW 20, 28–30, 46 (Cynthia L. Estlund & Michael L. Wachter. eds., 2012).

58. See Charles H. Heying, *Civic Elites and Corporate Delocalization: An Alternative Explanation for Declining Civic Engagement*, 40 AM. BEHAV. SCIENT. 657 (1997).
59. *See* Henry Hansmann & Reinier Kraakman, *The End of History for Corporate Law*, *in* CONVERGENCE AND PERSISTENCE IN CORPORATE GOVERNANCE 33 (Jeffrey N. Gordon & Mark J. Roe eds., 2004).
60. Milton Friedman, *A Friedman Doctrine—The Social Responsibility of Business Is to Increase Its Profits*, N.Y. TIMES MAG., Sept. 13, 1970, at 33.
61. *Business Roundtable Redefines the Purpose of a Corporation to Promote 'An Economy That Serves All Americans,'* BUSINESS ROUNDTABLE (Sept. 19, 2019), https://perma.cc/K49Y-2JJY.
62. Tania Branigan, *Chinese Workers Link Sickness to N-Hexane and Apple iPhone Screens*, GUARDIAN (May 7, 2010), https://perma.cc/G8SG-9BSB; Charles Duhigg & David Barboza, *In China, Human Costs Are Built into an iPad*, N.Y. TIMES (Jan. 25, 2012), https://perma.cc/VZG8-RBUM; Nick Statt, *iPhone Manufacturer Foxconn Plans to Replace Almost Every Human Worker with Robots*, VERGE (Dec. 30, 2016, 5:07 p.m. EST), https://perma.cc/KH26-GY53.
63. *See, e.g.*, Rich Blake, *In Coronavirus Fight, Robots Report For Disinfection Duty*, FORBES (Apr. 17, 2020), https://perma.cc/EAM4-GGXC.
64. *See* Jiaxing & Yangon, *A Tightening Grip: Rising Chinese Wages Will Only Strengthen Asia's Hold on Manufacturing*, ECONOMIST (Mar. 12, 2015), https://perma.cc/GU6C-QKN7.
65. Jeffrey Rothfeder, *Why Donald Trump Is Wrong About Manufacturing Jobs and China*, NEW YORKER (Mar. 14, 2016), https://perma.cc/AB4R-XW8W; Peter S. Goodman, *Globalization Is Moving Past the US and Its Vision of World Order*, N.Y. TIMES (June 19, 2019), https://perma.cc/5BTU-SEHD.
66. KARL POLANYI, THE GREAT TRANSFORMATION: THE POLITICAL AND ECONOMIC ORIGINS OF OUR TIME (2d ed. 2001).
67. *See* CYNTHIA ESTLUND, A NEW DEAL FOR CHINA'S WORKERS? 99–122 (2017); ELI FRIEDMAN, INSURGENCY TRAP: LABOR POLITICS IN POSTSOCIALIST CHINA (2014).
68. Kate Taylor, *Fast-Food CEO Says He's Investing in Machines Because the Government Is Making it Difficult to Afford Employees*, BUS. INSIDER (Mar. 16, 2016, 5:30 p.m.), https://perma.cc/HT2N-44CX.
69. MARTIN FORD, RISE OF THE ROBOTS: TECHNOLOGY AND THE THREAT OF A JOBLESS FUTURE (2015).
70. On the role of intellectual property law in that race, *see* Camilla A. Hrdy, *Intellectual Property and the End of Work*, 71 FLA. L. REV. 303 (2019).
71. *See, e.g.*, David H. Autor, *Why Are There Still So Many Jobs? The History and Future of Workplace Automation*, 29 J. ECON. PERSP. 3 (2015); Paul Krugman, *Democrats, Avoid the Robot Rabbit Hole*, N.Y. TIMES (Oct. 17, 2019), https://www.nytimes.com/2019/10/17/opinion/democrats-automation.html.

72. For an excellent collection of theoretical, comparative, and historical perspectives on the "right to work," *see* THE RIGHT TO WORK: LEGAL AND PHILOSOPHICAL PERSPECTIVES (Virginia Mantouvalou ed.) (2015).
73. That is distinct from the anti-union "right-to-work" slogan that is more familiar in US public discourse.
74. *See* Katherine V.W. Stone, *A Right to Work in the United States: Historical Antecedents and Contemporary Possibilities*, in THE RIGHT TO WORK, *supra* note 72, at 275.
75. Michael Hiltzik, *Andy Puzder, Trump's Choice for Labor Secretary, Is a Good Spokesman for Fast-Food Restaurant Owners. For Their Employees, Not So Much*, L.A. TIMES (Dec. 8, 2016, 1:40 p.m.), https://perma.cc/9P7T-JQBW.
76. Daniel Shaviro, *The Minimum Wage, the Earned Income Tax Credit, and Optimal Subsidy Policy*, 64 U. CHI. L. REV. 405, 406 (1997). For more recent evidence for that conclusion, *see, e.g.*, David Neumark, *Employment Effects of Minimum Wages*, IZA WORLD. LAB. (2018), https://perma.cc/Q4L5-3GFW; David Neumark, *The Effects of Minimum Wages on Employment*, FED. RES. BANK S.F. (Dec. 21, 2015), https://perma.cc/WEP2-S3PD.
77. *See* DAVID E. CARD & ALAN B. KRUEGER, MYTH AND MEASUREMENT: THE NEW ECONOMICS OF THE MINIMUM WAGE (1995).
78. *See* David Cooper, *Raising the Federal Minimum Wage to $15 by 2024 Would Lift Pay for Nearly 40 Million Workers*, ECON. POL'Y INST. (Feb. 5, 2019), https://perma.cc/N7JU-S8Z6 (citing many studies). Among major studies, *see* Doruk Cengiz et al., *The Effect of Minimum Wages on Low-Wage Jobs*, 134 Q. J. ECON. 1405 (2019). For a round-up of studies finding little or no employment impact, *see* Holly Sklar, R*esearch Shows Minimum Wage Increases Do Not Cause Job Loss*, BUS. FOR FAIR MINIMUM WAGE, https://perma.cc/VJ5X-HMYE.
79. *See* Lloyd Corder, *Survey of US Economists on a $15 Federal Minimum Wage*, EMP'T POLICIES INST. (2019), https://perma.cc/RRC4-NLT4.
80. See Jared Bernstein, *Minimum Wages and Capital/Labor Substitution*, ON THE ECON.: JARED BERNSTEIN BLOG (Aug. 17, 2015, 3:43 p.m.), https://perma.cc/U7FU-GYSL; Alan B. Krueger, *The Minimum Wage: How Much Is Too Much?*, N.Y. TIMES (Oct. 10, 2015), https://perma.cc/62NC-AHWA. *See also* Cong. Budget Office, *The Effects on Employment and Family Income of Increasing the Federal Minimum Wage* 1, 3 (2019), https://perma.cc/K5NR-5TVX.
81. *Economists in Support of a Federal Minimum Wage of $15 by 2024*, ECON. POL'Y INST. (Feb. 6, 2019), https://perma.cc/LUR8-QTMZ.
82. Cooper, *supra* note 78, at 16.
83. Alina Selyukh, *Biden to Call for Raising Federal Minimum Wage to $15 an Hour*, NPR, Jan. 15, 2021, https://www.npr.org/2021/01/15/957371280/biden-to-call-for-raising-federal-minimum-wage-to-15-an-hour.
84. *See* Isaac Sorkin, *Are There Long-Run Effects of the Minimum Wage?*, 18 REV. ECON. DYN. 306 (2015). Sorkin observes that many studies, including Card & Kreuger, *supra* note 77, "focus[] on estimating the short-run employment response to minimum wage increases"; they "capture the part of the employment response that operates through the change in output (the *scale* effect), and very little of the substitution

of labor for capital (the *substitution* effect)," which Sorkin finds is much larger in simulations. *Id.* at 312.

85. Daniel Aaronson et al., *Industry Dynamics and the Minimum Wage: A Putty-Clay Approach*, 59 INT'L ECON. REV. 51 (2018).
86. *Id.* In other words, new entrants' capital-labor mix is moldable like putty, while that of incumbents hardens like clay.
87. *Id.* at 69. *See also* Grace Lordan & David Neumark, *People Versus Machines: The Impact of the Minimum Wages on Automatable Jobs* (NBER, Working Paper No. 23667, 2017), http://www.nber.org/papers/w23667; Cengiz, et al., *supra* note 78, at 1409, 1438.
88. *See* Lordan & Neumark, *supra* note 87, at 14; Cengiz et al., *supra* note 78, at 1409.
89. *See* Daniel Aaronson & Brian J. Phelan, *Wage Shocks and the Technological Substitution of Low-Wage Jobs*, 129 ECON. J. 1 (2019).
90. *See* WEIL, *supra* note 2 [1].
91. *See* GUY DAVIDOV, A PURPOSIVE APPROACH TO LABOUR LAW 115–16 (2016); WEIL, *supra* note 2 [1], at 236–37; Richard R. Carlson, *Why the Law Still Can't Tell an Employee When It Sees One and How It Ought to Stop Trying*, 22 BERKELEY J. EMP. & LAB. L. 295, 306–14 (2001); *Independent Contractor Misclassification Imposes Huge Costs on Workers and Federal and State Treasuries*, NAT'L EMP. L. PROJECT (July 2015), https://perma.cc/84NX-FUC6.
92. *See* JEREMIAS PRASSL, THE CONCEPT OF THE EMPLOYER (2015). A more modest reform that could be adopted by US courts would treat as "independent contractors" only those who actually operate an independent business, see AMERICAN LAW INSTITUTE, RESTATEMENT OF EMP'T LAW § 1.01.
93. *See* Judy Fudge et al., *Changing Boundaries in Employment: Developing a New Platform for Labour Law*, 10 CANAD. LAB. & EMP. L.J. 329, 336 (2003).
94. *See* DAVIDOV, *supra* note 91; Harry W. Arthurs, *The Dependent Contractor: A Study of the Legal Problems of Countervailing Power*, 16 U. TORONTO L.J. 89 (1965); Seth D. Harris & Alan B. Krueger, *A Proposal for Modernizing Labor Laws for Twenty-First-Century Work: The "Independent Worker,"* HAMILTON PROJECT (Dec. 2015), http://perma.cc/66AB-G82M.
95. Under Cal. Lab. Code § 1182, a firm seeking to escape employer status must show that the worker (A) . . . is free from the control and direction of the hirer . . ., both under the contract . . . and in fact; (B) . . . performs work that is outside the usual course of the hiring entity's business; and (C) . . . is customarily engaged in an independently established trade, occupation, or business of the same nature as the work performed for the hiring entity. For analysis, *see* Anna Deknatel & Lauren Hoff-Downing, *ABC on the Books and in the Courts: An Analysis of Recent Independent Contractor and Misclassification Statutes*, 18 U. PA. J. L. SOC. CHANGE 54, 65–71 (2015).
96. That is because the work of Uber drivers is not "outside the usual course of the hiring entity's business," which is one element of the ABC test. *See* Noam Scheiber, *Gig Economy Business Model Dealt a Blow in California Ruling*, N.Y. TIMES (Apr. 30, 2018), https://perma.cc/W736-XN4H.

97. Dara Khosrowshahi, Logan Green, & John Zimmer, *Open Forum: Uber, Lyft Ready to Do Our Part for Drivers*, S.F. Chron. (June 12, 2019), https://perma.cc/4FBK-NR8Q.
98. *See* Megan Rose Dickey, *This Is the Gig Worker Ballot Initiative Uber, Lyft, DoorDash and Instacart are Backing*, TechCrunch (Oct. 29, 2019), https://perma.cc/7BS2-ZDSG; Nayantara Mehta, *Flexible Work Hours and Employee Status: The Truth About AB 5*, Nat'l Emp. L. Project (June 21, 2019), https://perma.cc/W4SJ-CYN8.
99. *See* Kate Conger, *Uber and Lyft Drivers in California Will Remain Contractors*, N.Y. Times (Nov. 7, 2020), https://www.nytimes.com/2020/11/04/technology/california-uber-lyft-prop-22.html.
100. Eli Rosenberg, *Gig Economy Bills Move Forward in Other Blue States, After California Clears the Way*, Wash. Post (Jan. 17, 2020), https://perma.cc/GWF5-8LQV.
101. *See* Noam Scheiber, *Labor Department Clarifies Employment Guidelines*, N.Y. Times (Jan. 20, 2016), https://perma.cc/VL92-DW8S; Noam Scheiber, *Labor Dept. to Curb Lawsuits by Franchise Workers*, N.Y. Times (Jan. 12, 2020), https://perma.cc/F79Z-D3P2.
102. See, for example, the US Chamber of Commerce critiques of Obama-era expansions of "joint-employment" in the NLRB, *Establish a Proper Definition of Joint Employer*, US Chamber Com. (Feb. 26, 2018), https://perma.cc/D9ED-H6K4; and in the Labor Department, *Wage and Hour's Joint Employer Pile-on*, US Chamber Com. (Feb. 10, 2016), https://perma.cc/6FLK-LYEA.
103. *See* Alan Hyde, *To What Duties Do Global Labour Rights Correlate?: Responsibility for Labour Standards Down the Production Chain*, in Global Justice and International Labour Rights 209, 209–36 (Yossi Dahan et al. eds., 2016); *see also* Cynthia Estlund, *Enforcement of Private Transnational Labor Regulation: A New Frontier in the Anti-Sweatshop Movement?*, *in* Enforcement of Transnational Regulation 237 (Fabrizio Cafaggi ed., 2012). One recent initiative would use arbitration to enforce brand agreements with suppliers over labor conditions. *See* Clean Clothes Campaign et al., *Four Major Civil Society Groups Release Dispute Resolution System and Model Arbitration Clauses for Disputes Arising Under Enforceable Brand Agreements*, Int'l Lab. Rts. Forum. (June 24, 2020), https://perma.cc/ZN4Z-QG2M.
104. *See, e.g.*, Int'l Labour Org. [ILO], *Giving Globalization a Human Face: International Labour Conference, 105th Session*, 2016, ILO Doc. ILC.105/IV (2016), https://perma.cc/S7VE-YSN6; Kishanthi Parella, *Improving Human Rights Compliance in Supply Chains*, 95 Notre Dame L. Rev. 727 (2019).
105. *See, e.g.*, Associated Press, *Nike Reveals Overseas Factory Names, Locations*, NBC News (Apr. 13, 2005), https://perma.cc/RL4M-XJ3A.
106. *See* Karen McVeigh, *Cambodian Female Workers in Nike, Asics and Puma Factories Suffer Mass Faintings*, Guardian (June 24, 2017), https://perma.cc/3ZZH-DXWS; Anna Fifield, *China Compels Uighurs to Work in Shoe Factory that Supplies Nike*, Wash. Post (Feb. 29, 2020), https://perma.cc/8XRL-9ZB3.
107. *See* Rebecca Greenfield, *How Apple Fixed Its Foxconn Problem*, Atlantic (May 10, 2012), https://perma.cc/G4KX-R6S5; Paul Harris, *Apple Hit by Boycott Call over*

Worker Abuses in China, GUARDIAN (Jan. 28, 2012, 19:07 EST), https://perma.cc/8XNV-5AG5.

108. *See, e.g.*, Reed Albergotti, *Apple Accused of Worker Violations in Chinese Factories*, WASH. POST (Sept. 9, 2019), https://perma.cc/TN2C-YYCR; Annie Kelly, *Apple and Google Named in US Lawsuit Over Congolese Child Cobalt Mining Deaths*, GUARDIAN (Dec. 16, 2019), https://perma.cc/6AAX-28L9.
109. *See* Estlund, *supra* note 7 [77], at 241.
110. David Barboza, *After Suicides, Scrutiny of China's Grim Factories*, N.Y. TIMES (June 6, 2010), https://www.nytimes.com/2010/06/07/business/global/07suicide.html.
111. For a review of the empirical literature, *see* HRISTOS DOUCOULIAGOS, RICHARD B. FREEMAN & PATRICE LAROCHE, THE ECONOMICS OF TRADE UNIONS 46–51 (2017).
112. *See* Brishen Rogers, *The Law and Political Economy of Workplace Technological Change*, forthcoming, 55 HARV. CIV. RTS-CIV. LIB. L. REV ___ (2020).
113. FREEMAN & MEDOFF, *supra* note 43, at 169, 183–84, 190; DOUCOULIAGOS et al., *supra* note #, at 130–46.
114. FREEMAN & MEDOFF, *supra* note 43, at 180.
115. Rogers, *supra* note 112.
116. *See* Walther Müller-Jentsch, *Germany: From Collective Voice to Co-management*, *in* WORKS COUNCILS: CONSULTATION, REPRESENTATION, AND COOPERATION IN INDUSTRIAL RELATIONS (Joel Rogers & Wolfgang Streek eds., 1995), at 58–60.
117. Sandrine Cazes et al., *Collective Bargaining Systems and Workers' Voice Arrangements in OECD Countries*, *in* OECD, NEGOTIATING OUR WAY UP: COLLECTIVE BARGAINING IN A CHANGING WORLD OF WORK 22–84 (2019).
118. Oliver Denk et al., *The Role of Collective Bargaining Systems for Labour Market Performance*, *in* NEGOTIATING OUR WAY UP, *supra* note 117, at 105, 110–15.
119. *See* WEILER, *supra* note 5, at 283–90. Both are given prominent play in the 2020 Harvard report, *Clean Slate for Worker Power*, which attempts to chart a course for fundamental labor law reform in the United States. Benjamin Sachs & Sharon Block, *Clean Slate for Worker Power: Building a Just Economy and Democracy*, Labor and Worklife Program, Harvard Law School, https://www.cleanslateworkerpower.org/clean-slate-agenda.
120. *See* Jason Heyes, *Training, Social Dialogue and Collective Bargaining in Western Europe*, 28 ECON. & INDUS. DEMOCRACY 239 (2007), available at https://journals.sagepub.com/doi/abs/10.1177/0143831X07076116.

Chapter 4

1. That includes so-called "socialist market economies," such as China.
2. *See* JOHN RAWLS, JUSTICE AS FAIRNESS: A RESTATEMENT §13(1)(b) at 42–43, §18.3 at 63–64 (Erin Kelly ed., 2001). I don't mean to either adopt or reject Rawls's exacting "difference principle" for judging how much inequality is justified.

3. *E.g.*, Areeba Haider & Justin Schweitzer, *The Poverty Line Matters, But It Isn't Capturing Everyone It Should*, Ctr. for Am. Progress (Mar. 5, 2020), https://perma.cc/C3Z5-5RF8; Natalia A. Kolesnikova & Yang Liu, *Understanding Poverty Measures and the Call To Update Them*, Fed. Res. Bank of St. Louis (July 1, 2012), https://perma.cc/E6UD-K9T3.
4. Two points: Prevailing standards of decent housing or education, like prevailing labor standards, might be too low; they are and should be the subject of ongoing political contestation. Second, the focus here is on what a society owes its own members, not what a rich society might owe others as a matter of transnational justice.
5. *See* McKinsey Global Institute, *Jobs Lost, Jobs Gained: Workforce Transitions in a Time of Automation*, 30, 102 McKinsey & Co. 33, 37 (Dec. 2017), https://perma.cc/58PT-L4Q5.
6. In earlier elaborations of these ideas, I use the term "leisure" as shorthand for time outside of paid work. But I have been persuaded (by, among others, David Estlund) that the term "free time" better captures what I am after here and poses less risk of misunderstanding.
7. For a thoughtful essay on the essential yet undervalued nature of domestic work in the COVID era, *see* Alexandra Finley, *Women's Household Labor Is Essential. Why Isn't It Valued?*, Wash. Post (May 29, 2020), https://www.washingtonpost.com/outlook/2020/05/29/womens-household-labor-is-essential-why-isnt-it-valued/.
8. Tim Kasser & Kennon M. Sheldon, *Time Affluence as a Path Toward Personal Happiness and Ethical Business Practice: Empirical Evidence from Four Studies*, 84 J. Bus. Ethics 243 (2009).
9. *Id.*; Ashley V. Whillans et al., *Buying Time Promotes Happiness*, 114 Proc. Nat'l Acad. Sci. 8523 (2017).
10. *See* Robert E. Lane, *Work as "Disutility" and Money as "Happiness": Cultural Origins of a Basic Market Error*, 21 J. Socio-Econ. 43, 48–51 (1992).
11. Ian Goldin, *Opinion, Five Reasons Why Universal Basic Income Is a Bad Idea*, Fin. Times (Feb. 11, 2018), https://perma.cc/V3BS-M5HN; Matthew Continetti, *A UBI Would Undermine Work*, Nat'l Rev. (July 25, 2019), https://www.nationalreview.com/magazine/2019/08/12/a-ubi-would-undermine-work/ Among conservative fans of work, *see* Oren Cass, The Once and Future Worker: A Vision for the Renewal of Work in America (2018); further to the left, *see* Michael J. Sandel, The Tyranny of Merit: What's Become of the Common Good? (2020); Russell Muirhead, Just Work (2004).
12. Max Weber, The Protestant Ethic and the Spirit of Capitalism (Stephen Kalberg trans., Oxford Univ. Press 2010) (1920).
13. *See, e.g.*, Nick Srnicek & Alex Williams, Inventing the Future: Postcapitalism and a World Without Work (2015); Kathi Weeks, The Problem with Work: Feminism, Marxism, Antiwork Politics, and Postwork Imaginaries (2011).
14. *See* Muirhead, *supra* note 11; Alain de Botton, Status Anxiety 90–93 (2004); David Graeber, Bullshit Jobs, A Theory (2018); David Graeber, *On the*

Phenomenon of Bullshit Jobs: A Work Rant, STRIKE! MAGAZINE (2013), https://perma.cc/Q695-FHUL.

15. *See, e.g.*, PHILIPPE VAN PARIJS & YANNICK VANDERBORGHT, BASIC INCOME: A RADICAL PROPOSAL FOR A FREE SOCIETY AND A SANE ECONOMY 100–32 (2017); SRNICEK & WILLIAMS, *supra* note 13, WEEKS, *supra* note 13, at 155–71.
16. For several recent overviews of the history of these ideas, see JAMIE K. MCCALLUM, WORKED OVER: HOW ROUND-THE-CLOCK WORK IS KILLING THE AMERICAN DREAM (2020); MUIRHEAD, *supra* note 11; WEEKS, *supra* note 13.
17. On the role of work in promoting human capabilities, *see* MARTHA C. NUSSBAUM, CREATING CAPABILITIES: THE HUMAN DEVELOPMENT APPROACH 34 (2011); Brian Langille, *What Is Labour Law? Implications of the Capability Approach*, *in* THE CAPABILITY APPROACH TO LABOUR LAW 122 (Brian Langille ed., forthcoming); Virginia Mantouvalou, *Work, Human Rights, and Human Capabilities*, *in* THE CAPABILITY APPROACH, *id.* at 137.
18. Muirhead holds that, for work that is necessary but not fulfilling or a good "fit" for anybody, less of it—shorter hours—should be required in order to make a living. MUIRHEAD, *supra* note 11, at 174–76.
19. Karl Marx, *Critique of the Gotha Programme*, *in* MARX: LATER POLITICAL WRITINGS 215 (Terrell Carver ed., Cambridge Univ. Press 1996) (1875).
20. Jon Elster, *Comment on Van der Veen and Van Parijs*, 15 THEORY AND SOC'Y 709, 719 (1986).
21. DAVID G. BLANCHFLOWER, NOT WORKING: WHERE HAVE ALL THE GOOD JOBS GONE? 42–45 (2019).
22. *See generally* ROBERT D. PUTNAM, BOWLING ALONE: THE COLLAPSE AND REVIVAL OF AMERICAN COMMUNITY (2000); *see* Matthew Modini et al., *The Mental Health Benefits of Employment: Results of a Systemic Meta-Review*, 24 AUSTRALASIAN PSYCHIATRY 331 (2016); Anthony Winefield & Marika Tiggemann, *Employment Status and Psychological Well-Being: A Longitudinal Study*, 75 J. APP. PSYCHOL. 455 (1990).
23. Daiga Kamerade et al., *A Shorter Working Week for Everyone: How Much Paid Work Is Needed for Mental Health and Well-Being?*, 241 SOC. SCI. & MED. 1 (2019). *See also* Jennie E. Brand, *The Far-Reaching Impact of Job Loss and Unemployment*, 41 ANN. REV. OF SOC. 359 (2015); Frances McKee-Ryan et al., *Psychological and Physical Well-Being During Unemployment: A Meta-Analytic Study*, 90 APP. PSYCHOL. 53 (2005).
24. *See* Peter Butterworth et al., *The Psychosocial Quality of Work Determines whether Employment Has Benefits for Mental Health: Results from a Longitudinal National Household Panel Survey*, 68 OCCUP. & ENVIR. MED. 806 (2011).
25. *See* CYNTHIA ESTLUND, WORKING TOGETHER: HOW WORKPLACE BONDS STRENGTHEN A DIVERSE DEMOCRACY 56–59, 114–18 (2003) (reviewing evidence).
26. GRAEBER, BULLSHIT JOBS, *supra* note 14, at 240–44.
27. *See* Anca Gheaus & Lisa Herzog, *The Goods of Work (Other Than Money!)*, 47 J. OF SOC. PHIL. 70 (2016).
28. SANDEL, *supra* note 11. The argument about work and contributive justice is also recapitulated in Michael J. Sandel, *What Liberals Get Wrong About Work*, ATLANTIC

(Sept. 2, 2020), https://perma.cc/3JKY-HN5D. Quotes below are taken from the article.

29. *Id.*
30. *Id.*
31. For an extended version of this argument, featuring Tocqueville, Durkheim, and others, see ESTLUND, *supra* note 25, at 105–24.
32. On the many and varied contributions of associational life to democracy, see Archon Fung, *Associations and Democracy: Between Theories, Hopes, and Realities*, 29 ANN. REV. SOCIOL. 515 (2003).
33. *See, e.g.*, JEAN L. COHEN & ANDREW ARATO, CIVIL SOCIETY AND POLITICAL THEORY ix (1992); JOHN EHRENBERG, CIVIL SOCIETY: THE CRITICAL HISTORY OF AN IDEA 235 (1999); JÜRGEN HABERMAS, BETWEEN FACTS AND NORMS 366–67 (1996); Robert C. Post, *Racist Speech, Democracy, and the First Amendment*, 32 WM. & MARY L. REV. 267, 289 (1991). *See also* HANNAH ARENDT, THE HUMAN CONDITION 122–35, 159–167 [1958] (2d ed. 1998).
34. PUTNAM, *supra* note 22. To be sure, not all social capital is virtuous. *See* E. Villalonga-Olives & I. Kawachi, *The Dark Side of Social Capital: A Systematic Review of the Negative Health Effects of Social Capital*, 194 SOC. SCI. & MED. 105 (2017); Alejandro Portes, *Social Capital: Its Origins and Applications in Modern Sociology*, 24 ANN. REV. SOC. 1 (1998).
35. PUTNAM, *supra* note 22.
36. For further elaboration, *see generally* ESTLUND, *supra* note 25.
37. Alexander Hertel-Fernandez, *Power and Politics in the US Workplace*, ECON. POL'Y INST. 14 (Oct. 7, 2020), https://perma.cc/2LGR-Y8N9.
38. On work as a source of "weak ties," *see* Gillian M. Sandstrom & Elizabeth W. Dunn, *Social Interactions and Well-Being: The Surprising Power of Weak Ties*, PERSONALITY & SOC. PSYCH. BULL. (Apr. 25, 2014), https://journals.sagepub.com/doi/abs/10.1177/0146167214529799.
39. See Ashley Fetters, *Your Work Friends Knew Exactly What Kind of Week You'd Had*, N.Y. TIMES (Oct. 21, 2020), https://www.nytimes.com/2020/10/21/opinion/work-from-home-loneliness.html?action=click&module=Opinion&pgtype=Homepage.
40. I explore this theme in a recent book chapter, *Coming Apart: How Union Decline and Workplace Disintegration Imperil Democracy*, forthcoming in LABOR AND CHALLENGES TO DEMOCRACY (Mark Barenberg & Angela Cornell, eds., 2021))[hereinafter Estlund, *Coming Apart*].
41. *See generally* BILL BISHOP, THE BIG SORT: WHY THE CLUSTERING OF LIKE-MINDED AMERICA IS TEARING US APART (2008). *See also Political Polarization in the American Public*, PEW RES. CTR. 42–55 (June 12, 2014), https://perma.cc/PHQ8-6UTS; John Kelly & Camille François, *This Is What Filter Bubbles Actually Look Like*, MIT TECH. REV. (Aug. 22, 2018), https://perma.cc/KEV5-WY35.
42. Hertel-Fernandez, *supra* note 37, at 7–9.
43. *Id.* at 9.
44. *See* SIDNEY VERBA ET AL., VOICE AND EQUALITY: CIVIC VOLUNTARISM IN AMERICAN POLITICS 312–20 (1995); ESTLUND, *supra* note 25, at 116.

45. Hertel-Fernandez, *supra* note 37, at 12–13.
46. *Id.* at 6–7.
47. *Id.* at 1, 10 (emphasis added).
48. *See* ESTLUND, *supra* note 25, at 7–10, 61–69. Putnam recognizes this, too. *See* PUTNAM, *supra* note 22, at 87.
49. *See* KEVIN STAINBACK & DONALD TOMASKOVIC-DEVEY, DOCUMENTING DESEGREGATION (Russell Sage Foundation, 2012).
50. See Xavier de Souza Briggs, "Some of My Best Friends Are . . .": Interracial Friendships, Class, and Segregation in America, 6 CITY & COMMUN. 263 (2007).
51. ESTLUND, *supra* note 25, at 77–83 (citing studies). For meta-analyses, see Thomas Tropp & Lind Pettigrew, *A Meta-Analytic Test of Intergroup Contact Theory*, 90 J. PERSONALITY & SOC. PSYCH. 751 (2006), and the more mixed assessment of Elizabeth Levy Paluck et al., *The Contact Hypothesis Reevaluated,* 3 BEHAV. PUB. POL'Y 29 (2018). One recent study finds that white individuals who work with at least one Black co-worker manifest significantly less racial bias than those who do not, and finds clues that the link is causal, not just coincidental. *See* Sean Darling-Hammond, Rodolfo Mendoza-Denton, & Randy Lee, *Interracial Contact at Work: Can Workplace Diversity Reduce Bias?*, GROUP PROCESSES & INTERGROUP RELATIONS (July 2020), https://journals.sagepub.com/doi/10.1177/1368430220932636.
52. *See* ESTLUND, *supra* note 25, at 77–83.
53. STAINBACK & TOMASKOVIC-DEVEY, *supra* note 49, at 20–10, 278.
54. Given that my focus here is on the egalitarian spillover effect of workplace relations between men and women, I have in mind primarily heterosexual cohabitating couples comprising cisgender individuals.
55. On the complexity of that project, see ESTLUND, *supra* note 25, at 84–96.
56. *See* Mick Cunningham, *Influences of Women's Employment on the Gendered Division of Household Labor over the Life Course: Evidence from a 31-Year Panel Study*, 28 J. FAM. ISSUES 422 (2007). *See also* Cynthia Estlund, *Women in the Workplace*, 4 TEX. J. WOMEN & L. 1 (1995).
57. ELIZABETH ANDERSON, PRIVATE GOVERNMENT: HOW EMPLOYERS RULE OUR LIVES (AND WHY WE DON'T TALK ABOUT IT) (2017). For my review, *see* Cynthia Estlund, *Rethinking Autocracy at Work*, 131 HARV. L. REV. 795 (2018).
58. Some theorists hold that associations can promote democracy only if they are themselves democratically organized. *See, e.g.*, JOSHUA COHEN & JOEL ROGERS, ASSOCIATIONS AND DEMOCRACY (1995). Others take a more pluralistic view of how associations can be democracy-enhancing; *see* Nancy Rosenblum, MEMBERSHIP AND MORALS: THE PERSONAL USES OF PLURALISM IN AMERICA (1998). I have more to say on these issues in ESTLUND, *supra* note 25, at 105–24.
59. *See* CHARLES MOSKOS & JOHN BUTLER, ALL THAT WE CAN BE: BLACK LEADERSHIP AND RACIAL INTEGRATION THE ARMY WAY (1996). This is hardly a complete success story; the top layers of the military hierarchy are still overwhelmingly white (and male). Helene Cooper, *African-Americans Are Highly Visible in the Military, but Almost Invisible at the Top,* N.Y. TIMES (May 25, 2020), https://perma.cc/S98W-L46D.

60. Cohen & Rogers, *supra* note 58; ESTLUND, *supra* note 25, at 40–42; Estlund, *Coming Apart*, *supra* note 40. At least that is so once unions were compelled to break with patterns of exclusion that had long infected parts of the labor movement.
61. Race is not necessarily submerged in those campaigns; successful unions have instead learned to appeal to racial and ethnic loyalties in ways that unite workers rather than divide them. *See* LANI GUINIER & GERALD TORRES, THE MINER'S CANARY (2002).
62. For an extended discussion of how to strike a constructive balance between civility constraints in the interest of equality and mutual respect among co-workers and some modicum of liberty in those relationships, see ESTLUND, *supra* note 25, at 157–59.
63. For a relatively favorable view of those programs, *see* Stacy L. Hawkins, *The Long Arc of Diversity Bends Towards Equality: Deconstructing the Progressive Critique of Workplace Diversity Efforts*, 17 U. MD. L.J. RACE, RELIGION, GENDER & CLASS 61 (2017). For more critical views, *see* Nancy Leong, *Racial Capitalism*, 126 HARV. L. REV. 2151, 2165 (2013); Soohan Kim et al., *Progressive Corporations at Work: The Case of Diversity Programs*, 36 REV. OF L. & SOC. CHANGE 171 (2012); Astrid Kersen, *Diversity Management*, 13 J. OF ORG. CHANGE MANAGEMENT 235 (2000).
64. I return to this point in Chapter 5's discussion of UBI as a response to a future of less work.
65. *See, e.g.*, Markus Jäntti et al., *The Double Role of Ethnic Heterogeneity in Explaining Welfare-State Generosity* (Cowles Foundation Discussion Paper No. 1972, Dec. 2014); ALBERTO ALESINA & EDWARD GLAESER, FIGHTING POVERTY IN THE US AND EUROPE: A WORLD OF DIFFERENCE (2004); Dora L. Costa & Matthew E. Kahn, *Civic Engagement and Community Heterogeneity: An Economist's Perspective*, 1 PERSP. ON POL. 103 (2003); Alberto Alesina et al., *Why Doesn't the United States Have a European-Style Welfare State?* (NBER Working Paper No. 8524, Oct. 2001).
66. *See* Alberto Alesina et al., *Immigration, Diversity, and Economic Prosperity*, VOX CEPR POLICY PORTAL (Aug. 2013), https://perma.cc/AT3W-H5G4.
67. Estlund, *Coming Apart*, *supra* note 40.
68. *See* PAUL COLLIER, THE FUTURE OF CAPITALISM (2018); SANDEL, *supra* note 11.
69. *See* BRISHEN ROGERS, DATA AND DEMOCRACY AT WORK (forthcoming, 2021). *Cf.* J.C. Pan, *Unionizing the Office in an Age of Remote Work*, THE NEW REPUBLIC (May 28, 2020), https://perma.cc/2C68-G6TT.
70. Courtney Connley, *Why Many Employees Are Hoping to Work from Home Even After the Pandemic Is Over*, CNBC (May 4, 2020), https://perma.cc/US7E-E84D.
71. Deb Perelman, *In the Covid-19 Economy, You Can Have a Kid or a Job. You Can't Have Both*, N.Y. TIMES (July 2, 2020), https://perma.cc/F5RD-GX86.
72. Caitlyn Collins et al., *Covid-19 and the Gender Gap in Work Hours*, GENDER, WORK & ORG. (2020), https://doi.org/10.1111/gwao.12506.
73. Melissa Mazmanian et al., *The Autonomy Paradox: The Implications of Mobile Email Devices for Knowledge Professionals*, 24 ORG. SCI. 1337. 1350 (2013); Michelle F. Davis & Jeff Green, *Three Hours Longer, the Pandemic Workday Has Obliterated Work-Life Balance*, BLOOMBERG (Apr. 23, 2020), https://perma.cc/3H68-8VT8; Irina Ivanova, *Coronavirus Lockdowns are Making the Workday Longer*, CBS NEWS (Aug. 5. 2020), https://perma.cc/9B9K-DUAW/.

74. See Fetters, *supra* note 39.
75. For an overview and taxonomy of many of these efforts, *see* Thomas A. Kochan, *Worker Voice, Representation, and Implications for Public Policies*, MIT Work of the Future Taskforce 6–8 (2020), https://perma.cc/C398-VY9T.
76. Kamerade et al., *supra* note 23.
77. Nor did the study control for the idiosyncratic circumstances that allowed some research subjects to work eight hours per week or less.

Chapter 5

1. On COVID-19 responses, see Int'l Monetary Fund, *Policy Responses to COVID-19*, https://www.imf.org/en/Topics/imf-and-covid19/Policy-Responses-to-COVID-19#C (last updated Sept. 25, 2020), https://perma.cc/6HPN-53YH. Depression-era responses are discussed later.
2. What Is Basic Income?, *Stanford Basic Income Lab* (2019), https://perma.cc/W7EX-68VR.
3. *See* Philippe Van Parijs & Yannick Vanderborght, Basic Income: A Radical Proposal for a Free Society and a Sane Economy 51–98 (2017).
4. There have been pilot studies, but none meets all of the definitional criteria for true UBI. *See infra* notes 37 and 38.
5. *See* Andy Stern & Lee Kravitz, Raising the Floor: How a Universal Basic Income Can Renew Our Economy and Rebuild the American Dream (2016).
6. Eric Newcomer, *Yang's Pet Issue Could Outlive His Campaign*, Bloomberg (Jan. 29, 2020), https://perma.cc/77MT-MY29.
7. For an overview of recent academic research on the psychological effects of poverty, *see* Ben Fell & Miles Hewstone, Joseph Rowntree Found., Psychological Perspectives on Poverty (2015).
8. Left-libertarian philosopher Robert S. Taylor argues that guaranteed basic income, if coupled with measures to ensure labor market competition, would be *sufficient* to counter employer domination and abuse. *See* Robert S. Taylor, Exit Left: Markets and Mobility in Republican Thought 12–25 (2017).
9. Stern & Kravitz, *supra* note 5, Taylor, *supra* note 8; Albert Wenger, Work After Capital (forthcoming), https://perma.cc/YDU8-ALYX.
10. Wenger, *supra* note 9.
11. *See* Van Parijs & Vanderborght, *supra* note 3, at 177–78.
12. *See id.* at 4–28.
13. Annie Miller et al., *The Gender Effects of a Basic Income*, *in* The Palgrave International Handbook of Basic Income 133 (Malcolm Torry ed., 2019); Almaz Zelleke, *Institutionalizing the Universal Caretaker Through a Basic Income?*, 3 Basic Income Stud. 1 (2008).
14. Taylor, *supra* note 8, at 11–26.

15. Milton Friedman and Friedrich Hayek supported basic income schemes (discussed in Van Parijs & Vanderborght, *supra* note 3, at 84–87. *See also* Matt Zwolinski, *Property Rights, Coercion, and the Welfare State: The Libertarian Case for a Basic Income for All*, 19 The Independent Rev. 515 (2015); David Frum, *A Rule for Conservative Anti-Poverty Plans: Keep It Simple*, The Atlantic (July 31, 2014), https://perma.cc/GX9B-U6UP; Matt Zwolinski, *The Pragmatic Libertarian Case for a Basic Income Guarantee*, Cato Unbound (Aug. 4, 2014), https://perma.cc/KQ84-78DJ.
16. For a thoughtful analysis of varied political views on UBI, *see* Peter Frase, *On the Politics of Basic Income*, Peter Frase (July 16, 2018), https://perma.cc/M528-LQZ5. *See also* George Zarkadakis, *The Case Against Universal Basic Income*, HuffPost (Feb. 27, 2017, 6:34 a.m.), https://www.huffpost.com/entry/the-case-against-universal-basic-income_b_58b0178ee4b02f3f81e44612.
17. *See* Alyssa Battistoni, *The False Promise of Universal Basic Income*, Dissent (2017), https://perma.cc/59SC-C8E2; Daniel Zamora, *The Case Against a Basic Income*, Jacobin (Dec. 28, 2017), https://perma.cc/UYK5-5Y7C.
18. *See* Alex Gourevitch, *The Limits of a Basic Income: Means and Ends of Workplace Democracy*, 11 Basic Income Stud. 17 (2017).
19. Anca Gheaus, *Basic Income, Gender Justice and the Costs of Gender-Symmetrical Lifestyles*, 3 Basic Income Stud. 1 (2008).
20. *See* Battistoni, *supra* note 17. Combining several of these critiques, *see* Brishen Rogers, *Basic Income in a Just Society*, Boston Review (May 15, 2017), available at http://bostonreview.net/forum/brishen-rogers-basic-income-just-society
21. Editorial, *Chicago's Next Really Bad Idea: A Guaranteed Basic Income*, Inv. Bus. Daily (July 20, 2018), https://www.investors.com/politics/editorials/guaranteed-basic-income/. On the inflation problem, compare Pavlina R. Tcherneva, *What Are the Relative Macroeconomic Merits and Environmental Impacts of Direct Job Creation and Basic Income Guarantees?*, Levy Econ. Inst. of Bard Coll. (2007), https://perma.cc/EF6P-P7CK, with Van Parijs & Vanderborght, *supra* note 3, at 133–34; Dylan Matthews, *A New Study Debunks One of the Biggest Arguments Against Basic Income*, Vox (Sept. 20, 2017), https://perma.cc/N3CC-J9CX; Scott Santens, *Wouldn't Unconditional Basic Income Just Cause Massive Inflation?*, Medium (Nov. 22, 2014), https://perma.cc/VD6K-WAXA.
22. Of course, a progressive income tax would more than tax away UBI at higher incomes.
23. These issues have been well-vetted by others. *See, e.g.*, Van Parijs & Vanderborght, *supra* note 3, at 133–69; Benjamin M. Friedman, *Born to Be Free*, The New York Review of Books 39 (Oct. 12 2017), https://perma.cc/RJK5-67M8; Jordi Alcarons et al., *Feasibility of Financing a Basic Income*, 9 Basic Income Stud. 79 (2014). Zamora, *supra* note 17, estimates the costs of different versions of UBI in different countries. For example, in Britain, a monthly grant of £284 would cost 6.5 percent of annual GDP; in France, a basic grant of €1,100 would cost 35 percent of annual GDP. Van Parijs's plan for Belgium, with a monthly basic income of €600, would cost 6 percent of that country's annual GDP.
24. *See* Van Parijs & Vanderborght, *supra* note 3.

25. US Dep't of Health & Human Servs., *HHS Poverty Guidelines for 2019* (Jan. 11, 2019), https://aspe.hhs.gov/poverty-guidelines. This ignores wide variations in the cost of living.
26. *See, e.g.*, Michalis Nikiforos et al., *The Roosevelt Inst., Modeling the Macroeconomic Effects of a Universal Basic Income* 9 (Aug. 2017).
27. *See* Van Parijs & Vanderborght, *supra* note 3, at 9.
28. *Id.* at 130–70; *see also* Dylan Matthews, *The 2 Most Popular Critiques of Basic Income are Both Wrong*, Vox (July 20, 2017), https://perma.cc/S22W-CD7H; Robert Greenstein, *Commentary: Universal Basic Income May Sound Attractive But, if It Occurred, Would Likelier Increase Poverty Than Reduce It*, Ctr. on Budget and Pol'y Priorities: Pol'y Futures (Sept. 18, 2017), https://www.cbpp.org/poverty-and-opportunity/commentary-universal-basic-income-may-sound-attractive-but-if-it-occurred; Jessica Wiederspan et al., *Expanding the Discourse on Antipoverty Policy: Reconsidering a Negative Income Tax*, 19 J. of Poverty 218 (2015).
29. *See* Van Parijs & Vanderborght, *supra* note 3, at 147–58.
30. Friedman, *supra* note 23, at 39; Zamora, *supra* note 17; Greenstein, *supra* note 28.
31. *See* Van Parijs & Vanderborght, *supra* note 3, at 134–37.
32. *See id.* at 138–47. See also Guy Standing, *Basic Income as Common Dividends: Piloting a Transformative Policy: A Report for the Shadow Chancellor of the Exchequer*, Progressive Economy Forum (May 7, 2019), https://perma.cc/Q9KB-KCHH.
33. *See* Friedman, *supra* note 23, at 41.
34. *See* Zamora, *supra* note 17. Note, however, that major proponents of the JG rely on Modern Monetary Theory, which rejects the notion that a JG must be paid for by new taxes or budget cuts elsewhere. *See* Chapter 8.
35. *See* Van Parijs & Vanderborght, *supra* note 3, at 100–32; Philippe Van Parijs, *Why Surfers Should Be Fed: The Liberal Case for an Unconditional Basic Income*, 20 Phil. & Publ. Affairs 101 (1991).
36. Van Parijs & Vanderborght, *supra* note 3, at 41, 159-160. For a thorough theoretical and empirical overview of the work incentive controversy, *see generally* Ed Dolan, *A Universal Basic Income and Work Incentives. Part 1: Theory*, EconoMonitor (Aug. 18, 2014), https://perma.cc/9YK9-LRNS; Ed Dolan, *A Universal Basic Income and Work Incentives. Part 2: Evidence*, EconoMonitor (Aug. 25, 2014), https://perma.cc/MP5L-AEKR.
37. *See* Dolan, *Part 2*, *supra* note 36; Karl Wilderquist, A Critical Analysis of Basic Income Experiments for Researchers, Policymakers, and Citizens 43–70 (2018).
38. *See* Wilderquist, *supra* note 37, at 43–70. Guy Standing proposes a pilot program to address that empirical gap. *See* Standing, *supra* note 32.
39. Indeed, one of UBI's virtues is that it favors marriage or cohabitation over living alone, unlike means-tested programs that are keyed to household income. *See, e.g.*, Spencer Rand, *The Real Marriage Penalty: How Welfare Law Discourages Marriage Despite Public Policy*, 18 UDC-DCSL L. Rev. 93, 122–37 (2015).
40. Jon Elster, *Comment on Van der Veen and Van Parijs*, 15 Theory and Soc'y 709, 719 (1986).

41. *Compare* Van Parijs, *supra* note 35; *with* Michael W. Howard, *Exploitation, Labor, and Basic Income*, 37 ANALYSE & KRITIK 281, 299 (2015).
42. *See* Van Parijs, *supra* note 35; VAN PARIJS & VANDERBORGHT, *supra* note 3, at 100–32.
43. *See* Van Parijs, *supra* note 35, at 121–24.
44. *Id.* at 124.
45. Michael J. Sandel, *What Liberals Get Wrong About Work*, ATLANTIC (Sept. 2, 2020), https://perma.cc/3PYE-HSYW.
46. That might include addictions to drugs, video games, or pornography. *See* Dieter Henkel, *Unemployment and Substance Use: A Review of the Literature (1990-2010)*, 4 CURRENT DRUG ABUSE REV. 4 (2011); Xavier Carbonell et al., *Trends in Scientific Literature on Addiction to the Internet, Video Games, and Cell Phones from 2006 to 2010*, 7 INT'L J. PREV. MED. 63 (2016); Todd Love et al., *Neuroscience of Internet Pornography Addiction: A Review and Update*, 5 BEHAV SCI. (BASEL) 388 (2015).
47. Though some UBI advocates have suggested it would serve as a built-in strike fund. *See* STERN & KRAVITZ, *supra* note 5, at 188; Erik Olin Wright, *Basic Income as a Socialist Project* 4 (Mar. 2005) (paper presented at the annual US-BIG Congress, March 4–6, 2006), available at https://perma.cc/MPN7-5PFG.
48. Brishen Rogers, *Basic Incomes in a Just Society*, BOSTON REV. (May 15, 2017), http://bostonreview.net/forum/brishen-rogers-basic-income-just-society.
49. For a proposal to couple a partial UBI with a guaranteed job *at below minimum wage*, *see* Felix FitzRoy & Jim Jin, *Basic Income and a Public Job Offer: Complementary Policies to Reduce Poverty and Unemployment*, IZA INST. OF LABOR ECON., 6–11 (2017).
50. Philip Harvey, *Wage Policies and Funding Strategies for Job Guarantee Programs*, *in* THE JOB GUARANTEE: TOWARD FULL EMPLOYMENT 39, 40 (Michael J. Murray & Mathew Forstater eds., 2013); *see also* Peter-Christian Aigner & Michael Brenes, *The Long, Tortured History of the Job Guarantee*, THE NEW REPUBLIC (May 11, 2018), https://perma.cc/D3VL-RJQ2.
51. *See, e.g.*, Senator Huey P. Long, *Statement of the Share Our Wealth Movement* (May 23, 1935), *in* 74 CONG. REC. 8,040–43 (1935)
52. *See* Margaret Weir, *Full Employment as a Political Issue in the United States*, 54 SOC. RES. 377, 383–91 (1987).
53. *Id.*
54. Dr. Martin Luther King, Jr., *Showdown for Nonviolence*, LOOK, at 24 (Apr. 16, 1968), https://perma.cc/UEE9-JTYH.
55. *See generally* DEAN BAKER, ET AL., CTR. FOR POPULAR DEMOCRACY, THE FULL EMPLOYMENT MANDATE OF THE FEDERAL RESERVE: ITS ORIGINS AND IMPORTANCE (2017).
56. Gregory Krieg, *Why a "Federal Jobs Guarantee' Is Gaining Steam with Democrats*, CNN.COM (April 26, 2018, 8:30 a.m.), https://perma.cc/PC7S-SNWS.
57. *See Recognizing the Duty of the Federal Government to Create a Green New Deal*, H. RES. 109 S. 1, 116th Cong. (2019), https://perma.cc/Q574-FZ7D.
58. The job guarantee was left out of the "unity task force recommendations" that emerged out of discussions between the Biden and Sanders campaigns. *See* Biden-Sanders

Unity Task Force Recommendations, Biden for President (2020), https://perma.cc/XHC3-XX8Y; Ella Nilsen, *How Joe Biden and Bernie Sanders Joined Forces to Craft a Bold, Progressive Agenda*, Vox (July 9, 2020), https://perma.cc/XZP2-H9N6.

59. A Civis poll asked about a federal JG, paid for by a 5 percent tax increase for those earning over $200,000 a year; it was "one of the most popular issues we've ever polled," with 52 percent of respondents in support and only 29 percent opposed. *See* Sean McElwee, Colin McAuliffe, & Jon Green, *Why Democrats Should Embrace a Federal Jobs Guarantee*, The Nation (Mar. 20, 2018), https://perma.cc/PM9D-FWS3.
60. Mark Paul et al., Ctr. on Budget and Policy Priorities, The Federal Job Guarantee—A Policy to Achieve Permanent Full Employment (2018) [hereinafter CBPP Proposal], https://perma.cc/37JJ-F9CB; L. Randall Wray et al., Levy Econ. Inst. of Bard Coll., Public Service Employment: A Path to Full Employment (2018) [hereinafter, LEI Proposal], https://perma.cc/P5P6-N5AT] Unlike the CBPP proposal, in which the federal government would administer jobs directly, the LEI proposes federal funding but job creation and administration by state and local governments and non-profit organizations. A third proposal by the Center for American Progress (CAP) is described as a job guarantee, but it is really a more conventional jobs program, with "a target of maintaining the employment rate for prime-age workers without a bachelor's degree at the 2000 level of 79 percent." Neera Tanden et al., *Toward a Marshall Plan for America: Rebuilding Our Towns, Cities, and the Middle Class*, Ctr. for Am. Progress (May 16, 2017), https://perma.cc/F535-XZUU.
61. That is, fully-funded health coverage, child care, and paid family leave. On the LEI's estimated cost of benefits, see *infra* note 64.
62. Specifically, health insurance (for full timers), retirement contributions, paid family and sick leave, and paid vacation amounting to four weeks per year. The average direct payroll cost would be $26.92 per hour for full-time workers. CBPP Proposal, *infra* note 73, at 12 table 1.
63. *See* L. Randall Wray, *A Consensus Strategy for a Universal Job Guarantee Program*, Levy Econ. Inst. of Bard College, Policy Note 2 (2018), https://perma.cc/LC97-CL5C; and CBPP report, *supra* note 60, at 10.
64. The CBPP proposal is backed by more realistic estimates of participation levels and costs. For example, LEI estimates benefit costs at just 20 percent of wage costs, for a total direct payroll cost per hour of $18 per hour, LEI Proposal, *supra* note 60, at 49. That is much less than actual benefit costs in the private sector and much less than the CBPP's estimate of benefit costs for its job guarantee, see *supra* note 62. For my critique of the LEI estimates, see Cynthia Estlund, *Three Big Ideas for a Future of Less Work and a Three-Dimensional Alternative*, 82 L. & Contemp. Probl. 1, 21 (2019).
65. *See*, e.g., Max Gulker, PhD, American Institute for Economic Research, The Job Guarantee: A Critical Analysis (Oct. 18, 2018), https://www.aier.org/wp-content/uploads/2018/10/JobGuarantee.pdf. *See also* Stern & Kravitz, *supra* note 5, at 164–65.
66. CBPP Proposal, *infra* note 73, at 11.

67. *See* Gulker, *supra* note 65, at 6. To be sure, some workers might prefer a non-JG job that pays less but offers more opportunity for advancement. And if a JG excluded undocumented workers, those workers would presumably work for less. Immigration poses knotty questions for either a UBI or a JG. *See generally* James Davis, *Opinion, Reconciling UBI with Immigration Concerns*, Basic Income Earth Network (Sept. 21, 2016), https://perma.cc/N99Z-STMM; Kevin D. Williamson, *The UBI and Immigration*, Nat'l Rev. (June 10, 2016, 7:59 p.m.), https://perma.cc/N4JG-GLNS.
68. The LEI Proposal assumes that *none* of the full-time workers currently making more than $7.25 but less than $15 plus benefits would enter the JG program; rather, *all* of those jobs would be upgraded to the JG threshold. See LEI Proposal, *supra* note 60, at 16–17. That is in some tension with evidence on the impact of large minimum wage increases on employment. *See supra* Chapter 3 [nn. 75–90].
69. For such a proposal, and a supporting rationale, see Rosalind Dixon & Richard Holder, Fair Markets: Liberalism After COVID (forthcoming). *See also* FitzRoy & Jin, *supra* note 49, which proposes a job guarantee at slightly below the prevailing minimum wage along with a partial UBI.
70. CBPP Proposal, *infra* note 73, at 2–3, 13–14.
71. *See* Dylan Matthews, *Modern Monetary Theory, Explained*, Vox (Apr. 16, 2019), https://www.vox.com/future-perfect/2019/4/16/18251646/modern-monetary-theory-new-moment-explained. *See also* Cullen O. Roche, *Understanding the Modern Monetary System*, Orcam Fin. Group (Aug. 5, 2011), https://perma.cc/6CEH-LUQ8.
72. As with UBI, some critics predict inflation from the massive infusion of purchasing power into the economy. The LEI predicts only a temporary and manageable inflationary effect, *see* LEI Proposal, *supra* note 60, at 6.
73. CBPP Proposal, *supra* note 60.
74. *See supra* at note 34. *But see* FitzRoy & Jin, *supra* note 49 (proposing to combine a partial UBI with a low-wage JG). Pavlina Tcherneva of the LEI favors the JG over UBI (Pavlina R. Tcherneva, *The Job Guarantee: Design, Jobs, and Implementation* 48–50 (Levy Econ. Inst., Working Paper No. 902, Apr. 2018), https://perma.cc/3M8H-RMA6; but she suggests that UBI could complement the JG for those who cannot work or who are still in poverty. *See* David Roberts, *30 Million Americans Are Unemployed. Here's How to Employ Them*, Vox (May 4, 2020). https://www.vox.com/science-and-health/2020/5/4/21243725/coronavirus-unemployment-cares-act-federal-job-guarantee-green-new-deal-pavlina-tcherneva.
75. Josh Bivens, *How Do Our Job Creation Recommendations Stack up against a Federal Jobs Guarantee?*, Econ. Policy Inst.: Working Econ. Blog (April 12, 2018, 10:00 a.m.), https://perma.cc/J6BJ-ARKH.
76. Anne Kim, *Guaranteed Jobs: Too Big to Succeed*, Progressive Pol'y Inst. (May 4, 2018), https://perma.cc/Z48X-35GL.
77. *See* Jonathan Chait, *Democrats Are Rushing Into a Job Guarantee. It Could Be a Huge Mistake*, N.Y. Mag. (Apr. 25, 2018), https://perma.cc/4RGU-UWRY.

78. The CBPP Proposal would offer a range of wage rates based on skill level in lieu of a uniform wage level; that makes the program more complex but in other ways stronger. CBPP Proposal, *supra* note 73.
79. Gulker, *supra* note 65, at 14–15; Wendell Gordon, *The Job Guarantee Revisited*, 31 J. ECON. ISSUES 826, 832–33 (1997).
80. On the Depression-era appeal of work spreading, *see* Deborah C. Malamud, *Engineering the Middle Classes: Class Line-Drawing in New Deal Hours Legislation*, 96 MICH. L. REV. 2212, 2223 (1998).
81. BENJAMIN KLINE HUNNICUTT, FREE TIME: THE FORGOTTEN AMERICAN DREAM, 148–53 (2013) [hereinafter FREE TIME].
82. *See* Matthew Dimick, *Better Than Basic Income? Liberty, Equality, and the Regulation of Working Time*, 50 IND. L. REV. 473 (2017).
83. JAMIE MCCALLUM, WORKED OVER: HOW ROUND-THE-CLOCK WORK IS KILLING THE AMERICAN DREAM (2020).
84. *The Shorter Work Week: A Radical and Pragmatic Proposal* (Will Stronge & Aidan Harper, eds.) (2019), https://perma.cc/M97M-Y8AT.
85. Robert Whaples, *Hours of Work in US History*, ECON. HISTORY ASS'N, https://perma.cc/SNM2-D35W.
86. BENJAMIN KLINE HUNNICUTT, WORK WITHOUT END: ABANDONING SHORTER HOURS FOR THE RIGHT TO WORK (1988) [hereinafter, WORK WITHOUT END]; *see also* FREE TIME, *supra* note 81. MCCALLUM, *supra* note 83, also surveys the history of this movement and contends for its revival in his recent book.
87. Scott D. Miller, *Revitalizing the FLSA*, 19 HOFSTRA LAB. & EMP. L.J. 1, 1 (2001); *see* HUNNICUTT, WORK WITHOUT END, *supra* note 86, at 9–36.
88. *See* HUNNICUTT, FREE TIME, *supra* note 81, at 70–71; William E. Forbath, *The Ambiguities of Free Labor: Labor and the Law in the Gilded Age*, 1985 WIS. L. REV., 767, 805–6.
89. *See* Forbath, *supra* note 88, at 800–17.
90. *See* SCHOR, *infra* note 9, at 107–38; *see* HUNNICUTT, FREE TIME, *supra* note 81, at 114–15.
91. *See generally* HUNNICUTT, FREE TIME, *supra* note 81, at 1–12; *see also* John Maynard Keynes, *Possibilities for Our Grandchildren*, *in* ESSAYS IN PERSUASION 321, 327 (Palgrave Macmillan, 2010); Sherman Gwinn, *Days of Drudgery Will Soon Be Over: An Interview with Walter S. Gifford*, AM. MAG., Nov. 1928, 25.
92. *See generally* HUNNICUTT, FREE TIME, *supra* note 81, at 48–69; Robert T. Rhode, *Culture Followed the Plow, However Slowly*, 15 KY. PHILOLOGICAL REV. 49 (2001); David D. Anderson, *Walt Whitman: Nineteenth-Century Man*, WALT WHITMAN BIRTHPLACE BULLETIN 3–5 (Apr. 1960).
93. *See* HUNNICUTT, FREE TIME, *supra* note 81, at 6–7.
94. *See* Keynes, *supra* note 91, at 327.
95. HUNNICUTT, WORK WITHOUT END, *supra* note 86, at 148–90; *see also* FREE TIME, *supra* note 81, at 109–21; Malamud, *supra* note 80, at 2233–36.
96. *See* HUNNICUTT, WORK WITHOUT END, *supra* note 86, at 251–65; FREE TIME, *supra* note 81, at 114–21.

97. *See* Free Time, *supra* note 81, at 115; *see also* Constant Southworth, *Can There Be General Overproduction? No!*, 32 J. Pol. Econ., 722–23 (1924).
98. 29 U.S.C. § 201.
99. Malamud, *supra* note 80, at 2318–19; *Hours Worked*, OECD Data (2017), https://perma.cc/9XYB-TXLX.
100. Congress extended minimum wage guarantees to agricultural workers, albeit at a lower level, in 1966. *See* Phyllis Palmer, *Outside the Law: Agricultural and Domestic Workers under the Fair Labor Standards Act*, 7 J. Pol'y Hist., 416, 420–26 (1995).
101. *See generally* Marc Linder, *Farm Workers and the Fair Labor Standards Act: Racial Discrimination in the New Deal*, 65 Tex. L. Rev. 1335 (1987); Joseph Fishkin & William F. Forbath, The Anti-Oligarchy Constitution (forthcoming 2022).
102. West Coast Hotel Co. v. Parrish, 300 US 379 (1937).
103. In particular, the female-dominated Communications Workers of America pushed back against the labor movement's abandonment of the shorter hours cause. *See, e.g.*, Hunnicutt, Free Time, *supra* note-- 156–57.
104. *See* David R. Roediger & Philip S. Foner, Our Own Time: A History of American Labor and the Working Day, 265–66 (1989).
105. Hunnicutt, Free Time, *supra* note 81, at 156–61; *see also* Marion Crain, *Where Have All the Cowboys Gone?: Marriage and Breadwinning in Postindustrial Society*, 60 Ohio St. L.J. 1877, 1917–21 (1999); Lizabeth Cohen, A Consumers' Republic 154 (2003).
106. *See* Hunnicutt, Free Time, *supra* note 81, at 161–65; Cohen, *supra* note 105, at 124–25.
107. *See The Productivity-Pay Gap*, Econ. Policy Inst. (Aug. 2018), https://perma.cc/ZFJ8-YT7P.
108. On the economically driven scramble for hours of work among below-median-income workers, see McCallum, *supra* note 83.
109. *See* Daniel Markovits, The Meritocracy Trap 81–99 (2019); Heather Boushey & Bridget Ansel, *Overworked America: The Economic Causes and Consequences of Long Work Hours*, Wash. Ctr. Equitable Growth 15 (2016), https://perma.cc/C7TY-UNZK; Juliet Schor, The Overworked American: The Unexpected Decline of Leisure, 17–82 (1991).
110. Markovits *supra* note 109, at 79–86; Boushey & Ansel, *supra* note 109, at 13–18.
111. Lawrence Mishel, *Vast Majority of Wage Earners Are Working Harder, and For Not Much More*, Econ. Pol'y Inst. (Jan. 30, 2013), https://perma.cc/BJ9T-7M2P.
112. Heather Boushey, Finding Time: The Economics of Work-Life Conflict 58–60 (2016); Elizabeth Warren & Amelia Warren Tyagi, The Two-Income Trap xix–xx (2004).
113. *See* Claudia Goldin, *The Quiet Revolution That Transformed Women's Employment, Education, and Family*, 15–22 (NBER Working Paper No. 11953, 2006), https://perma.cc/7RJR-33G4.
114. *See* Council of Econ. Advisers, Families and the Labor Market, 1969-1999: Analyzing the "Time Crunch" 3–6 (1999) [hereinafter, Time Crunch].

115. *See generally* ARLIE HOCHSCHILD, THE SECOND SHIFT (1989).
116. *See* ROBERT GORDON, THE RISE AND FALL OF AMERICAN GROWTH 1–24 (2016).

Chapter 6

1. For example, on the relative merits of single-payer models versus public options, *compare* GANESH SITARAMAN, THE PUBLIC OPTION: HOW TO EXPAND FREEDOM, INCREASE OPPORTUNITY, AND PROMOTE EQUALITY (2019), *with Improved Medicare for All Quality, Guaranteed National Health Insurance*, HEALTHCARE-NOW! (2019), https://perma.cc/WLE4-9G6F.
2. Rockefeller Found. & Deutsche Bank Grp. Climate Change Advisors, UNITED STATES BUILDING ENERGY EFFICIENCY RETROFIT 7, 31 (2012), https://perma.cc/M3HD-WKVH.
3. Amanda Novello & Greg Carlock, *Redefining Green Jobs for a Sustainable Economy*, CENTURY FOUND. (Dec. 2, 2019), https://perma.cc/9SFE-7BJF.
4. Megan Cassidy, *Plum Gig or Slave Labor? California Inmates Fight Wildfires for $1 an Hour*, S.F. CHRON. (Aug. 11, 2018), https://perma.cc/L5HW-YG4D; Melody Gutierrez & Megan Cassidy, *As California Burns, Volunteer Firefighters Become Harder to Find*, S.F. CHRON. (Aug. 11, 2018), https://perma.cc/3P5N-X9HS.
5. *See* Chapter 5; Anne Kim, *Guaranteed Jobs: Too Big to Succeed*, PROGRESSIVE POL'Y INST. (May 4, 2018), https://perma.cc/UQ4N-LS3X.
6. *See* McKinsey Global Inst., *The Future of Work in America: People and Places, Today and Tomorrow*, MCKINSEY & COMPANY vi, 47–56 (2019), https://perma.cc/3ZVL-5XQK. *See also* Mark Muro et al., *Automation & Artificial Intelligence: How Machines are Affecting People and Places*, BROOKINGS 26–28, 37–43 (Jan. 2019), https://perma.cc/NEH5-754W.
7. Clara Hendrickson et al., *Countering the Geography of Discontent: Strategies for Left-Behind Places*, BROOKINGS 28–29, 32 (2018), https://perma.cc/BL9L-T7RJ.
8. A recent proposal by US Representatives Watson-Coleman and Omar suggests this template. Their bill would create "a job guarantee program through grants to states, localities and tribal entities where unemployment is greater than 10 percent OR double the national unemployment rate." *See* Press Release, Rep. *Watson-Coleman, Omar Introduce Bill for Direct Job Creation as Millions Continue to Reel from Coronavirus Unemployment* (July 2, 2020), https://perma.cc/B56T-G6UW.
9. *See* Laura Tatum et al., *The Youth Opportunity Guarantee: A Framework for Success*, GEORGETOWN CTR. ON POVERTY & INEQUALITY 12, 19 (2019), https://perma.cc/VXR9-UW5V.
10. *See generally id.*
11. NATIONAL COMMISSION ON MILITARY, NATIONAL, AND PUBLIC SERVICE, INSPIRED TO SERVE 44–48 (2020), available at https://www.inspire2serve.gov/reports (the average living allowance in 2018 was $15,370, modestly above the national poverty line for an individual; and the AmeriCorps education award was $6,195 for 2019–2020, or about 60 percent of average in-state college tuition).

12. John M. Bridgeland & John J. DiIulio, Jr., *Will America Embrace National Service?*, BROOKINGS INST. 7 (2019), https://perma.cc/HQ3Y-YG7N.
13. Tatum et al. *supra* note 9, at 50–51.
14. Bridgeland & DiIulio, *supra* note 12, at 1.
15. *Id.* (emphasis added).
16. *Id.*
17. That might be on the order of one year of in-state public tuition per year of service or—in case we were to adopt a broader guarantee of free public higher education—a continued living allowance for those continuing their education.
18. *See* ULRICH BECK, THE BRAVE NEW WORLD OF WORK (2000).
19. AmeriCorps, *What Is AmeriCorps Seniors?*, https://www.nationalservice.gov/programs/senior-corps/what-senior-corps.
20. Americorps, *Americorps Seniors & Health Benefits*, https://www.nationalservice.gov/programs/senior-corps/senior-corps-and-health-benefits.
21. Marc Linder, *The Minimum Wage as Industrial Policy: A Forgotten Role*, 16 J. LEGIS. 151, 152–56 (1990).
22. On regulated self-regulation as an example of regulatory reform, *see* CYNTHIA ESTLUND, REGOVERNING THE WORKPLACE 79–82, 139–50 (2010); Orly Lobel, *Interlocking Regulatory and Industrial Relations: The Governance of Workplace Safety*, 57 ADMIN. L. REV. 1071 (2005).
23. *See, e.g.*, Michael Grabell & Howard Berkes, *The Demolition of Workers' Comp*, PROPUBLICA (Mar. 4, 2015), https://perma.cc/2F2D-626F; US DEP'T OF LABOR, DOES THE WORKERS' COMPENSATION SYSTEM FULFILL ITS OBLIGATIONS TO INJURED WORKERS? (2016), https://perma.cc/3YEH-7396.
24. *See* Lobel, *supra* note 22, at 1080–86.
25. *See* Jonathan Timm, *Why Fair Scheduling Could Be Labor's Next Big Fight*, IN THESE TIMES (Nov. 25, 2016), https://perma.cc/6VFV-XHJ6.
26. Brishen Rogers also suggests that "employment-related duties should be limited to those that advance goals that can only be achieved through changes to employer policies," and that some employee benefits and their funding should be "socialized." Brishen Rogers, *Employment Rights in the Platform Economy: Getting Back to Basics*, 10 HARV. L. & POL'Y REV. 479, 517–18 (2016). He emphasizes gains for economic equality and worker mobility; the goal of avoiding unnecessary job losses is one more good reason to do that.
27. The point was underscored by the MIT Work of the Future Task Force in its final report in 2020, at p. 51. A 2020 survey of employers found that annual premiums for family health coverage was $21,342, with workers paying $5,558 of that cost on average. *2020 Employer Health Benefits Survey: Abstract*, KAISER FAMILY FOUND. (Oct. 8, 2020), https://perma.cc/77PC-2F5W.
28. *See* Charlotte S. Alexander, *Legal Avoidance and the Restructuring of Work*, *in* THE STRUCTURING OF WORK IN ORGANIZATIONS 311, 318 (Lisa E. Cohen et al. eds., 2016).
29. *See* Marcus Dillender, Carolyn J. Heinrick, & Susan Houseman, *Effects of the Affordable Care Act on Part-Time Employment, Early Evidence* (Upjohn Inst., Working Paper No. 16-258, 2016), https://perma.cc/3ACA-PUGK; William E. Even & David

A. Macpherson, *The Affordable Care Act and the Growth of Involuntary Part-Time Employment*, 72 Indus. & Lab. Rel. Rev. 955 (2019). Other studies have shown limited effects. *See, e.g.*, Jean Abraham & Anne Beeson Royalty, *How Has the Affordable Care Act Affected Work and Wages?*, Leonard Davis Inst. Health Econ. (Jan. 19, 2017), https://perma.cc/L59D-BTMS; Bowen Garrett et al., *Recent Evidence on the ACA and Employment: Has the ACA Been a Job Killer? 2016 Update* (2017), https://perma.cc/3BDN-24UR.

30. *See* Even & Macpherson, *supra* note 29.
31. Casey B. Mulligan, *The Employer Penalty, Voluntary Compliance, and the Size Distribution of Firms: Evidence from a Survey of Small Businesses* (NBER Working Paper No. 24037, 2017), https://perma.cc/9EXH-6SVN.
32. On why much of the cost of employment mandates falls on employers, see *supra* Chapter 3 [nn. 49–53].
33. One diverse group of stakeholders has declared that "[e]veryone, regardless of employment classification, should have access to the option of an affordable safety net that supports them when they're injured, sick, in need of professional growth, or when it's time to retire." *See* Byron Auguste et al., *Common Ground for Independent Workers: Principles for Delivering a Stable and Flexible Safety Net for All Types of Work*, WTF? Economy (Nov. 9, 2015), https://perma.cc/JLL5-TSFT.
34. Among OECD countries, the United States has by far the lowest level of *public* health care coverage (under 35 percent compared to 100 percent coverage in most countries); including private health care coverage, the United States is still next to last (ahead of Greece) in coverage, and one of the few that has not achieved universal health coverage. *Universal Health Coverage and Health Outcomes*, OECD (2016), https://perma.cc/6AUY-7F2J; *see also* Special Report, *America Is a Health-Care Outlier in the Developed World*, Economist (Apr. 26, 2018), https://perma.cc/8FTT-LFPS.
35. *See supra* Chapter 3 [n. 17].
36. *See* Katherine V.W. Stone, *A Fatal Mismatch: Employer-Centric Benefits in a Boundaryless World*, 11 Lewis & Clark L. Rev. 451, 460 (2007).
37. *See* Alain Supiot, Beyond Employment: Changes in Work and the Future of Labour Law in Europe (2001); David Charny, *The Employee Welfare State in Transition*, 74 Tex. L. Rev. 1601 (1996); Nicolas Colin & Bruno Palier, *The Next Safety Net: Social Policy for a Digital Age*, Foreign Aff. (July–Aug. 2015), https://perma.cc/3DWT-62JA; Stone, *supra* note 35, at 464.
38. It also impairs worker mobility, as quitting one job for another, or for making a go at independent self-employment, may put a whole family's health coverage at risk. *See* Dean Baker, *Job Lock and Employer-Provided Health Insurance: Evidence from the Literature*, AARP Pub. Pol'y Inst. (Mar. 2015), https://perma.cc/R9AD-7NMN.
39. *See* T.R. Reid, The Healing of America: A Global Quest for Better, Cheaper, and Fairer Health Care 17–19 (2009). The so-called "Bismarck Model" (used in Germany, France, and Japan, *inter alia*), achieves universal coverage while relying on private insurers and mostly private providers, and on funding through mandatory employer contributions. It taxes employment, but insurers are regulated non-profits and costs are lower.

40. Akilah Johnson, *Medicare-for-All Is Not Medicare, and Not Really for All. So What Does It Actually Mean?*, ProPublica (Sept. 6, 2019), https://perma.cc/D962-F58R; Kevin Uhrmacher et al., *Where 2020 Democrats Stand on Health Care*, Washington Post (Apr. 8, 2020), https://perma.cc/9U9H-XWLG; John Cassidy, *Elizabeth Warren's Medicare for All Dilemma*, New Yorker (Oct. 17, 2019), https://perma.cc/W2SK-FZBB.
41. Gretchen Livingston, *Among 41 Nations, US Is the Outlier When It Comes to Paid Parental Leave*, Pew Res. Ctr. (Sept. 26, 2016), https://perma.cc/P5RA-XWB4.
42. So far, California, New Jersey, New York, Rhode Island, and Washington (and the District of Columbia).
43. *See* Julie Kashen, *The Future of Work? Paid Leave for All*, Century Found. (Mar. 8, 2018), https://perma.cc/6N83-J6P9.
44. *See* AEI-Brookings Working Group on Paid Family Leave, *Paid Family and Medical Leave: An Issue Whose Time Has Come*, Brookings 4–7 (May 2017), https://perma.cc/TMC6-B5NJ.
45. The Family and Medical Leave Act, 29 U.S.C. § 2601 (2018), already requires that to a limited extent.
46. *See FMLA and Its Impact on Organizations: A Survey Report by the Society for Human Resource Management*, Soc'y for Hum. Res. Mgmt. 26 figure12 (July 2007), https://perma.cc/CYG7-6MME; Jacob Alex Klerman et al., *Family and Medical Leave in 2012: Technical Report*, Abt Assocs., Inc. 157 exhibits 8.5.1 & 8.5.2 (Apr. 18, 2014), https://perma.cc/NN4A-F939.
47. Of course, that would be illegal, but it might not be detectable, provable, or likely to trigger a lawsuit. *See* Samuel Issacharoff & Elyse Rosenblum, *Women and the Workplace: Accommodating the Demands of Pregnancy*, 94 Colum. L. Rev. 2154, 2172–89 (1994).
48. *See Overview of Paid Family & Medical Leave Laws in the United States*, A Better Balance 5 (July 1, 2020), https://perma.cc/GD4X-9WA3.
49. Paid family leave might foster employee retention and loyalty. That is presumably why some employers voluntarily offer paid such benefits. It is less clear that *mandatory* paid family leave does that. *See supra* Chapter 3 [n. 57].
50. *See* Kelly Bedard & Maya Rossin-Slater, *The Economic and Social Impacts of Paid Family Leave in California*, Cal. Emp't. Dev. Dep't (Oct. 13, 2016), https://perma.cc/MU6V-D3AP; Harry J. Holzer, *Paid Family Leave: Balancing Benefits and Costs*, Brookings (Jan. 30, 2017), https://perma.cc/A33C-ENQ4.
51. Holzer 2017.
52. *Id.*; Eileen Appelbaum & Ruth Milkman, *Paid Family Leave Pays Off in California*, Harv. Bus. Rev. (Jan. 19, 2011), https://perma.cc/KNU3-T945; *The Economics of Paid and Unpaid Leave*, Council of Econ. Advisers 19–20 (June 2014), https://perma.cc/9RVB-GRWP.
53. *See* Erin Killian, *Parental Leave: The Swedes Are the Most Generous*, NPR (Aug. 8, 2011 3:59 PM EST), https://perma.cc/Y3GE-9EG5.
54. *See* Chapter 3 [nn. 85–89].

55. *See* Living Wage Calculator (2020): for Holmes County, Mississippi, https://perma.cc/7DKD-6R58; for Atlanta-Sandy Springs-Roswell, GA, https://perma.cc/3YS4-CCK7.
56. *See* Living Wage Calculator (2020): for New York County, NY, https://perma.cc/4QXB-3GZA.
57. *Earned Income Tax Credit Overview*, Nat'l Conf. St. Legislatures (July 15, 2020), https://perma.cc/N5RR-ZU8T.
58. David Callahan, *Why Not Peg EITC Benefits to the Local Cost of Living?*, Demos (Mar. 9, 2014), https://perma.cc/HFT7-T4Q4.
59. 26 U.S.C. § 32(c)(2)(A)(ii) (2018).
60. Daniel Shaviro, *The Minimum Wage, the Earned Income Tax Credit, and Optimal Subsidy Policy*, 64 U. Chi. L. Rev. 405, 459–66 (1997).
61. Isabel V. Sawhill & Quentin Karpilow, *Raising the Minimum Wage and Redesigning the EITC*, Econ. Pol'y Inst. (Jan. 30, 2014), https://perma.cc/QV69-BBZB; Alan B. Krueger, *The Minimum Wage: How Much Is Too Much?*, N.Y. Times (Oct. 10, 2015), https://perma.cc/34ZG-DK29 (both recommending increases in EITC *and* the minimum wage).
62. Oren Cass, *The Wage Subsidy: A Better Way to Help the Poor*, Manhattan Inst. for Pol'y Res. 12 (2015), https://perma.cc/V54K-U25U.
63. For an empirical assessment of some relatively narrow wage subsidy programs, see Lawrence F. Katz, *Wage Subsidies for the Disadvantaged* (NBER Working Paper No. 5679, 1996), https://perma.cc/4VTD-UJ66. For a more polemical endorsement from a business-friendly think tank, *see The Case for a Targeted Living Wage Subsidy*, Emp. Policies Inst. (2001), https://perma.cc/6RUT-ME3H.
64. Shaviro finds these "even better" than the EITC on efficiency grounds. Shaviro, *supra* note 60, at 410.
65. West Coast Hotel v. Parrish, 300 US 379, 399 (1937).
66. Soc. Sec. Admin., Fact Sheet: Social Security (2020), https://perma.cc/XM2V-MP22.
67. As of 2018, only the first $125,400 of income is subject to the tax. *Maximum Taxable Earnings (1937–2018)*, Soc. Security Admin., https://perma.cc/QJ8Y-JGHQ.
68. Elizabeth Newman, Downhill from Here: Retirement Insecurity in the Age of Inequality (2019).
69. *See* Daniel S. Hamermesh, *Do Labor Costs Affect Companies' Demand for Labor?*, IZA World Lab. (2014), https://perma.cc/5PRU-NXGR. *Cf.* Lawrence H. Summers, *What Can Economics Contribute to Social Policy?: Some Simple Economics of Mandated Benefits*, 79 Am. Econ. Rev. 177, 181 (1989).
70. Daron Acemoglu, Andrea Manera, & Pascual Restrepo, *Taxes, Automation, and the Future of Labor*, Mit Work Of The Future Taskforce (2020), https://perma.cc/2YZX-WUTJ.
71. *Id.* at 2.
72. *See* William E. Forbath, *The Ambiguities of Free Labor: Labor and the Law in the Gilded Age*, 1985 Wis. L. Rev. 767, 769 (1985); Elizabeth Anderson, Private Government: How Employers Rule Our Lives (and Why We Don't Talk

ABOUT IT) (2017). Some were also struggling to retain their domination of unfree members of their own households—wives, children, apprentices, servants, slaves.

73. *See* SUPIOT, *supra* note 37, at 57.
74. The 1999 "Supiot Report" was later published in book form. SUPIOT, *supra* note 37.
75. Judy Fudge et al., *Changing Boundaries in Employment: Developing a New Platform for Labour Law*, 10 CANADIAN LAB. & EMP. L.J. 329, 331–32, 363 (quoting Brian Langille, *Labour Policy in Canada—New Platform, New Paradigm*, 28 CANADIAN PUB. POL'Y 133 (2002)).
76. *See generally* ARUN SUNDARARAJAN, THE SHARING ECONOMY: THE END OF EMPLOYMENT AND THE RISE OF CROWD-BASED CAPITALISM (2016); David Shadpour, *The Gig Economy: Pioneering The Future*, FORBES (Jan. 19, 2018), https://perma.cc/5LPJ-ARS3.
77. McKinsey Glob. Inst., *Independent Work: Choice, Necessity, and the Gig Economy*, MCKINSEY & COMPANY 1, 7 (2016), https://perma.cc/9D4K-AAEU.
78. *Id. See also* Harry Campbell, *Lyft & Uber Driver Survey 2019: Uber Driver Satisfaction Takes a Big Hit*, RIDESHARE GUY (Oct. 1, 2020), https://perma.cc/FX3C-RAJ3 (66 percent of drivers surveyed said they wanted to be independent contractors, for reasons including flexibility, "control/autonomy," "independence/freedom," and "not wanting to be 'micromanaged' or assigned specific shifts, hours to work, etc.").

Chapter 7

1. For example, in January 2020 the Finnish prime minister announced potential legislation mandating a four-day week for all employees. André Spicer, *Will Finland Introduce a Four-Day Week?*, GUARDIAN (Jan. 6, 2020), https://perma.cc/S4DJ-8Z77. *See also Achieving a Shorter Working Week Across Europe*, NEW ECON. FOUND. (Mar. 2019), https://perma.cc/6MH3-3B8R; *The Shorter Work Week: A Radical and Pragmatic Proposal* (Will Stronge & Aidan Harper eds., 2019), https://perma.cc/M97M-Y8AT.
2. Stefano Scarpetta et al., *Job Retention Schemes During the Covid-19 Lockdown and Beyond*, OECD (Aug. 3, 2020), https://perma.cc/57S4-RCB5.
3. The bottom 40 percent of *households* are those that that make less than $50,000 as of 2018. *Household Income Quintiles*, TAX POL'Y CTR. (Mar. 24, 2020), https://perma.cc/T74Y-BZWK.
4. I have more to say about those issues in CYNTHIA ESTLUND, REGOVERNING THE WORKPLACE: FROM SELF-REGULATION TO CO-REGULATION (2010).
5. That income level satisfies the "salary" test for the white-collar exemptions, making the more subjective "duties" test determinative. An estimated 11.5 percent of salaried workers are misclassified as exempt by their employers. Susann Rohwedder & Jeffrey B. Wenger, *The Fair Labor Standards Act: Worker Misclassification and the Hours and Earnings Effects of Expanded Coverage*, RAND CORP. WR-1114 (2015), https://perma.cc/36LE-9QMK.

6. Alex Andonovska, *Understanding the Biglaw Salary Scale*, JD J. (Apr. 22, 2020), https://perma.cc/LA88-KP7G.
7. This assumes a billable target of 2,200 hours a year and includes the non-billable hours that lawyers work. *The Truth About the Billable Hour*, YALE LAW SCHOOL CAREER DEV. OFFICE (last visited Aug. 27, 2020), https://perma.cc/EJ2X-2QGV.
8. *See* Janet Walsh, *Not Worth the Sacrifice? Women's Aspirations and Career Progression in Law Firms*, 19 GENDER, WORK & ORG. 508 (2012); Veta T. Richardson & Robin Meyers, *Cause and Effect: Why Women Leave the Legal Profession*, ASS'N CORP. COUNS. DOCKET 78 (Jan./Feb. 2017), https://perma.cc/329D-EJWG.
9. For evidence that work has become more intense in the last few decades, apart from longer hours, see ARNE L. KALLEBERG, GOOD JOBS, BAD JOBS 154–58 (2011).
10. *See* Simon Deakin et al., *How Do Labour Laws Affect Unemployment and The Labour Share of National Income? The Experience of Six OECD Countries, 1970–2010,* 154 INT'L LAB. REV. 1, 5 (2014).
11. Some of those quasi-fixed costs consist of mandatory benefits, the cost of which would be reduced under the unburdening strategy described in Chapter 6.
12. *Briefing: The Future of the Office*, ECONOMIST (Sept. 12, 2020), https://perma.cc/C6DV-TAQ3.
13. For a recent exploration of the problem, see JAMIE K. MCCALLUM, WORKED OVER (2020).
14. Andre Zimmerman, *New EU Directive on Transparent and Predictable Working Conditions Will Give Gig Workers More Rights*, ORRICK EMP'T LAW & LITIG. (July 19, 2019), https://perma.cc/3W9H-ZBY2.
15. US workers exceed those in most EU countries in both average weekly and annual hours. Alexander Bick et al., *Hours Worked in Europe and the US: New Data, New Answers* (IZA, Discussion Paper No. 10179, Aug. 2016). And in the United States, unlike other rich countries, average annual and weekly hours have increased over the past century. SANGHEON LEE ET AL., WORKING TIME AROUND THE WORLD 25–26 (2007); Kuhn & Lozano, *infra* note 43, at 311–12. Moreover, one in three US workers works on weekends, and one in four does work between 10 p.m. and 6 a.m. Daniel S. Hamermesh & Elena Stancanelli, *Long Workweeks and Strange Hours*, 68 INT'L LABOR REV. 1007, 1009 (2015).
16. Paul M. Secunda, *The Employee Right to Disconnect*, 9 NOTRE DAME J. INT'L & COMP. L. 1, 27–30 (2019) (comparing French and German approaches to the right to disconnect).
17. Press Release, Dep't of Labor, US Department of Labor Issues Final Overtime Rule (Sept. 24, 2019), https://perma.cc/6XVQ-RLAG.
18. For evidence that overtime premiums tend to reduce working hours, *see* Daniel Hamermesh & Stephen Trejo, *The Demand for Hours of Labor: Direct Evidence from California*, 82 REV. ECON. & STAT. 38 (2000).
19. *See* Joan C. Williams et al., *Cultural Schemas, Social Class, and the Flexibility Stigma*, 69 J. SOC. ISSUES 209, 213–15 (2013). On white-collar workers' resistance to working time regulations, *see* Deborah Malamud, *Engineering the Middle Classes: Class Line-Drawing in New Deal Hours Legislation*, 96 MICH. L. REV. 2212 (1998).

20. One in five workers said they would take a 20 percent pay cut in exchange for one less day of work. Lonnie Golden, *FLSA Working Hours Reform: Worker Well-Being Effects in an Economic Framework*, 54 Indus. Relations 717, 733 (2015). And many say they would accept a 20 percent wage cut to secure hours that are steady and predictable, or to avoid evening and weekend hours. Alexandre Mas & Amanda Pallais, *Valuing Alternative Work Schedules* 17 (NBER Working Paper No. 22708, 2016), https://perma.cc/7GBW-DW7W.
21. Council Directive 2003/88/EC, of the European Parliament and of the Council of 4 November 2003 Concerning Certain Aspects of Working Time, Art. 6, 2003 O.J. (L 299) 9.
22. Most EU states guarantee maternity leaves of several months (with at least two-thirds pay), with some as high as twelve months (not all paid); and most also provide two to three weeks or more of paid paternity leave. Peter Moss & Fred Deven, *Leave Policies in Europe*, 40 Int'l J. Soc. & Soc. Pol'y 429, 432–33 (2019). EU law requires at least four months of total parental leave for a new child, including at least ten days of paid paternity leave. Council of the European Union Press Release IP 10/19, *Better Work-Life Balance for Parents and Carers in the EU: Council Adopts New Rules* (June 13, 2019), https://perma.cc/G5BW-VTYD.
23. On the potential work-spreading benefits of paid leave policies, *see* Per Kongshøj Madsen, *Working Time Policy and Paid Leave Arrangements: The Danish Experience in the 1990s*, 4 Euro. Rev. of Lab. & Res. 692, 710–11 (1998).
24. Cynthia Estlund, *Wrongful Discharge Protections in an At-Will World*, 74 Tex. L. Rev. 1655 (1996).
25. Laura Carlson, *Sweden's Experience in Combatting Employment Discrimination* 10 (unpublished manuscript presented at the Institute of European and American Studies, Academica Sinica, 2007), https://perma.cc/K2QU-YT4V.
26. For a proposal to expand employers' duty to make reasonable accommodations, see Michael Ashley Stein et al., *Accommodating Every Body*, 81 U. Chi. L. Rev. 689 (2014).
27. *See* Pam Walton et al., *Appendix 1: Job Sharing—Literature Review* 47–54, *in* Lucy Daniels, *Job Sharing at Senior Level: Making it Work*, The Job Share Project (2011), https://perma.cc/YEB3-Q8BQ. See also Rosalind Dixon & Richard Holder, Fair Markets: Liberalism After COVID (forthcoming 2021).
28. European Union, *Your Europe/Part-Time Work*, https://perma.cc/9638-PVKW; Center for Economic and Policy Research, *The US and Europe: Different Approaches on Work-Life Balance*, Nov. 2016, https://perma.cc/46KZ-42ET.
29. *See* Bailey et al., *infra* note 31, at 25; Marianne Bertrand et al., *Gender Identity and Relative Income within Households*, 130 Q. J. Econ. 571, 592–94 (2015). Even single women in an MBA program express less willingness to work long hours or travel, perhaps because it signals "less availability for home production." Leonardo Bursztyn et al., *'Acting Wife': Marriage Market Incentives and Labor Market Investments*, 107 Am. Econ. Rev. 3288, 3290–91 (2017).
30. *See* Mallika Thomas, *The Impact of Mandated Maternity Benefits on the Gender Differential in Promotions: Examining the Role of Adverse Selection* 31–32 (Cornell

ILR, Inst. for Compensation Stud., Paper No. 2016-0001, 2016), https://perma.cc/Z4L5-62VV.

31. *See, e.g.*, Heather Antecol et al., *Equal But Inequitable: Who Benefits from Gender-Neutral Tenure Clock Stopping Policies?* 18–22 (Inst. for Study of Lab., Discussion Paper No. 9904, Apr. 2016), https://perma.cc/BQ99-XDKP; Martha Bailey et al., *The Long Term Effects of California's 2004 Paid Family Leave Act on Women's Careers: Evidence from US Tax Data* 2-4 (NBER, Working Paper No. 26416, 2019); Thomas, *supra* note 30, at 31–32.
32. *See, e.g.*, Gozde Corekcioglu et al., *Do Generous Parental Leave Policies Help Top Female Earners?* (Nor. Sch. of Econ., Disc. Paper No. 07/2020, May 2020), https://perma.cc/KH3E-PUYA; Antecol, et al., *supra* note 31.
33. See Ásdís A. Arnalds et al., *Equal Rights to Paid Parental Leave and Caring Fathers—The Case of Iceland*, 9 Ice. Rev. Pol. & Admin. 323 (2013); Lenna Nepomnyaschy & Jane Waldfogel, *Paternity Leave and Fathers' Involvement with Young Children*, 10 Cmty., Work & Fam. 427 (2007); Ankita Paknaik, *Reserving Time for Daddy: The Consequences of Fathers' Quotas*, 37 J. Lab. Econ. 1009 (2019).
34. *EU Plans to Move Closer to the Swedish Model for Parental Leave*, Economist (Nov. 23, 2017), https://perma.cc/TWL7-DHUD; Anne Chemin, *Norway, the Fatherland*, Guardian (July 19, 2011), https://perma.cc/NW8X-PVVQ.
35. On US law's lower tolerance for gender preferences, *see* Jens Dammann, *Place Aux Dames: The Ideological Divide Between US and European Gender Discrimination Laws*, 45 Cornell J. Int'l L. 25 (2012).
36. *See* Scott Coltrane et al., *Fathers and the Flexibility Stigma*, 69 J. Soc. Issues 279, 288–89 (2013); Alina Ewald et al., *Fathering and Flexible Working Arrangements*, 12 J. Fam. Theory & Rev. 27 (2020); Claire Cain Miller, *Men Say They Want Paid Leave But Then Don't Use All of It. What Stops Them?*, N.Y. Times (Dec. 4, 2019), https://perma.cc/Q6QU-FA6X.
37. *See* Williams et al., *supra* note 19.
38. Karl Marx, *A Critique of the German Ideology*, Marxists Internet Archives [1845] (last visited Aug. 28, 2020), https://perma.cc/4YDD-UE4X.
39. The idea echoes Alain Supiot's idea of "social drawing rights," in which everyone would be entitled to a source of funds to support a range of socially valued activities. Alain Supiot, Beyond Employment 56–57 (2001). Others have expanded on this idea. Lionel Maurel et al., *Common Labour Rights and the Right of the Commons*, 13 J. Peer Prod. 1, 4–6 (2018).
40. Heather Boushey, Finding Time: The Economics of Work-Life Conflict 96–111 (2016); Kalleberg, *supra* note 9, at 151–56; Bridget Ansel & Heather Boushey, *Overworked America: The Economic Causes and Consequences of Long Work Hours*, Wash. Ctr. Econ. Growth 22–23 (2016), https://perma.cc/J9VR-LBM4; Claudia Goldin, *A Grand Gender Convergence: Its Last Chapter*, 104 Am. Econ. Rev. 4 1091, 1094 (2014); Cha & Weeden, *infra* note 43.
41. Goldin, *supra* note 40, at 1094.
42. *See* Kalleberg, *supra* note 9, at 105–31.

43. Goldin, *supra* note 40, at 1094. The wage premium for long hours has increased in recent decades. Youngjoo Cha & Kim A. Weeden, *Overwork and the Slow Convergence in the Gender Gap in Wages*, 79 AM. SOC. REV. 457, 468 (2014). *See also* Peter Kuhn & Fernando Lozano, *Understanding Trends in Long Work Hours Among US Men, 1979–2004*, 26 J. LAB. ECON. 311 (2008).
44. Ansel & Boushey, *supra* note 40.
45. Debra Cassens Weiss, *Would Millennial Lawyers Trade Pay for Better Work-Life Balance? A Significant Percentage Say Yes*, ABA J. (Apr. 4, 2019), https://perma.cc/Q5AS-PAH3.
46. Goldin, *supra* note 40, at 1117.
47. *Id.*
48. This move would raise the cost of some labor versus machines, but these jobs are among the least automatable. And if we got far enough along in the project of work spreading for this idea to be thinkable—nearing the goal of less work for all versus little or no work for many—less work is less worrisome.
49. *See* Rocky Mengle, *Election 2020: Joe Biden's Tax Plans*, KIPLINGERS (Aug. 26, 2020), https://perma.cc/LE56-VQ2E.
50. That rate kicked in at $200,0000 for single filers, or $1.5 million in 2020 dollars. *Historical Highest Marginal Income Tax Rates*, TAX POL'Y CTR. (Feb. 4, 2020), https://perma.cc/KJ8K-ZQNJ; Nick Kasprak, *Some Historical Tax Stats*, TAX FOUND. (Sept. 29, 2011), https://perma.cc/AV55-A5SY.
51. James Fallows, *When the US Tax Rate was 70 Percent—Or Higher*, ATLANTIC (Jan. 25, 2019), https://perma.cc/ZR47-FCJ6. The Reagan administration enacted the biggest changes in this realm. For a succinct history of twentieth-century tax policy, *see* Sven Steinmo, *The Evolution of Policy Ideas in the 20th Century*, 5 BRITISH J. POL. & INT'L REL. 206 (2003).
52. Thomas Piketty & Emmanuel Saez, *Income Inequality in the United States, 1913–1998,* 118 Q. J. ECON. 1 (2003).
53. *The Shorter Work Week: A Radical and Pragmatic Proposal* (Will Stronge & Aidan Harper, eds.) (2019), https://perma.cc/M97M-Y8AT.
54. *Id.* at 49.
55. Mark Muro et al., *Automation & Artificial Intelligence: How Machines are Affecting People and Places*, BROOKINGS 52–56 (2019), https://perma.cc/XKZ9-XRPM.
56. *See id.* at 55–56.
57. *See* Paul Osterman, *Skill Training for Adults*, MIT WORK OF THE FUTURE TASKFORCE 6–7 (2020), https://perma.cc/48GA-GZJH.
58. Annalies Goger, *Desegregating Work and Learning Through "Earn-and-Learn" Models*, BROOKINGS (Dec. 9, 2020), https://www.brookings.edu/research/desegregating-work-and-learning/.
59. *See* Jonathan Harris, *Unconscionability in Contracting for Worker Training*, 72 ALA. L. REV. (forthcoming, 2021).
60. See Harris, *id.* at 47. The idea of income share agreements, or of selling "stock" in oneself, was first floated by Milton Friedman; the high returns have made them popular

investment instruments in Silicon Valley, but also reflect the usurious character of some of these agreements. *Id.* at 47–51.

61. *See generally* LYNDA GRATTON & ANDREW SCOTT, THE 100 YEAR LIFE (2016); Anne Alstott, *Law and the Hundred-Year Life*, 26 ELDER L.J. 131 (2016).
62. For recent calls for protections against unjustified dismissal, *see* Benjamin Sachs & Sharon Block, *Clean Slate for Worker Power: Building a Just Economy and Democracy*, HARV. L. SCH. LAB. & WORKLIFE PROGRAM 46–50 (Jan. 23, 2020), https://perma.cc/G3JG-SCDE; Alexander Hertel-Fernandez, *American Workers' Experiences with Power, Information, and Rights on the Job: A Roadmap for Reform*, ROOSEVELT INST. 10, 34 (2020), https://perma.cc/L5NU-ZDAW.
63. *See* Zoe Adams et al., *The Economic Significance of Laws Relating to Employment Protection and Different Forms of Employment: Analysis of a Panel of 117 Countries, 1990–2013*, 158 INT'L LAB. REV. 1, 2 (2019).
64. *See* Deakin et al., *supra* note 10, at 5–6.
65. *See* Adams et al., *supra* note 63, at 2.
66. *Id.*
67. According to MIT's Living Wage Calculator as of March 2020 (https://livingwage.mit.edu/articles/61-new-living-wage-data-for-now-available-on-the-tool#:~:text=The%20living%20wage%20in%20the,wage%20for%20most%20American%20families). That does not take into account the contribution of universal basic benefits or more public goods on what counts as adequate income.
68. *See* Richard B. Freeman, *Who Owns the Robots Rules the World*, IZA WORLD LAB. 1 (2015), https://perma.cc/V8R9-7PRX.
69. *Id.*
70. See JOSEPH R. BLASI ET AL., THE CITIZEN'S SHARE: PUTTING OWNERSHIP BACK INTO DEMOCRACY (2013); DOUGLAS KRUSE ET AL., SHARED CAPITALISM AT WORK: EMPLOYEE OWNERSHIP, PROFIT AND GAIN SHARING, AND BROAD-BASED STOCK OPTIONS, NBER Books (2010), https://econpapers.repec.org/bookchap/nbrnberbk/krus08-1.htm.
71. BLASI, FREEMAN & KRUSE, *supra* note 70.
72. *Id.*
73. There might be some optimal balance between diversification and concentration of workers' portfolios. *See* Joseph R. Blasi et al., *Risk and Lack of Diversification Under Employee Ownership and Shared Capitalism*, in KRUSE, FREEMAN & BLASI, *supra* note 70, https://www.nber.org/system/files/chapters/c8088/c8088.pdf.
74. See *id.* for some efforts to solve this puzzle.

Chapter 8

1. Payroll taxes in general are the most regressive large category of taxes in Europe as well as in the United States. *See Briefing Book*, TAX POL'Y CTR. 61 fig.2 (2016), https://perma.cc/66M8-UC2K; *Policy Basics: Federal Payroll Taxes*, CTR. ON BUDGET &

Pol'y Priorities (Mar. 23, 2016), https://perma.cc/5L9U-HTJ8; John H. Cochrane, *Europe's Payroll Taxes*, Grumpy Economist (Sept. 22, 2012, 3:28 p.m.), https://perma.cc/36RE-REC3.

2. For a close look at the politics and social psychology of redistribution, with some implications for funding of social programs, *see* Gillian Lester, *Can Joe the Plumber Support Redistribution? Law, Social Preferences, and Sustainable Policy Design*, 64 Tax L. Rev. 313 (2011); Gillian Lester, *"Keep Government Out of My Medicare": The Search for Popular Support of Taxes and Social Spending*, *in* Working and Living in the Shadow of Economic Fragility 176 (Marion Crain & Michael Sherraden eds., 2014).
3. Social Security and Medicare also have the political advantage of mainly benefiting older or disabled individuals, as opposed to adults capable of working.
4. *See* Theda Skocpol, *Targeting within Universalism: Politically Viable Policies to Combat Poverty in the United States*, *in* The Urban Underclass 411 (Christopher Jencks & Paul E. Peterson eds., 1991).
5. Of course, Social Security (and Medicare) are also highly resistant to reform, even when it is needed. Indeed, Social Security is so resistant to reform it is often called the "third rail of politics, touch it and you die." *See The Third Rail*, Economist (Oct. 7, 2004), https://perma.cc/ZH74-KNN7. But we're likely facing a long-term and growing need for redistributive programs; securing their enactment and insulating them against backlash seems worth the risk of excessive entrenchment against needed reforms.
6. *See generally* Lawrence F. Katz, *Wage Subsidies for the Disadvantaged* (NBER Working Paper No. 5679, 1996), https://perma.cc/4VTD-UJ66.
7. Cass, *supra* note 6, at 15.
8. Robert E. Prasch, *What Is Wrong with Wage Subsidies?*, 36 J. Econ. Issues 357, 360–61 (2002).
9. *See* Anne Roder & Mark Elliott, *Stimulating Opportunity: An Evaluation of ARRA-Funded Subsidized Employment Programs*, Econ. Mobility Corp. (2013), https://perma.cc/86PF-UZ9J; Katz, *supra* note 6, at 18–23, 26–27.
10. As we saw in asking whether employers or employees actually bear the cost of existing payroll taxes; *see* Chapter 3 [nn. 49–53].
11. *See* Dylan Matthews, *Modern Monetary Theory, Explained*, Vox (Apr. 16, 2019), https://www.vox.com/future-perfect/2019/4/16/18251646/modern-monetary-theory-new-moment-explained.
12. *See id.*
13. *See* Milton Ezrati, *What Is Modern Monetary Theory?*, Forbes, May 28, 2019, https://www.forbes.com/sites/miltonezrati/2019/05/28/what-is-modern-monetary-theory/#221b20613186.
14. *See* Matthews, *supra* note 11.
15. *See id.*; Patricia Cohen, *Modern Monetary Theory Finds an Embrace in an Unexpected Place, Wall Street*, N.Y. Times (Apr. 5, 2019), https://perma.cc/5N5F-BJA9.
16. For recent critiques of MMT from the left side of the spectrum, *see* Matt Bruenig, *Just What Is a Job Guarantee*, Jacobin (May 13, 2018), https://perma.cc/

7K4A-VVY5; Paul Krugman, Opinion, *MMT, Again*, N.Y. Times, Aug. 15, 2011, https://perma.cc/F23D-V5A7. Nearer the middle, see Lawrence Summers, *The Left's Embrace of Modern Monetary Theory Is a Recipe for Disaster*, Washington Post (March 4, 2019), https://perma.cc/3K57-GD7X; and from the right, *see* Warren Coats, *Modern Monetary Theory: A Critique*, 39 Cato J. 3 (2019), https://perma.cc/2GYV-FQBU.

17. Laura Tyson & Michael Spence, *Exploring the Effects of Technology on Income and Wealth Inequality*, *in* After Piketty: The Agenda for Economics and Inequality 170, 171 (Heather Boushey, J. Bradford DeLong, & Marshall Steinbaum eds., 2017).
18. Edward D. Kleinbard, We Are Better Than This: How Government Should Spend Our Money xxi (2015).
19. *Id. See also* Tax Policy Center, *How Do U.S. Taxes Compare Internationally?*, https://www.taxpolicycenter.org/briefing-book/how-do-us-taxes-compare-internationally.
20. *See* Kevin J. Delaney, *The Robot That Takes Your Job Should Pay Taxes, Says Bill Gates*, Quartz (Feb. 17, 2017), https://perma.cc/G3KD-WVX5; *see also* Abbott & Bogenschneider, *infra* note 26; Orly Masur, *Taxing the Robots*, 46 Pepp. L. Rev. 277, 297 (2019)
21. *See, e.g.*, Masur, *supra* note 20, at 298–304 (criticizing "robot tax" proposals); Daron Acemoglu, Andrea Manera, & Pascual Restrepo, *Taxes, Automation, and the Future of Labor*, MIT Work of the Future Taskforce 13 (2020) [hereinafter, Acemoglu, Manera, & Restrepo, *Future of Labor*], https://perma.cc/2YZX-WUTJ.
22. Masur, *supra* note 20, at 298–99
23. *See id.* at 299; Acemoglu, Manera, & Restrepo, *Future of Labor, supra* note 21, at 13.
24. Though that argument might reflect a more sanguine view of technological innovation than I have taken here. *See* Yanis Varoufakis, *A Tax on Robots? Bill Gates' Proposal for a "Robot Tax" Highlights Technological Risks to Jobs – and also to the Income Tax Base*, Acuity (June–July 2017), at 35–36; James Bessen, Commentary, *Bill Gates Is Wrong That Robots and Automation Are Killing Jobs*, Fortune (Feb. 25, 2017), https://perma.cc/QU3B-46DZ.
25. Daron Acemoglu, Andrea Manera & Pascual Restrepo, *Does the US Tax Code Favor Automation?* 10–13 (NBER, Working Paper No. 27052, April 2020), https://perma.cc/T44S-QXM4.
26. Daron Acemoglu & Pascual Restrepo, *Artificial Intelligence, Automation and Work* 14 (NBER, Working Paper No. 24196, 2018), https://perma.cc/L768-6NSV. *See also* Ryan Abbott & Bret Bogenschneider, *Should Robots Pay Taxes? Tax Policy in the Age of Automation*, 12 Harv. L. & Pol'y Rev., 145, 150 (2018).
27. Acemoglu, Manera, & Restrepo, *Future of Labor, supra* note 21, at 14.
28. Greater progressivity could be achieved in part by eliminating some highly regressive tax expenditures, including "around $100 billion of outright subsidies every year to various business interests—subsidies that never would pass muster as cash outlays." Kleinbard, *supra* note 18, at 242.
29. *Historical Highest Marginal Income Tax Rates*, Tax Pol'y Ctr. (Feb. 4 2020), https://perma.cc/KJ8K-ZQNJ.

30. THOMAS PIKETTY, CAPITAL IN THE TWENTY-FIRST CENTURY 515–39 (Arthur Goldhammer trans., 2014).
31. *See* Leonard E. Burman et al., *Financial Transaction Taxes in Theory and Practice*, 69 NAT'L TAX J. 171 (2016). For a critique of the FTT, see Tim Worstall, *The Monstrous Idiocy of the Robin Hood Tax Rears Its Ugly Head Again*, FORBES (Mar. 20, 2015), https://perma.cc/7JPF-5TYR.
32. *See* Lily L. Batchelder, *What Should Society Expect from Heirs:? A Proposal for a Comprehensive Inheritance Tax*, 63 TAX L. REV. 1 (2009); Lily L. Batchelder, *Tax the Rich and Their Heirs*, N.Y. TIMES (June 24, 2020), https://perma.cc/2LHB-GNAH.
33. *See* Michael J. Graetz, *100 Million Unnecessary Returns: A Fresh Start for the U.S. Tax System*, 112 YALE L.J. 261, 281–90 (2002). Consumption taxes tend to be regressive, but that could be offset either by other taxes or, on the spending side, by using increased revenues to fund redistributive programs.
34. *See* KLEINBARD, *supra* note 18, Lily L. Batchelder & David Kamen, *Taxing the Rich: Issues and Options*, available at https://papers.ssrn.com/sol3/papers.cfm?abstract_id=3452274. *See also* ROSALIND DIXON & RICHARD HOLDER, FAIR MARKETS: LIBERALISM AFTER COVID (forthcoming, OUP, 2022).
35. The gamesmanship that can be set off by changes in tax laws is illustrated (in the context of the Trump tax legislation) in an extraordinary report by thirteen leading tax law scholars. *See* David Kamin et al., *The Games They Will Play: Tax Games, Roadblocks, and Glitches Under the 2017 Tax Legislation*, 103 MINN. L. REV. 1439 (2019).

Chapter 9

1. SYLVIA NASAR, GRAND PURSUIT: THE STORY OF ECONOMIC GENIUS xiii–xiv (2011) (discussing Thomas Robert Malthus, *An Essay on the Principle of Population* (1798)).
2. Bayard Rustin, *From Protest to Politics: The Future of the Civil Rights Movement*, COMMENTARY (Feb. 1965), available at https://perma.cc/D28A-NTJZ. Rustin was not alone among civil rights leaders who perceived that automation would have a disparate impact on Black workers. *See* Charlton McIlwain, *The Three Civil Rights-Era Leaders Who Warned of Computers and Racism*, SLATE (Jan. 30, 2020), https://perma.cc/2CNJ-TQZ4.
3. Rustin, *supra* note 2.
4. *Id.*
5. *See* Karen Tumulty & Kennedy Elliott, *Evaluating the Success of the Great Society*, WASH. POST (May 17, 2014), https://perma.cc/ZU99-YYR9 (charting key pieces of legislation by month and year).
6. For one persuasive take on that complex question, *see* EZRA KLEIN, WHY WE'RE POLARIZED (2020).
7. For two engaging origin stories of this concerted campaign, featuring Friedrich Hayek, Milton Friedman, and others, *see* JOSEPH FISHKIN & WILLIAM E. FORBATH,

THE ANTI-OLIGARCHY CONSTITUTION [coda] (forthcoming 2021); and DAVID HARVEY, A BRIEF HISTORY OF NEOLIBERALISM 19–30 (2007). Especially in the United States, businesses, large and small, and their organizations mobilized aggressively and effectively to push political, legal, and judicial institutions to the right. *See* JACOB HACKER & PAUL PIERSON, WINNER-TAKE-ALL POLITICS 116–26 (2011). A famous 1971 memo by soon-to-be Justice Lewis Powell for the Chamber of Commerce, available at https://scholarlycommons.law.wlu.edu/powellmemo/1/) exhorted the business community to action and pointed the way.

8. President Ronald Reagan, *First Inaugural Address* (Jan. 20, 1981), https://perma.cc/TV6N-NUHC.
9. *See generally* HACKER & PIERSON, *supra* note 7.
10. See, for example, Milton Friedman's analysis of unions in 1962, MILTON FRIEDMAN, CAPITALISM AND FREEDOM 115–17, 123–25 (1962).
11. For one excellent recent account, *see* SOPHIA Z. LEE, THE WORKPLACE CONSTITUTION FROM THE NEW DEAL TO THE NEW RIGHT 56–80 (2014).
12. *See* HACKER & PIERSON, *supra* note 7, at 129–32.
13. Alberto Alesina et al., *Why Doesn't the United States Have a European-Style Welfare State?*, 2 BROOKINGS PAPERS ON ECON. ACTIVITY 187 (2001), https://perma.cc/L7RC-MFJN.
14. *See, e.g.*, JOSEPH E. STIGLITZ, GLOBALIZATION AND ITS DISCONTENTS REVISITED xxxix–xli, 3–4, 9 (2018); Cohen, *Populism*, *infra* note 15, at 20; David Autor et al., *Importing Political Polarization: The Electoral Consequences of Rising Trade Exposure* (NBER Working Paper No. 22637, 2016), https://perma.cc/8NRB-9TM4.
15. On this function of unions, *see* Jean L. Cohen, *Populism and the Politics of Resentment*, 1 JUS COGENS 5, 20–23 (2019) [hereinafter Cohen, *Populism*]; Seymour Martin Lipset, *Democracy and Working-Class Authoritarianism*, 24 AM. SOC. REV. 482, 484 (1959); Karen Nussbaum, *Unions and Democracy*, 44 LAB. STUD. J. 365 (2019).
16. I do that at greater length in Cynthia Estlund, *Coming Apart: How Union Decline and Workplace Disintegration Imperil Democracy*, in THE CAMBRIDGE HANDBOOK OF LABOR AND DEMOCRACY (Mark Barenberg & Angela Cornell eds., forthcoming 2021).
17. *See* Chapter 4, *supra* [Sec. B.4].
18. *See* Heidi Shierholz & Margaret Poydock, *Continued Surge in Strike Activity Signals Worker Dissatisfaction with Wage Growth*, ECON. POL'Y INST. (Feb. 11, 2020), https://perma.cc/9JGU-LGSZ. On the role of young workers, *see* Steven Greenhouse, *The Faces of a New Union Movement*, NEW YORKER (Feb. 28, 2020), https://perma.cc/Z7NB-JTCJ.
19. *See* Sarita Gupta, Stephen Lerner, & Joseph A. McCartin, *Why the Labor Movement Has Failed—And How to Fix It*, BOSTON REVIEW (June 6, 2019), https://perma.cc/EDC4-ESF4.
20. See Kate Andrias, *The New Labor Law*, 126 YALE L.J. 2 (2016); Michael M. Oswalt, *Alt-Bargaining*, 82 LAW & CONTEMP. PROB. 89 (2019).
21. Mike Elk, *Justice in the Factory: How Black Lives Matter Breathed New Life into Unions*, GUARDIAN (Feb. 10, 2018), https://perma.cc/BU3Z-9Q52.

22. Eli Day, *Labor Unions Battle for Working-Class Georgians*, AMERICAN PROSPECT (Dec. 15, 2020), https://prospect.org/politics/labor-unions-battle-for-working-class-georgians/.
23. *See, e.g.*, Elise Gould & Valerie Wilson, *Black Workers Face Two of the Most Lethal Preexisting Conditions for Coronavirus—Racism and Economic Inequality*, ECON. POL'Y INST. 4 (June 1, 2020), https://perma.cc/G2HQ-2UVF; Hye Jin Rho et al., *A Basic Demographic Profile of Workers in Frontline Industries*, CTR. FOR ECON. & POL'Y RES. (2020), https://perma.cc/4PQU-YVZ4.
24. Clean Slate Project, *Clean Slate for Worker Power: Building a Just Economy and Democracy*, Labor and Worklife Program, Harvard Law School, https://www.cleanslateworkerpower.org/. The full report (https://perma.cc/R7JC-P3VQ) gained national attention. *See, e.g.*, Emily Bazelon, *Why Are Workers Struggling? Because Labor Law is Broken*, N.Y. TIMES MAG. (Feb. 19, 2020), https://perma.cc/FHZ2-W9EE; Steven Greenhouse, *Overhaul US Labor Laws to Boost Workers' Power, New Report Urges*, GUARDIAN (Jan. 23, 2020), https://perma.cc/H732-S2DL
25. Justin Worland, *America's Long Overdue Awakening to Systemic Racism*, TIME (June 11, 2020), https://perma.cc/DW7T-6U8K; *The Ezra Klein Show: Why Ta-Nehisi Coates Is Hopeful*, Vox (June 5, 2020), available at https://www.vox.com/2020/6/5/21279530/ta-nehisi-coates-ezra-klein-show-george-floyd-police-brutality-trump-biden.
26. In 1932, 7.8% of employed workers belonged to unions. Gerald Mayer, *Union Membership Trends in the United States*, CONG. RESEARCH SERV. 23 (2004), https://perma.cc/N6CM-LAXZ.
27. On the role of the Congress of Industrial Organizations in particular, see LIZBETH COHEN, MAKING A NEW DEAL: INDUSTRIAL WORKERS IN CHICAGO 1919–1939 (1990).
28. Brishen Rogers, *Data and Democracy at Work* (Manuscript, forthcoming 2021).
29. Thanks to Brishen Rogers for emphasizing this advantage of my proposals.
30. Rustin, *supra* note 2,
31. *See generally* VARIETIES OF CAPITALISM: THE INSTITUTIONAL FOUNDATIONS OF COMPARATIVE ADVANTAGE (Peter A. Hall & David Soskice eds., 2001); DEBATING VARIETIES OF CAPITALISM (Bob Hancké ed., 2009).
32. Frank Newport, *The Meaning of "Socialism" to Americans Today*, GALLUP (Oct. 4, 2018), https://perma.cc/572A-M3BQ.
33. *Id.*
34. *See* Randall Collins, *The End of Middle-Class Work: No More Escapes*, *in* IMMANUEL WALLERSTEIN ET AL., DOES CAPITALISM HAVE A FUTURE? (2013).
35. *See, e.g.*, ANTHONY GIDDENS, THE THIRD WAY: THE RENEWAL OF SOCIAL DEMOCRACY (1998); MARQUIS WILLIAM CHILDS, SWEDEN: THE MIDDLE WAY (1936); Thomas B. Edsall, *Clinton and Blair Envision a 'Third Way' International Movement*, WASH. POST (June 28, 1998), https://perma.cc/NP6S-CAQT.

Index

For the benefit of digital users, indexed terms that span two pages (e.g., 52–53) may, on occasion, appear on only one of those pages.